No Momma's Boy

No Momma's Boy

✦

How I Let Go of My Past and Embraced the Future

A Memoir

Dominic Carter

iUniverse, Inc.
New York Lincoln Shanghai

No Momma's Boy
How I Let Go of My Past and Embraced the Future

iUniverse books may be ordered through booksellers or by contacting:

iUniverse
2021 Pine Lake Road, Suite 100
Lincoln, NE 68512
www.iuniverse.com
1-800-Authors (1-800-288-4677)

ISBN: 978-0-595-42839-7 (pbk)
ISBN: 978-0-595-87178-0 (ebk)

Printed in the United States of America

This book is dedicated to the memory of my grandmother,
Anna Pearl Carter.

To my Aunt Inez Carter.

And, finally,

To my mother, Laverne Carter.

After all these years, I have forgiven you.

May you rest in peace.

Contents

Acknowledgements

I am forever grateful to my wife, Marilyn, my college sweetheart, who for more than 25 years has stood by me through thick and thin. She was my rock as I uncovered the shocking details of my little known past—and she has been the voice of compassion and and more importantly, reason, throughout the writing of this book.

Of course there is my beautiful daughter, Courtney Ann Carter, who is blossoming into a brilliant young lady. She has already traveled the world, and is the reason why I keep pushing for the best. She is showing the potential to be twice as good a TV journalist as her Dad ever was. There's Dominic Jr., whose warm smile is contagious. My son's exuberance is a constant reminder of what is truly important in life.

To my sisters Malika, and Antoinette, I send you love and wish you both the best life has to offer. And the same goes to my nieces Makia, Beatrice, and Stephanie.

To my dear late Mother-in-Law Ruby Stevens, we came into each others life at an ideal time. She tragically had to bury several of her sons and did so, with such dignity and class, and I in turn had another mother figure. I became her new son. Rest In Peace.

For my friends at NY1. First, my longtime boss Steve Paulus, who has given me extraordinary opportunities—and has trusted my instincts. He has stood by me for more than 15 years, and I will never forget our trip together to Japan. To my News Director, Bernadine Han, thanks for always being a good listener, and to my Assistant News Director, Dan Jacobson; we worked together shoulder to shoulder as reporters during New York's Crown Heights riots in 1991, and at City Hall. I have always valued your friendship.

I am indebted to the entire Time Warner family—and particularly Chairman and CEO Richard Parsons, for championing my work since 1992, and for protecting me from powerful politicians who wanted my head on a platter. I also thank the Rev. Al Sharpton. A man I cover as a newsmaker, and have known him for more than 20 years.

I'd also like to thank my colleagues in the political unit: Political Director, Robert Hardt—who was a great advisor during the development of this book. Thanks also go out to Michael Nitzky, Cefaan Kim, Sandra Endo, Rita Nissan, Josh Robin, Molly Kroon and Michael Scotto. I'd also like to thank staffer Clover Lalehzar for her support.

I am very grateful to Howard Rubenstein and Jim Grossman for their words of encouragement. Also many thanks to Ivy Cohen, Ann Marie Nieves, Barbara Seaman, Joanna Perlman, Jeff Simmons, Jamie McShane, Taina Hernandez, Luisa Doyle, Tim Scheld, Peter Noel, Curtis Taylor, Charles Warfield, Albert Stevens Jr., Scott Levinson, Roma Torre, and Kristen Shaughnessy. I'd also like to thank New York City Schools Chancellor Joel Klein.

There is a strong possibility this book would not exist if not for longtime friends Ronald Johnson and Debra Pointer. They gently prodded me to write a book for almost 20 years, and then demanded that I do so. Thanks to webmaster Loretta Wilkins, who turned www.nomomommasboy.com into an eye popping and intriguing website.

During the writing of this book, the support of one childhood friend has been rock solid: Randolph Codrington. I also send my heartfelt appreciation to my other buddies: Ty Caldwell, John Williams, Steven Brandon, "Wes", and Johnny Brown.

Finally, many thanks to the millions of faithful TV viewers and Radio Listeners, over the years—from bus drivers to college professors and especially young people who tell me they pay more attention to politics because of my show, And to all of the kind people who have stopped me on the street to share a word and a thumbs up. I am indebted to you all.

Preface

My Aunt Inez fought strongly against me writing this book. My sister Malika pointedly asked, "You're not going to demonize Laverne, are you?" During the development of this memoir, I, in turn, have asked myself that very question repeatedly. And I can confidently say that this memoir does not demonize my late mother Laverne, even though much of our experience together may be hard for you, the reader, to digest. My mother, as you will learn, did some despicable things to me, but she was no demon.

She was a woman, indeed a vulnerable woman, who battled mental illness. Regrettably, she fought against a taboo sickness that too many people were afraid to understand, especially in the 1950s and 1960s. And, as a result, I was caught in the cycle of denial, rejection, and shame.

My upbringing is the flip side of the American Dream: the story of a mother and son who came of age in the most prosperous nation on Earth. We are the stuff of which living nightmares are made; however, I've had the great honor of transforming my cross into a crown. Through sheer determination and the grace of God, I have flipped the script of what was destined to become another American Tragedy.

I've had an amazing career in television news, which has seen many highs and very few lows. Heralded as one of most influential political journalists in New York, it's been a long road from the streets of the Bronx to the halls of power. I've interviewed some of the most famous people in the world—from Nelson Mandela to Bill Clinton and so many more. I have moderated high-profile political debates with Hillary Clinton, and I have certainly had more than my share of news-making exclusive interviews.

Lights, camera, and action aside, hardly a day goes by where I am not tempted to pinch myself and say, "Can you believe how far you've come?" Other than my grandmother, Anna Pearl, and my dear Aunt Inez, few, if any, predicted that I would be anything more than a convict or a drug dealer—or dead.

More than a few people who witnessed my antics during my troubled teenaged years thought for sure they were seeing a dead kid walking. But I was merely confused. It wasn't easy living with the fact that I remembered "things" about my mother and my childhood. Puberty and poverty were hard enough, but, when I tried to face my past, life became pretty much unbearable. But Aunt Inez made sure I stayed on the right path. Sure enough, I came out on the other side of despair.

That is one of the main reasons I am now baring my soul to the world. My message for every person, young and old, who have been told they can't achieve their goals and are tempted to give up: see my life as an example to prove the critics wrong.

I titled this book *No Momma's Boy*. My relationship with my mother was the polar opposite of a traditional mother-son relationship. Laverne had birthed me, but I did not really feel like her son. During my childhood, my grandmother and aunts kept Laverne at arm's length to protect me from her episodes of madness. While I could never bring myself to hate her, my pride wouldn't allow me to address her as mom, or anything of the sort. I simply called her Laverne. Sadly, I was never a momma's boy.

It is often said, "The truth shall set you free," and uncovering these mysteries in my life has released the shackles of shame. I hope my life story will empower others who have lived through the tangled web of mental illness, sex abuse, and despair. Keep in mind, however, that the truth is still a bitter pill to swallow. For years, my past was an embarrassing secret lodged deep in my soul. But in my heart, I now know I have nothing to be ashamed of. Tearful and sleepless nights coupled with painstaking research have forced me to confront the memories that I had pushed to the farthest corners of my mind.

No, my mother was not a demon, but she saw demons, and, at times, she confessed that she heard them tell her to do terrible things. Sometimes she obeyed those voices; other times, she turned a deaf ear. I am thankful for the times she ignored those voices.

As a man in my forties, I never understood how much emotional pain my mother must have been in. It breaks my heart to think about as a teenager, when she should have been going to the school dance like everybody else, she was being institutionalized in psychiatric hospitals. Her world consisted of very powerful psychiatric medications, electrical shock treatment, and straightjackets.

I will never forget the first batch of my mother's mental records that I received in the mail after her death. Much of this book is based on those documents, along with five long years of research. Imagine reading that your mother wanted to kill you before you even learned how to recite the alphabet. I'm not sure a person can ever get over such a disclosure of mental madness. It's a mind-numbing shock.

If a demon exists in this story, it is society's collective mistreatment and misunderstanding of mental illness in the mid-twentieth century. Doctors documented my mother's murderous thoughts against me, and yet somehow I was still left in her sole custody. My mother, in a very strange way, was innocent. She was a victim of her own illness. She was poorly educated, confused, angry, and depressed. Most of the time, my mother literally didn't know whether she was coming or going. She was in no way, shape, or form prepared to raise a child. She was, in many ways, a child herself. Lucky for me, I was surrounded by three women who loved me very much as a child: my grandmother, Aunt Inez, and Aunt Joann.

My climb up the ladder of success has not been easy. There have been rungs missing, tacks in it, places where I have held on for dear life. But I have kept climbing up, amazed at how grace has lifted me.

I wish I could say hindsight is 20/20—but in my case it's not. There are many answers that my mother took with her to the grave, and many questions, I suppose, that I will take to my own resting place. But at least now I can one day rest in peace. And I pray that Laverne Carter, my mother, is resting peacefully, too.

Truth be told, I blame her for nothing. I have some regrets, but I have no shame. Somewhere I pray she is an angel. I hope she's proudly looking down on me because I have emerged from our collective misery—not unscathed, but unbowed. Bloodied, but unbowed.

1

On a warm spring day in 1997, the sun was shining, some kids were playing in the park, and the birds were chirping. I arrived home and greeted my wife, Marilyn, and my mother-in-law, better known as Grandma Ruby. As I approached the kitchen in our Manhattan apartment, I noticed someone sitting in a chair in the shadows. It was my mother, Laverne Carter. My smile began to fade, and my mood immediately changed.

For years, my wife and my mother-in-law had pressured me to establish a mother-son relationship with Laverne. They could not fathom why a son and his mother had never bonded. For me, a mother-son relationship would have to happen over my dead body.

As we all engaged in small talk, it became time for the traditional verbal sparring session into why I had not embraced my mother. The conversation would normally go something like this: My wife and my mother-in-law would tell me to embrace Laverne, while my mother sat there wearing the look of the perfect victim.

What my wife and my mother-in-law were saying became background noise, and this time I felt almost like a professional athlete, tuning out the fans in order to perform. I looked into my mother's eyes. I noted how she held her mouth. She sat quietly, but her manner seemed to imply that she enjoyed the sympathy.

"Come here for a minute," I finally said to my mother, glaring at her and motioning with my head for her to follow me down the hall and into the living room. I hadn't planned this conversation in advance, but this was our moment of truth. As we walked down the long hallway, I felt that I was walking in slow motion. This was the same hallway that I would hear Grandma Ruby's slippers sashay down in the wee hours of the morning to wake me up when I began my journalism career in radio. Now I heard my mother's slow footsteps behind me on the wooden floor. When I was a little boy, the sounds of her footsteps had frightened me as I followed behind her when she was on one of her rampages. She was now following me, her footsteps sounding as if she were walking her last mile. I was in control this time, and I wanted justice.

Glancing over my shoulder, I strongly suspected from her body language that she sensed what was ahead. I wasn't leading her into the living room to talk about sugar and spice and everything nice. We were going to lift the scab off a wound that had refused to heal until the air of truth got to it.

My mind raced. At last, I would make her talk about the past. Those events weren't just in my imagination. Many times I had tried to tell myself that maybe I'd made everything up, but my memory would indict my attempt at denial. My mother had indeed sexually abused me years before, and now was the time for her to face that fact.

I had walked this familiar hallway ten thousand times, yet on this afternoon I was acutely aware of every inch of it. My peripheral vision caught my many professional awards for excellence in journalism hanging neatly along Grandma Ruby's beige hallway. After each honors ceremony, I turned over the award to Aunt Inez or Grandma Ruby, who cherished them as if they had been formed from her own flesh and blood.

Technically, these awards should have hung on my mother's walls, but, because of our tarnished past, I was unwilling to share such joys with her. I wondered how my mother felt about having her son's honors hanging on another woman's wall. Did she care? Was she jealous? She had walked down that hallway many times and had to have noticed.

When we arrived in the living room, I motioned for my mother to sit down on the couch. I felt like a lawyer indicating that she should take the witness stand. With her head bowed, she sank down onto the long, cream-colored sofa covered in plastic. As my mother settled herself, the plastic softly crackled beneath her thin, frail body.

I sat upright on a chair that I turned so it was directly in front of her. My posture screamed power. I held my head high. My feet were planted on the floor, and my hands were firmly on the armrests. I looked directly into Laverne's eyes, though she didn't look into mine.

For a brief moment, I could not speak. Laverne looked straight ahead, not at me, but through the window behind me. Her eyes reflected the trees of Morningside Park. I didn't take my eyes off her because I had a strong feeling that in this conversation her body language would speak louder than her words.

She placed one hand on top of the other and crossed her ankles. Over the years, I have interviewed hundreds, perhaps thousands, of people, and this was the most important interview of my life. I had interviewed presidents, mayors, governors, and civil rights leaders; all of them paled in comparison to this one-on-one with my mother. This time, there were no cameras or microphones. The only recording was playing in my mind—the same mind that had recorded those horrific events long ago.

Her face was a bit drawn, and she didn't lock eyes with me until I cleared my throat.

"Laverne," I said, my voice strong, "why did you do that to me?"

She seemed calm, but I could see a look of sheer panic deep in her eyes. She quickly looked away. I felt certain that she knew what "that" had meant. In one word, I had summed up years of abuse and neglect.

When she peeked at me from her downcast eyes, I suspected that she was hoping I'd been too young to remember her abusing me. Now she cleared her throat and spoke at last.

"Boy, leave me alone with that." She looked at the floor. She seemed to be studying the brown, wood-grain linoleum tiles, inch by inch. I had actually installed those tiles myself.

My mind raced even faster. Not only did my mother not want to talk about what she had done, but she was avoiding my question, perhaps banking on the hope that I might have forgotten everything. But I hadn't forgotten, and I wasn't letting her off that easily. I decided to cross-examine her further. If I could grill Rudy Giuliani, New York City's tough-as-nails former mayor, I could certainly grill her.

"No, Laverne, seriously," I countered. "Why?"

I couldn't even bring myself to speak about the details of our past encounter, but she must have known exactly what I was talking about. And she repeated her same, sorry response.

"Boy, I *said* leave me alone with that."

She kept looking down, in my eyes indicted, tried, and sentenced in one instant. And in fact, she had been. Her body language told me clearly that she didn't want to talk about the past.

She was done. And so was I. The nerve of her! I'd given her a chance to confess to me and explain her sins, and she had refused.

I'd asked a simple question, but in that one question I had sent a lot of information to my mother. For one, I showed her that she wasn't off the hook. After years of pretending, I wanted her to look her son, her firstborn, dead in the eyes and acknowledge her crimes against me. When we looked at one another, I wanted her to see how many times I had cried myself to sleep because of her abuse.

I wanted her to answer my questions, and they were many: "Why did you play games with my fragile life, Laverne? Why did you dump me in foster care when there were relatives who were more than willing to take care of me? In family court, why did you try to take me from Grandma Anna Pearl when you knew you didn't want me? Why didn't you want me? What did I do to deserve your scorn?" All these questions and more were raging inside me, and I wanted her answers.

We sat quietly for another minute or so. My eyes left her slumped shoulders and scanned the pictures on the mantle above the fireplace. One of my favorite pictures of my wife sat there, when she had been no more than three years old. She looked very cute in the faded black and white photograph, her arms stretched wide and her mouth open, probably calling for her mother. I knew that my wife loved me, and I was sure that my mother-in-law loved me, too. But I feared that the one person who had birthed me would never say, "Son, I love you, and I'm sorry."

After giving her several minutes to say something, anything else, I abruptly stood up and began my long walk back down the hallway. I heard Laverne get up and walk behind me, but now I no longer cared what she did. My wife told me later that, when I got back to the kitchen, she could tell by the looks on our faces that something had gone wrong during our talk. She said I looked calm, but I was very quiet. My mother-in-law, seeing the solemn expressions on my mother's face and on mine, said, "What's the matter? You guys were doing so well."

I gave my mother-in-law a half smile, walked out of the apartment, rode down seven stories in the elevator, and hurried out into the noonday sun.

Boy, leave me alone with that. That was how my mother would sum up a lifetime of sick memories for me. I deserved more than a leave-me-alone answer.

I walked down Morningside Avenue to calm my spinning thoughts. I had given my mother a chance to redeem herself, and she had refused. Her actions had left the gaping hole in my heart that promised to haunt me until my death, and she apparently could not have cared less. Tears welled in my eyes. All I had wanted my mother to say was that she was sorry—to break down and to say that she loved me. I wanted her to tell me how proud she was that I'd made a success of my life in spite of all her abuse. I wanted her to say, "I didn't know what I was doing, son. I was mentally sick, and I couldn't control myself." If she had said anything like that, I would have embraced her, and maybe I could finally have had some sense of closure, some semblance of peace with myself. Once again, Laverne had left me heartbroken, and I was again that little boy waiting on the stoop after school, waiting in vain for my mother to come for me.

As heartbroken as I was, this time I also felt empowered. A big part of me had been afraid to confront Laverne, yet I had done it. Another part of me wanted to humiliate her the way she had humiliated me, and I did. I felt certain that Laverne had been thoroughly humiliated in front of my wife and Grandma

Ruby. I had let my mother know that although she'd left me for dead emotionally, many people had stepped in to fill her shoes.

My grandmother, my aunt, my friends, my wife, my children, even strangers on the street showed more affection to me than my mother had. I don't recall a single kiss on the cheek from her. When I graduated from Cortland College in New York State, everyone showered me with kisses. I had lipstick on both of my chubby cheeks, even on my collar. At that time, my mother gave me a limp embrace and briefly rested her wigged head against my chin. When my first child was born, my mother grabbed my arm and said something that I couldn't discern. She had never taken me aside and told me how proud she was.

"Boy, leave me alone with that." For years, I had left her alone in body, but not in spirit. Now for the rest of *her* life, I wanted her to know that she had really hurt me. I wanted her to understand that I had never forgotten what she did to me.

At the time of this confrontation, I did not know of her extensive battle with mental illness. If I had known, I would have asked more questions: "Why didn't you let Grandma or Aunt Inez take care of me from the very start?" Later I understood and respected the fact that my mother was mentally incapacitated and had been so for years. I sympathized with her illness because I understood that she could not control herself. I also slowly realized that my mother was dealing with her own sad history of rejection.

She had been in pain, and she had passed that pain along to me. Had she known better? In her younger days, probably not. These days, though, I could tell by her response when I had confronted her that she most certainly did know. Perhaps she suffered memory loss from years of electroconvulsive therapy (ECT), but, at the very least, she must have known that she'd failed as a mother. Perhaps she had been traumatized by her own memories of being in an asylum. Maybe thoughts raced though her head of the time in her young teens when she had apparently been raped. Maybe she had obsessed over reasons why her mother had raised her other two sisters and not her. Had she felt that she was different or unworthy of such care?

I realized that my mother was unlikely to speak candidly to me or probably anyone else about her mental illness. She would never talk about her childhood or the time she had spent in asylums. But I had given her an open invitation to speak or to forever hold her peace. She chose to hold her peace.

I'm thankful that I didn't hold mine.

Even after that non-conversation with Laverne, I vowed that I would never give up my quest for the truth. At that time, I had no idea that four short years later, my mother would speak the truth from the grave. After a long battle with diabetes and high blood pressure, Laverne died in 2001. I tried to get over her passing but had difficulty doing so. I could not rest until I got answers about the missing chapters of my life.

I asked one of my mother's sisters, Aunt Inez, for information about Laverne's past, but she gave me only bits and pieces. For my whole life, Inez and the few remaining people in my small family had kept my mother's past from me in an effort to protect me. They probably thought that what I didn't know couldn't hurt me. Now I was a grown man, and I wanted to know the full story. I felt I could take the truth.

I knew my mother, but I didn't *know* my mother. She had never confided in me. Instead, we had spent our time together merely chatting. We had never scratched below the surface. I had no idea what had made my mother tick. And what I didn't know far exceeded what I did know.

Laverne Carter was my birth mother, yet I had more information about my colleagues' upbringing than about my own mother's. Deep down, I knew there was something inherently wrong. Yet there were so many questions that I was afraid to ask, fearing what I might find out. As a newsman in New York City, I would grill the toughest politicians about their backgrounds and motives, but Laverne Carter had been off limits. Her past and mine were protected by our family's own "don't ask, don't tell" policy.

My family had shielded me from my mother as if she were some unholy creature. Laverne had been not a woman of honor but a woman of mystery. I learned that she was to be respected as my mother but not scrutinized. I spent much of my life ignoring my past and my mother's past. I viewed my family history as one big blur. After my mother passed away, all I wanted to do was learn about her. My need for information became almost an obsession. At last, I could probe into my mother's past and not worry about her reaction. *My* reaction, of course, I didn't consider.

What I knew to that point was that my mother had suffered with some sort of mental illness, but I didn't know exactly what or how she had been treated. Aunt Inez gave me background information about my mother's past treatment for mental illness at Mount Sinai Hospital in Manhattan, the same hospital in which I had been born. Armed with that fact, I had a concrete lead. In 2003, I finally worked up the nerve to contact the medical facility and request Laverne Carter's psychiatric medical records.

Mount Sinai's response was the beginning of what would be a roller coaster of emotions. The records department of Mount Sinai located my mother's files and requested a fee of $300 to cover the cost of copying the 620 pages and shipping them to me. Imagine—one psychiatric unit possessed that many pages about a life that I'd never known. And Mount Sinai was just one facility of what I would gradually discover were many.

I quickly mailed a check to the hospital and waited nervously for the package to arrive. As I had feared, the woman in Mount Sinai's records department recognized my voice and name as belonging to one of the most prominent faces in New York City television news. She said that her staff would expedite the process of copying and shipping my mother's files, but, from the tone of her voice, I realized that she felt badly for me. I would soon find out why.

On May 28, 2003, as I peeped out the front door of my suburban home, I saw a yellow slip stuck to my mailbox. I could feel my heart literally skip a beat. The slip stated that a package addressed to Dominic Carter from Mount Sinai Medical Center was waiting at the post office.

I ran back into the bedroom, jumped into the nearest pair of jeans and a T-shirt, yelled for my wife, Marilyn, and hurried with her into our SUV. My breakfast of blueberry pancakes and coffee would have to wait until we returned. We rushed to the tiny post office in Rockland County and found three people in line ahead of us. Before the postal worker could say, "Next," I was already walking toward him and preempted the "Can I help you?" by handing him my driver's license as identification, along with the yellow slip. He disappeared into the back room and returned holding a large, bulky yellow envelope.

My heart raced because I didn't know what I would find, but whatever it was, I knew it would be captivating. This was the biggest story of my life. It was a story that would change my life forever, only I didn't know it at the time. I carefully opened the package, handling it as carefully as I would a newborn baby.

Some of the 620 pages were typed, and some were barely legible, the writing scratched in various doctors' handwriting. Those pages contained my mother's case history. The fact that it was so voluminous made it that much more intimidating. I wanted to read those facts one page at a time. I walked away from the clerk and over to a side table, feeling that I was in for the shock of a lifetime. I picked up one sheet, placing the other 619 pages on the post office table. The dim, fluorescent light was not as bright as the morning sun that shone through the thick windows. But as my eyes scanned each line on that first page, the information somehow came more sharply into focus and made my skin crawl.

> On June 20, she beat him so hard that she raised "welts" on him. However, she wants to be a good mother and is quite alarmed by her recent angry outbursts and thoughts of strangling her son. On one occasion while feeling "strange and dead," she put her hands around his throat before he awakened, and she was frightened by his crying. She has more recently reported that while in a state of depersonalization, she has had frightening thoughts of pushing her son out the window and has heard a voice tell her to "do it."
>
> —Psychiatric Summary Report
> on Laverne Carter
> Dr. Robert Humphries
> Mount Sinai Hospital
> June 21, 1966

That page, that report, was talking about me! Reading the words quite literally took my breath away. With my wife peering over my shoulder, I read on, my mouth hanging open as if I were reading a suspense thriller. I thought to myself, I am the *he* in this psychiatric report, and my mother is the *she*.

I had absolutely no recollection of ever being beaten or nearly strangled. Until that moment, the information that I'd nearly been murdered by my own mother had never been revealed to me. My eyes opened wide as my mind struggled to create a picture of what I was reading. Numb with shock, I went deaf and blind to anything else going on around me. All I saw were the papers in front of me—the documents that showed me the lyrics to a sad song, a story that no one in my family ever wanted me to know. But I would soon find out this was only part of the information they had shielded from me all those years.

Marilyn must have driven us both home at some point that day, but I don't recall the drive. My attention was tightly focused on those pages. At the top of each page was 7N, which I learned stood for the northern wing of the hospital where Laverne Carter spent most of her time at Mount Sinai Hospital. The psychiatric unit, I found out, was housed in 7N.

Between 1963 and 1973, my mother was both an inpatient and an outpatient at the hospital. Ironically, during those years I had also been a frequent patient in Mount Sinai—beginning with my birth in 1964. I was delivered by caesarean section on June 18 at 2:52 PM, and I weighed nearly eight pounds. I was shocked to find out that Laverne visited the maternity ward one month, and not long after she was in the mental ward of the same hospital. As I continued to read the pages, I learned that my mother had been in and out of mental hospitals since she was a teenager. At first, I felt embarrassed—and then sad. These

620 pages helped me unlock doors that had been bolted shut by my relatives, and a troubled family history unfolded before my eyes.

Laverne hadn't talked with me about her past; she had rarely talked to her mother or to either of her two sisters, Inez and Joanne. But those pages showed that my mother had done plenty of talking to psychiatrists, therapists, and social workers, and all her words had been carefully recorded in the documents I now held in my sweaty hands. These documents gave me the power to know much of the truth about my mother and about myself. And I used this power to explain finally who I was. I was still something of a mystery, even to myself. By 2003, much had happened to me over the course of my forty years, but I couldn't understand why it had happened. I had never been allowed to get to the root of my problems and my history. That root was my mother, Laverne.

Some four months after the Beatles took the music world by storm in 1964, Laverne gave birth to me. My aunt remembered that she seemed proud to be a mother and to welcome me into her world. My mother's sister, Inez, was respected by everyone in the family and named me Dominic Fitzgerald, a name she picked out of a book. She liked the ring of Dominic and had no idea that it was a strong Italian name. She chose Fitzgerald for the beloved President John Fitzgerald Kennedy, who died seven months before my birth. Had I been a girl, I would have been named Michelle Germaine.

I was a black child, but you surely couldn't tell by looking at me; I was as white as a ghost. When my grandfather, Johnny Carter, looked for me in the nursery, he told his family, "Dominic ain't in there—ain't nothing in there but white babies." But I was there, and, even though I was rather pale, my grandfather was thrilled to finally have a boy in the family because he already had three daughters.

Nothing in life has come easy for me. I wasn't even born healthy. When I was about a month old, a runny nose turned into a cold and then into pneumonia. After numerous runs to the emergency room at Mount Sinai Hospital, where my mother was an outpatient in the mental unit, the doctors also discovered there was something seriously wrong with me. I was diagnosed with dextrocardia, a rare heart condition characterized by abnormal positioning of the heart. The tip of a normal heart is normally positioned on the left side of the chest, but my heart is positioned on the right side. An abnormality that accompanies dextrocardia is reversal, or situs inversus, of some abdominal organs such as the liver and the spleen. Dextrocardia is not a fatal condition, and, as an adult I have not had serious complications related to it, but obviously the condition can pose a potential problem should I ever need emergency surgery. For example, when I was a teen and developed appendicitis, my doctors had no idea where to find my appendix because of the situs inversus. They had to perform an X-ray and exploratory surgery to locate my appendix before removing it.

Reading the medical records, I realized that my most immediate and critical threat as a child had not been dextrocardia, but my mother's mental health and her impatience with her sick toddler. In an initial case note, also dated June 21, 1966, doctors wrote:

> Born at Mount Sinai two years ago (by Caesarian section), her son Dominic has a cardiac anomaly (possibly dextrocardia). She has found him difficult to cope with, particularly

because of his frequent pulmonary infections and hospital-izations. She feels he is spoiled and sometimes cries for no reason at all. When she gets angry, and particularly when she is in her dreamlike state, she beats him on the head and back with her hands.

Tears welled in my eyes and my hands trembled as I contin-ued to read the records outlining my past abuse, of which I had absolutely no memory. I wondered what I could possibly have done to provoke such rage. I judged from the psychiatric records that my survival during childhood was a miracle. The more I read, the more revolting the information became.

She was having visual hallucinations of people laughing at her. After several weeks at Mount Sinai, the patient was transferred to Rockland State [Hospital], where she spent several months.

I momentarily put the papers down. Now I really felt like crying, but, as I have always done, I fought the impulse to feel sorry for myself. I tried to make sense of the report as I read about a life I never knew. I flipped to another page, which said at the top:

Diagnosis: Chronic Paranoid Schizophrenia 295.3 with possible dyskinetic reaction second day to Prolixin.

That diagnosis was a real eye-opener for me. Finally, a justifi-cation for all of this insanity: paranoid schizophrenia. Wow! I didn't know much about mental illness, but I knew schizophre-nia was one of the most serious illnesses. All of those years that I spoke with my mother, and I'd never have guessed she had suffered from schizophrenia. She hadn't seemed strange to me as an adult. She had seemed pretty much just like everybody else in her low-income neighborhood, the housing projects of New York City. Life seemed very unfair to them, but most people in these communities were survivors. My mother hadn't lived well—she had been poor and sickly—but she had been alive.

As I continued to flip through the pages, another psychiatric description of my mother aroused my sudden compassion.

> IDENTIFICATION: This twenty-five-year-old, single, jobless, mother of one, a Negro female enters Mount Sinai Hospital psychiatric and the sixth psychiatric hospital admission with the chief complaint of increasing depression and fear of killing self.

I turned to another page and was startled by the number of psychiatric medications that she once took.

> Thorazine
> Prolixin Ethonate
> Artane

As I read this account of my mother's life, that in part was my beginning, my emotions seesawed from profound sadness to rage. Where had my protectors been? One line in a document stood out: "The homicidal impulses toward her child are said to have begun or at least to have been most acute during the last two weeks." This woman was spilling her guts about her desire to kill her firstborn. Yet in 620 pages, no one suggested removing me from harm's way. I had been caught in the crossfire of a dangerous world. I had lived within an unfortunate mix of poverty, insanity, and abuse, all of which occurred even as I wore training shoes.

Clutching my newfound family history cloaked in medical documents, I searched at home for old pictures of myself. I needed to see what I had looked like during that time. I had washed so much of my past from my memory that I wanted to see the old me again. I found a faded picture of myself with a dog. Hot damn! I had totally forgotten that I had had a German shepherd when I had lived with my mom on Vice Avenue in the Bronx. I could not have been more than eight years old. I had apparently washed the good memories away with the bad. In the photograph, I am seated on a plastic-covered, yellow floral couch, and the large puppy is sitting partly on my lap. I appear to be laughing, holding my arms up in front of my face as if to prevent the dog from licking me. Ironically, I am wearing a blue T-shirt with a peace symbol on the front. After reading my mother's medical history, I realized there had obviously been little peace in our household. But in that photo, I didn't appear to have a care in the world, seated there next to my dog. I almost wished I could reach into the photo and go back in time to that moment. Had my mother taken the picture? Had she been happy? Had she been medicated? Had she recently been to the psychiatric ward? The picture says so much more to me now than it did before.

Another school picture taken in the 1970s shows me with a big, cheesy smile and a partly combed afro. I must've been about ten years old, and my mother's sexual abuse had occurred by then. In the photo, my eyes seemed full of sunshine. Holding the photo, I looked deep into my young, naïve eyes and saw nothing there—not a clue of what I had lived through.

Other photos showed that as I grew older, my smiles only widened. The hair on my eyebrows thickened, my sideburns grew in, my face filled out, and my teeth became more even. And in every picture, I saw no trace of sadness or despair anywhere on my pleasant face. Now I realize that, as a child and a teenager, I had done a masterful job of covering up my inner pain.

Since those days, I have gone on to success beyond my wildest dreams. I find it hard to believe that, once in my life, I had been so vulnerable and unprotected. It's a wonder that I survived at all. I have managed to piece my life together, beginning with my birth.

My mother and I had first lived in a Harlem tenement on 201 West 121st Street with Grandma Anna Pearl, Grandpa Johnny, Aunt Inez, and Aunt Joann. I do recall the story of where and how I was conceived—in an apartment house not far from where we lived. In 1963, my mother was eighteen years old. She had a slender, brown body, doe eyes, and medium-length hair. She was about five feet two inches tall. And she was not afraid to do "it"—that is, to have sex.

My father, Dudley Hall, was nineteen and had been doing "it" for some time. He had been born in Jamaica and was handsome and brown-skinned. He had a head full of processed hair and a confident smile punctuated by a gold tooth. Dudley was a player, also known as a ladies' man, and Laverne was one of the girls he regularly played with.

On a crisp, autumn day, Dudley and Laverne went to a party in a dingy Harlem apartment. Laverne usually tried to do all the talking because she had a hard time deciphering Dudley's thick Jamaican accent. Thick accent or not, she liked the way he talked, and she especially liked the way he called her "girl." His accent made the word sound like "gull." According to what my mother told me, Dudley knew in a matter of minutes that he could do it with Laverne. The music at the party was too loud, so he asked to talk to her in a closet. Talking in that closet led to touching, touching led to caressing, and caressing led to penetration. Laverne didn't give much thought to the act or the consequences. She just enjoyed being held and loved. That certainly wasn't her first time, but it led to her first pregnancy, which produced me.

I have often thought it awful that my mother revealed to me, without hesitation, that I had been conceived in a closet. Even though she had told me this story when I was a grown man, I was still embarrassed. And she said it as if it were completely funny to her. My parents didn't lie together in a bed and caress each other. My conception resulted from sheer lust—damnable lust—the "right now" lust that won't wait and won't go away until it's satisfied.

It was bad enough that my parents were not married, but it was unthinkable that my life began in a dark, cramped closet full of coats, shoes, and mothballs. I knew that the story, which my mother related matter-of-factly, was true and that all I could do was shrug it off. According to Aunt Inez, any hopes my mother had of making Dudley part of her life were quickly dashed. "Hall," as Laverne called him, impregnated two women, one of whom was my mother, at about the same time. The other woman was fourteen years old, and her name was Opal. Hall openly squired Opal around on his arm, but he kept his relationship with Laverne a secret.

The first person Laverne told about her pregnancy was her sister, Inez. She grabbed Inez's arm as they were walking down 121st Street in Harlem. "Come walk with me," Laverne said. "I'm pregnant."

"Ooh! By whom?" Inez said, trying to contain herself but ready to burst.

"I don't know."

Inez later admitted that she was certain Laverne knew who the daddy was, but didn't want to tell Inez because the other girl in question, Opal, was Inez's best friend. Inez pried the father's name from her sister and promised not to tell a soul, though Inez knew the promise was one she wouldn't keep. The moment she got back home, she told their mother.

Trouble was on the way. When Opal told her parents she was pregnant, they threatened to have Hall arrested for statutory rape. Hall got out of that jam by promising to marry Opal right away, but he never told them he had another baby on the way—and that the two babies were only weeks apart. All Hall cared about was not going to jail, even if his silence meant I would be considered an illegitimate child. Hall's attitude exemplified a way of life for members of the underclass.

This family drama is confirmed in my mother's initial case history.

> The putative father impregnated a fourteen-year-old girl at about the same time and married her to avoid a statutory rape conviction. Following delivery, patient became depressed and was transferred to psychiatric service ... Her son, Dominic, remains in the care of her parents.

The report calls my father "putative." I had to look up what the word meant. The dictionary defines the word as "generally regarded as such." The psychiatrists could have written "so-called" father, but I assume that would have been deemed derogatory. Hall never denied being my father, but he married Opal, a fact that infuriated the Carters. My grandmother, Anna

Pearl, was so disgusted that she refused to let Hall sign my birth certificate. She took it as a slap in the face that he didn't marry her daughter. So, in a move that was clearly not well thought out, Anna Pearl "punished" Hall by stopping him from acknowledging me as his son.

Thus, my birth certificate is one of the saddest documents I own. No matter what I have accomplished thus far in life, from visiting the White House to traveling around the globe, my birth certificate always humbles me. The section for the signature of my "putative" father is noticeably empty. Full name: blank. Age at time of this birth: blank. Birthplace: blank. Usual occupation: blank. Kind of business or industry: blank. And that's just what he was to me until the day he died: one big blank. When I needed a dad to play catch with: blank. When I needed a man to teach me how to pee standing up: blank. When I needed someone to teach me how to fight back at the bullies in school: blank.

My father's absence didn't eat at me until I became a man. As a child, I hardly missed him. Sadly, fatherless children were the norm in my community. To me, it seems the simplest thing, putting a goddamned name on a birth certificate, and I couldn't get even that. In fact, a complete stranger signed my birth certificate: Peter Liebert, MD, a physician at Mount Sinai. This white man—who didn't know me or my mother—signed his full name, and my own father didn't. Dr. Liebert didn't have a problem acknowledging my birth, so why did Dudley Hall? I couldn't understand why there was even a debate about acknowledging who my sperm donor was. Essentially that's all Dudley Hall was—a sperm donor. Dominic "Hall" would never be my name, thanks to family politics.

Through the years, I would always feel that my father didn't give a damn about me. Even though my mother's family had allegedly pushed Dudley away, I have always believed that my father could not have cared less about me, anyway. He made no attempt to be involved in my life, and, now that I am a man, I resent him for that lack of effort. He is more mysterious to me than my mother. I don't know much about him or his upbringing in Jamaica, nor do I care. No one has given me the exact details of his death; I just know that Dudley Hall is no more. I heard through the family grapevine that he died an alcoholic. I didn't go to his funeral, and neither did anyone in my family.

He contributed only his DNA to my life. How did he live with himself? He had a young son who needed him, and he virtually thumbed his nose at me. If he couldn't give me money, then, at the very least, he could have given me his time. It would've been nice to know that my father cared about me, even just a little bit. Instead, my father lived up the reputation of so many daddies—he accomplished little more than to become an expert sperm donor.

I don't mean to appear sexist here, but a woman, Aunt Inez, stepped up to teach me how to handle the tough guys at school. She handled that challenge just like a man, especially in helping me protect myself from one young man who regularly stole my money as I walked home from school. I cannot recall his name, but he was the neighborhood bully. Whenever he needed a few extra dollars, he considered me his personal banker.

First came the intimidating stare, then a few menacing words, and, in the end, a physical attack in which he stole everything I had in my pockets. His predation became such a regular occurrence that Aunt Inez intervened one day, but not in the way that I hoped. As I made my way home from school, Inez hid behind a store that I regularly passed and watched as the bully approached me. As we were passing by, she jumped from behind the store and confronted me, as if I were the bully. She said, "Now, either you beat his ass, or I am going to beat yours."

That statement was her way of teaching me to defend myself, but for a split second, I was scared to death. But faced with the wrath of either Inez or the bully, I dropped my book bag to the ground and beat the bully senseless. Afterward, that bully never bothered me again. My beloved aunt had done a fine job of teaching me how to survive the rough streets.

As I grew up, I became the first of a new generation of Carters. My mother, in her fragile mental condition, had to be both my mother and my father. I would learn through the psychiatric documents that she could handle neither set of responsibilities; in fact, she couldn't even handle the responsibility for herself.

Laverne Carter was born on October 19, 1944, in Augusta, Georgia. During her birth, she nearly killed her mother, Anna Pearl. Folks around town said that the baby just didn't want to come out. Anna Pearl lost a great deal of weight during her pregnancy, and she writhed in constant pain. She was in labor for a very long time, and, when Laverne was finally born, she cried nonstop and wouldn't accept Anna Pearl's breast. Without milk, the baby would most certainly die, so Laverne's great grandmother, Mary Jessie, stepped in to raise her.

As a toddler, Laverne thrived under the care of Mary Jessie, who was proud that she'd saved her helpless great-granddaughter. But over the years, Mary Jessie never wanted to let Laverne go.

"Don't take her from me now," Mary Jessie would say when Anna Pearl and her husband, Johnny, tried to take Laverne home. They couldn't possibly repay Mary Jessie for saving their baby girl, and they didn't feel right removing the pretty, button-nosed girl from Mary Jessie's care. As a sort of awkward reward for saving their daughter's life, they let Mary Jessie keep Laverne. After all, Mary Jesse had raised numerous other family members. But they would live to regret their decision, as Laverne would never get over what she thought of as abandonment by her parents. In her initial case study, Laverne gave a psychiatrist a slightly different twist of events.

> The patient was raised by a great-grandmother from age two months to sixteen years. Although the family has never stated the reason for this arrangement, they have apparently implied to the social worker that it was made because the patient was illegitimate.

Here was yet another bombshell: this was the first time I'd heard that my mother was illegitimate, though my relatives vehemently deny this allegation and my mother's birth certificate backs up their claim. Laverne Carter's birth certificate identifies Johnny Carter as her father and Anna Pearl Carter as her mother. I am inclined to believe that this was my mother's way of justifying why she was the only child her parents didn't raise together. But it's clear that my mother was never happy being reared outside her immediate family. Like me, she apparently felt vulnerable and unprotected. How ironic, I thought, that this feeling would be transferred to her firstborn! She had felt left out as a child, and I felt that my mother had left me out as well.

Another thunderbolt from the psychiatric records: evidence indicated that my mother had been raped. She told a Mount Sinai psychiatrist on July 17, 1970, that her first sexual experience "occurred at an early age with two uncles." She did not elaborate, and no record can be found of what that early age was.

Could this event have been what drove my mother insane? My mind spun with questions. If the men were her uncles, did they trick her or seduce her, or was the rape violent? Was it one solitary incident, or had it happened again and again? I had many questions, but I would never get those answers. Not even Aunt Inez knew about the rape.

Mary Jessie, Laverne's caretaker, lived close to Laverne's parents, and Laverne often visited her two younger sisters, Inez and Joann. Laverne adjusted the best she could to living away from her family. She was an aggressive, rough girl who didn't start fights but loved to end them. She beat the devil out of kids, both black and white, who bothered her or her sisters. Everyone soon understood not to dare Laverne to do anything, because she would never back down.

As Laverne got older, whenever she became unhappy with Mary Jessie, she would return to her parents. When she was unhappy with her parents, she would demand to return to Mary Jesse. This back-and-forth behavior became a pattern for Laverne, and a suitcase was always kept packed and ready for Laverne's departures.

Laverne wasn't prissy, but she loved being a cheerleader. She also made the basketball team in junior high school. She became popular with an air of confidence that eluded many girls of color who grew up in the segregated South. Inez says she had a twinkle in her eye, and boys were always attracted to her. For a while, Inez and Joanne were simply known as Laverne's sisters. Laverne's initial case evaluation gives a glimpse of her chutzpah. She told psychiatrists that "at the age of six or seven, she wanted to grow up fast, which she tried to do by putting cotton in her mother's bra and attempting to wear it."

When Laverne was about thirteen years old and was living with her parents, her emotional troubles began to surface. One day, Laverne woke up without the energy to get out of bed. She didn't respond to anything or anybody. The only way her relatives knew she was alive was by her breathing and her blinking eyes. Anna Pearl and Johnny came into her room and screamed, "Laverne, get out of that bed!" Laverne didn't budge. Johnny pulled the sheets back and picked up his daughter. He said it was just like holding a rag doll, and her head bounced from side to side. He laid her back down, and she stared at the ceiling, her chestnut eyes fixed on something, but no one could tell what. Her parents thought she would sleep off her emotions, but she didn't. They called the local hospital in Augusta, and black attendants responded, as was the custom in the segregated South. In the charts, doctors documented her early psychotic episodes.

> She developed dream states in which she could not control her behavior and felt as though she were "out of this world." In these states, she did such things as walk out on the street clad only in underwear, threaten another person with an ice pick, and try to commit suicide by walking out into traffic or by slashing her arms and legs or by drinking alcohol. An additional symptom of this period, which she has more recently reported, is hallucinations of little people who would pull at her clothes.

Reading this account, I felt even more compassion for my mother, who as a young teen had lived this horrific nightmare. I must have looked at my mother's arms a thousand times, but I cannot ever recall seeing scars on her arms. And to think that she had drunk alcohol to try to end her life makes me nauseous. But my mother's problems would only worsen with time.

She was transferred to the Milledgeville State Hospital in Milledgeville, Georgia, located more than two hours from where she was living. In the 1950s, the state hospital was a seg-regated institution. During her stay in the asylum, not only was my mother heavily medicated, but she also received between thirty-five and forty sessions of electroconvulsive therapy (ECT), or electrical shock. A treatment that made me cringe, a treatment I had seen only in the movies, was real-life treatment for my mother.

Science had decided ECT was an effective form of therapy for schizophrenia, though to outsiders the treatment looks cruel. After the patient is put to sleep, one electrode is attached above the temple on one side of the head, and another electrode is attached on the forehead. A current is sent through the brain to induce seizures, which can continue for more than a minute. About fifteen minutes after the seizures conclude, the patient is awakened.

I cannot imagine a young girl getting this shock treatment forty times. My mother had barely been fifteen years old. Stud-ies show that patients sometimes calm down after getting this treatment, but evidently the treatment did not ease my mother's problems.

When Laverne was released from the mental hospital, the family acted almost as if nothing had happened. When folks asked how Laverne was, her family said she had been sick. Only white folks were crazy; Negroes just got sick. Privately, family members knew what was going on, but they would say Laverne suffered from her nerves and that she had to take "nerve pills," which, in the black community, was a euphemism for psychiatric drugs. Other than the nerve pills, however, Laverne's mental illness was largely ignored.

Despite Laverne's sickness, life wasn't bad for the Carters in Augusta. My grandfather, Johnny, always had money in his pocket, and theirs was a two-car family, a rare luxury for Negroes in the 1950s. Both Johnny and Anna Pearl drove, another rarity. Johnny knew how to wheel and deal; he had a buddy who worked at Motor Vehicles and worked out a scheme to get a driver's license for Anna Pearl.

Both Johnny and Anna Pearl were proud people. Johnny was the "fish man" in that rural black town; he didn't own the fish delivery business, but he might as well have. He delivered fish in crates to stores all over town, and, when he could, he would stash a crate full of fresh fish aside—first for his family, then others to sell to his neighbors. It was theft, but he believed that the white owner of the business severely underpaid him for working from sunup to sundown, so he didn't think twice about it.

Unlike most black men in Augusta, Johnny, a short, wiry man, was self-sufficient. His three pretty girls didn't want for anything, and they never had to wear white kids' hand-me-downs like some of the other kids in the neighborhood had to do. The girls occasionally got tired of eating fish, but they stopped complaining once they realized some of their friends ate only once a day during the years immediately following World War II.

Aunt Inez was especially proud of how her father had hustled to make money for the family. Inez would be the shining star of the Carters, much like her father—always the one with money, always the one with a plan. The youngest child, Joann, was a light-skinned, chubby girl. She was a homebody, preferring to stay in the house all day long.

Although Laverne was suffering, Grandma Anna Pearl kept her eyes on a big dream. Tens of thousands of Georgians fled to the big city, New York, during the Great Migration; which is the time when blacks in the South moved to northern cities like New York, Philadelphia, Chicago, and Detroit in search of a better living and jobs. Anna Pearl was awestruck by stories of big buildings and good jobs. Like many Negro women in the South at that time, Anna Pearl was a domestic and made fifteen dollars a week. Johnny made more than twice that, thirty-five dollars a week, not bad money for the 1950s—but it could've been better. Whenever Anna Pearl got her hair done, she read the magazine *Ebony* and fantasized about the Harlem Renaissance, the Cotton Club, Joe Louis, and the Apollo Theater, all in New York City.

Augusta was a quiet, cozy town, nothing like Harlem, and that was just fine with Johnny. He would often say, "As long as Negroes keep having fish fries, I'll always have a job." Anna Pearl tried to forget about Harlem, but, one by one, her relatives kept relocating there, and she soon knew she would follow in their footsteps. By mail, her newly crowned New Yorker relatives sent black-and-white photographs. She saw her cousins sitting on steps that seem to lead to heaven itself. In the background was a three-story brownstone with lots of windows, just like the ones she had seen in *Ebony*. In the photos, all the transplanted relatives were smiling much brighter than they had while living in Augusta.

Anna Pearl was preparing her escape to New York even as she cleaned floors in Georgia. She was a top-notch domestic and could clean a house from top to bottom in no time. Folks used to say you could eat off the floor when Anna Pearl was finished cleaning. She was so good that she signed up with a firm in New York City, and, one week after finding a job, Anna Pearl was in the back of a Greyhound bus bound for the Port Authority Bus Terminal in Manhattan. My grandfather and my aunts Joann and Inez couldn't believe she had finally worked up the nerve to go—especially by herself.

But the Carters were more than a little intrigued with Anna Pearl's trip to New York City. They were all delighted that she had set out on her own to discover the big city, yet they were fearful of what the North held for her. Would she make it up north, and would she send for her family? Anna Pearl, the rock of the Carter family, said she just wanted to test New York out, since she had a place to stay with her cousins. If she didn't like what she found, she'd come back to Augusta. But deep down inside, Anna Pearl knew she wouldn't return to Augusta. When she got off the bus at Port Authority, she admired the look and the feel of fast-talking, fast-walking New Yorkers. They stood proud and tall just like her family did in Augusta. She paid especially close attention to black people, particularly those who worked in the station, hauling bags. These men with big, bright smiles, wearing shiny shoes and uniforms, acted as if they made really good money. Anna Pearl instantly fell in love with New York, and she would later say, "One day the Carters gonna be a big deal in this city," though she had no idea that her baby grandson—me—would later grace the cover of the *New York Times* television guide and would be profiled in many publications.

Her cousin Jimmy picked her up from Port Authority in a shiny black Ford and took her to 201 West 121st Street. It was the same building she had seen in the picture her cousins had sent in the mail. As they pulled up out front, Jimmy blew the horn, and her cousins came running down those heavenly stairs like a real celebrity was in town. They hugged and kissed her and almost knocked each other over, taking turns to greet Anna Pearl. Inside, the house was bright and airy with high ceilings. Anna couldn't get over the number of rooms—seven rooms with a communal bath and a kitchen that they all shared. Everybody had a bed of his or her own. The house also had couches and looked like a scene in the movies—much nicer, Anna Pearl thought, than the three-room house her family rented in Augusta.

When the family asked how Laverne was, Anna Pearl simply said she was sick and was doing okay. When they pressed her, she revealed a little bit about Laverne's nerves acting up, but she would not talk badly about her daughter. I'm convinced my grandmother was a little ashamed of her daughter's illness, and, at the same time, she did not fully understand Laverne's medical diagnosis.

Anna Pearl's agency placed her in New Jersey as a domestic. She became a sleep-in, a maid who lives with a family, takes care of the children and the house, and resides in a tiny room with only one day off each week—Sunday.

Since she didn't have to worry about food or shelter, Anna Pearl saved all of her money, and, when she had twenty-five dollars, she sent for her husband, because she couldn't afford to move the whole family at once. She made more money in the North than she had in the South, but not enough to rent and furnish an apartment for her children. They would have to wait until she could save more money.

Anna Pearl made friends with a cook named Roberta. They were the perfect team; they laughed and kept each other entertained while doing their work. She also ended up doing domestic work in the Hamptons, a playground for the rich and famous on Long Island, New York. Anna Pearl was the domestic for the handsome actor Eli Wallach, who had appeared in movies like *The Misfits* and *The Magnificent Seven.*

My grandfather Johnny, now in New York, started work with the same couple that his wife worked for, except that he was the chauffeur. Later on, he also worked as a maintenance man for a local union on Wall Street.

The girls had stayed behind in Georgia and were under the strict supervision of an aunt. Anna Pearl planned to save more money and then send for her girls, but a phone call sent her rushing back to Augusta earlier than expected. Laverne, who was living with her great grandmother, was back in the mental hospital.

Anna Pearl and Johnny went back to Augusta to visit Laverne, and, while they were there, they packed up Inez and Joann and brought them to New York. Anna Pearl and Johnny wrote to Laverne from New York; but, when Laverne received a letter from Inez postmarked New York, New York, she was devastated. From a psychiatric ward, she fired off a letter to her father, saying, "You took Inez and Joann up to New York and left me here. How could you do that? I guess you have the two you love, so the hell with me, right? I'll just stay here in this crazy house until I drop dead, and then you'll really be happy."

The whole family read that letter over and over. For the first time, they realized that Laverne felt left out. Johnny was especially hurt because he believed he'd never showed favoritism to any of his daughters. Three months later, Anna Pearl and Johnny sent money for a bus ticket for Laverne, who came to New York on a Greyhound bus, alone. Now Anna Pearl felt she had succeeded in saving her family from what she called "a backwater town." The Carters were now New Yorkers and proud of it.

When they picked up Laverne from Port Authority, they thought she looked like a country girl. They teased her about her pointed blue sneakers and flowery skirt. But otherwise, they said, she looked good. Whatever torment went on in her mind, Laverne's face didn't show it.

Anna Pearl told her friends she was never going back to Augusta and that she didn't even want to be buried back home. "If I die, sprinkle my ashes along Seventh Avenue," she would tell Inez. But life in New York was not easy. With Anna Pearl and Johnny working so hard, the girls were pretty much on their own, a situation which proved dangerous for Laverne and her unstable mind. The secret of her mental illness came out when one day, at a cousin's apartment on Harlem's East Side, Laverne grabbed a knife, climbed out of the kitchen window, and walked feverishly up and down the fire escape, mumbling under her breath that she was going to kill somebody. The young girls, all in their mid to late teens, knew they were not strong enough to disarm Laverne, so they called the authorities, who tackled her and sent her directly to Bellevue's mental ward in Manhattan.

Bellevue is home to one of the oldest mental institutions in the United States. Laverne would often stay at places like Bellevue for weeks, if not months.

Laverne's sisters Inez and Joann were upset, but they weren't frightened, because Laverne never attacked them. Other signs of her mental illnesses were more subtle. She would sometimes abruptly say, "I gotta wash up." Then she would take baths over and over again in a single day.

When her father witnessed her bizarre behavior, he would tell Anna Pearl, "She's gotta go to the doctor."

Sometimes Laverne would go by herself to the mental unit at Mount Sinai Medical Center for a regular psychiatric check up. If she was truly acting strangely, like washing her hands and bathing excessively, the institution would keep her for a while.

The mental ward was a revolving door for my mother before I was born, and I am sad that her condition did not change much after my arrival. By the time I entered the world, my mother was hopelessly caught in a vicious cycle of inpatient status in mental wards, bizarre and violent behavior, and depression.

Even with her emotional problems, Laverne tried to get an education, despite being left back once in the fifth grade. She made it to the eleventh grade, but, unfortunately, her past came back to haunt her. While she was in high school in New York, her medical records arrived from Georgia. According to my mother's medical transcript, she was told that she had to leave school because of her mental instability. The report notes:

> After being discharged from Rockland State, she returned to high school but was told by the principal that, for reasons not clear to her, she was no longer welcome there.

While Inez and Joann were in school, Laverne stayed by herself and sat on the stoop of the apartment building. But my mother did try to work. For a short time, Laverne was a volunteer nurse. She also did sales work for a department store, a job that was short lived.

While looking for work and trying to get vocational training, Laverne had lots of free time. That's how she met Hall. He lived on 147th Street, but his friends lived across the street from Laverne.

Dudley Hall was involved in the illegal trade of "numbers running," and he always had money. He served as a lookout for the numbers man, the person who held the bets and the cash. Dudley was always looking left or right, peering down the street as far as his eyes could see, looking for the cops. If he saw a flat-foot, he gave a certain whistle, and the numbers man would hide his betting slips, stuff the money in his crotch, and disappear until the coast was clear.

When Dudley wasn't looking out for cops, he was looking at Laverne or some other woman. Laverne always stared at his gold teeth and his shoes. She wasn't one to look a man in the eye, even though she was, by many accounts, eye candy herself. She was an attractive woman who admired Diana Ross and the Supremes. She even bought a wig in the style of these popular singers. Her cocoa-brown complexion was clear and beautiful.

Hall was smitten. He called her a shy, little country girl. And she would snap back, "Who you callin' country? You ain't from here, neither." That remark would make Dudley laugh. Sometimes Dudley would take Laverne and her sisters to the corner store and buy them sodas, and Laverne's eyes would nearly pop out when he pulled out a wad of bills. Her father used to show money in that way, too, with funds from the maintenance jobs he worked around Harlem. Laverne liked men with money.

One of Dudley's friends had a room that Dudley borrowed to sleep with his girlfriends. Laverne knew she had to keep their relationship a secret, but she didn't care if everyone found out. She knew he was sleeping around with other women, but his other activities were not her major concern. Having him in her life was the top priority.

By the time I was born, the secret was out, and Hall was nowhere to be found. I joined my mother, my grandparents, and my two aunts in a crowded apartment on 121st Street. I shared a room with my mother and my aunts. Our room was very large, so my crib fit in fine. My grandparents had the other room, which also served as a living room. The apartment was clean but rat infested. Ultimately, the living arrangements became a time bomb because Anna Pearl second-guessed everything Laverne did with her baby.

I was the first person Laverne could claim as her own, and everybody kept telling her what to do. She tried to be a good mother, but she couldn't stand my aunts and her mother's second-guessing her.

"Burp Dominic this way, put on the diaper cloth that way, and don't let him sleep with that bottle in his mouth," her mother told her. Anna Pearl deeply loved me and showed her love—maybe because I was the first baby boy in her life or because she wanted to show love to her daughter through me.

I can remember Anna Pearl's warm bear hugs to this day. She used to call me "Grandma's little boy." I remember watching her cook. She wore a faded yellow housedress that always reeked of whatever she had cooked that day. A dented can of used grease stood on the back of the yellow stove. Cooking oil was recycled in many black households. Bacon grease could be used a hundred different ways. Grandma would oil the pan with grease before scrambling eggs, and I remember savoring the delectable taste of bacon and eggs cooked with the same oil.

No one fried a bologna sandwich like my grandmother. I stood next to her many times as she put a dollop of recycled cooking oil into a pan and tossed two round pieces of bologna into the pan. As the fire scorched the pan, the lunchmeat crackled and sizzled to a deep brown color, and Grandma flipped the pieces over, one by one, with a fork. The bologna was done when it bubbled in the middle. My meals were not always balanced, but they were always sprinkled with love.

Oh yes, I adored my grandmother, but my mother clearly did not, nor did she try to hide her lack of affection. Even as a child, I could detect their coldness toward each other. There was warmth between Anna Pearl, Inez, and Joann. But between my grandmother and Laverne, there were no hugs and kisses upon greeting or embraces upon parting. Whatever love and affection they felt for each other was given almost exclusively to me. My mother was a poster child for defying her mother. Apparently, Laverne interpreted my grandmother's affection toward me as a threat, and she called her own mother's bluff at my expense.

When I was about three years old, my mother, slowly unraveling emotionally again, dressed me in my best clothes and prepared to take me out.

"Where you going with that boy?" my grandfather said, as my grandmother glared at my mother.

"We're going out," my mother snapped back.

"Leave the boy here, then," my grandfather said.

"No, I'm taking him with me," my mother responded.

My grandparents told me later that they had a bad feeling about her taking me out, but they let us go. My mother and I got on the bus and went directly to the Bureau of Child Welfare. She dropped me off there and told the staff to place me in foster care because she could no longer handle me. She told the social worker she feared she would hurt me. And just like that, I became a foster child in the notorious New York City Child Welfare System, the same system about which I later reported sordid tales of neglect and abuse when I became a journalist.

Just as my mother returned home without me, my aunts and grandparents received a phone call from the agency, telling them about my placement in a shelter. The entire family began to scream at Laverne, who solemnly walked into her room. Aunt Inez says Laverne told her that she had heard voices telling her to give me away so that she could go back to school and make something of her life. Those voices were her mental illness at work, and, according to her psychiatric records, she deeply regretted doing this to me. She told her doctor later that "she felt guilty and … attempted suicide."

Fortunately, I have no recollection of my two-month stay in the shelter and then with a foster care family, but my imagination still sends chills down my spine. Why did my own mommy leave me in a strange place where I could get lost in the system or even be physically hurt? I must have longed for my dear grandmother, who dealt with a lot of red tape to get me out. Child welfare officials couldn't immediately turn me over to my grandmother because my mother still lived with her. The welfare officials had to conduct interviews with every member of the household before returning me to the family. Aunt Inez and Grandpa Johnny came to see me at the shelter once and were going to steal me away, but guards stayed with them the whole time. Thanks to my mother, I was under the protection of the child welfare system, and my family, for a time, could not do anything about my situation.

I was finally released to my grandmother, but things would never be the same between Anna Pearl and Laverne. My family generally believes that my mother gave me away to spite my grandmother, as if to say, "How dare you love him when you didn't love me?" That would not be the last time my mother used me as a pawn to get back at my grandmother. Throughout my life, their relationship resembled a chess match in which my mother tried to checkmate her own mother.

From that time on, my grandmother Anna Pearl treated me as if I were her own child. My aunt Inez and Joann pitched in a lot, too. When they returned from high school each afternoon, they took care of me until I fell asleep and then did their homework. But Laverne was sick of the crowded Harlem apartment on 121st Street and considered moving out on her own. She was frustrated with her family and the dilapidated building. Once, when I was asleep, Laverne and Inez saw a rat jump out from my crib. I couldn't even sleep in peace. If my mother wasn't trying to give me away, then a rodent was trying to nibble at my body. Perhaps seeing that rat had been the final straw for my mother.

Soon, Laverne found her own place to live, but she couldn't make a living on her own. She went on welfare and moved into a two-bedroom apartment in the Bronx, bordering the Cross Bronx Expressway. She got a kick out of the fact that it was on Carter Avenue. My mom and I first lived on our own at 1691 Carter Avenue. If anyone was worried about my mother living alone with a young child, they never said anything. No one ever talked badly about Laverne, but everyone understood the concept of "don't make her mad." The family feared that Laverne would take her anger out on me or further distance herself from her parents and sisters.

We lived on the fourth floor in another dilapidated tenement, but it was ours. Laverne could finally be a mother without anybody telling her what to do. But a short time later, her parents and sisters moved into a different apartment in the same building. The Carters were all living together again in the East Bronx. I was about three years old.

Harlem was no paradise, but it had been better than the Bronx. At least Harlem had a cultural history. The Bronx's biggest claim to fame was the Yankees; whereas Harlem seemed to have everything: theaters, soul food shacks, and music ringing in the air from someone's car or apartment. But nobody appeared to care about the Bronx, and their lack of concern showed. Nature had been evicted from this community, which was paved over with cement and stone. Strewn glass replaced green grass. Street signs stood where trees should have been. Rolling hills were paved over and made rocky streets. Food, obviously, could not be picked fresh from fields and could be bought only in a store. Even the stores were not markets, but were mostly bodegas or corner haunts where the store owners sold sometimes-spoiled food to poor blacks and Latinos who were more concerned with the price than the expiration date.

Even the air in the Bronx was spoiled and sometimes life threatening. Most kids in my area suffered from asthma because they were nearly strangled by the pollution from the many trucks and cars that packed the expressways and parkways cutting through the neighborhood. At night we never heard crickets chirp, and, in the morning, we never heard sparrows sing. The sounds of the Bronx were all mechanical: roaring subways, screeching buses, backfiring trucks, horn-blowing cars, humming elevators, and slamming doors.

These were the sights and sounds that framed my youth. I didn't tiptoe out onto a wooden porch to begin my day. Instead, as if I were some kind of prisoner, I peeked from behind windows protected by bars. It was certainly no surprise to me that many of my childhood friends later ended up in jail, because they'd been well prepared for incarceration. Our childhood, our precious childhood, was a landscape of despair, and, if a child allowed this poisonous environment to get into his system, he was doomed to a life of mediocrity.

Residents in the building literally had a bird's-eye view of one of the most congested highways in the city, the Cross Bronx Expressway, which often played host to nasty car accidents. The biggest ones involved trucks that spilled gas and sent everyone running, even the cops. Observing from the fire escape was like watching a movie.

Emotionally, my mother started to slip away again. Her family was interfering in her business. She saw less and less of Dudley and more and more of her sisters and her mother.

At this time, I was an inquisitive, bright little kid. Aunt Inez bought all of my clothes and would take me, her cute nephew, for walks. She had a good job with the city, and often spent her money on me. I had to have been the best-dressed child in the neighborhood. Some of my outfits were complete with bow ties and cashmere coats. My grandmother cooked all of my food to make sure her boy would "eat right." Everyone in the family, except my mother, saw something positive in me. My relatives invested in my appearance, determined that I would not look like the other kids. They took me on shopping sprees to department stores. All of my family's hopes were pinned to my little trench coats and shiny shoes. In a community that turned its back on the future, they held me up as their shining prince. In their eyes, I was as close to royalty as one could get, though my mother was no Queen Mum.

Indeed, I felt like a motherless child, even though my mother stood right before my eyes. I loved my mother, just like any other fresh-faced youngster does, but I sensed that she was turning on me. Or perhaps she was turning on herself. The tone of her voice terrified me, and she became more hostile with both her words and her actions. I could sense that she viewed me with scorn. Her behavior showed a sad reversal of motherhood that would play itself out to my disadvantage.

As if she were running from her family or from a landlord looking for her unpaid rent, Laverne took off with me again when I was about five years old. We moved a few miles away to 7487 Vice Avenue in the South Bronx. This address proved to be an ominous one. The South Bronx housing areas were among the worst ghettoes in the United States. But because of my mother's mental instability, she didn't work, so she didn't have much choice in where or how she lived.

In the late 1960s, Laverne wasn't looking so good any more, even though the psychiatrists at Mount Sinai noted numerous times in their official reports that she was an attractive woman. She didn't fix her hair all the time, and sometimes she stayed in her pajamas all day long and stared into space. I didn't know much at the time and I certainly don't remember much, but I do recall thinking that my mommy was not like the other mommies I saw in the neighborhood.

The other mothers held normal conversations, but my mother just stared at people, almost as if she had to concentrate hard on what a person was saying. The other mothers seemed to dress in the latest styles, and for a while my mother did as well. One of my favorite photographs of my mother in her prime was of the two of us at the Central Park Zoo. She looked like one of the Supremes, complete with a sexy, short black dress, a fashionable wig, and Diana Ross-style sunglasses. But that attractiveness didn't last for long. Not long after the trip to the zoo, my mother seemed to unravel in both appearance and mental state. She threw her clothes together, and she no longer wore dainty little dresses. The next time Mommy got sick, her mustard-colored boy with skinny legs and narrow eyes was caught in the middle of her psychotic world.

Sometimes during the day, my mother and I had lots of fun. With whatever was left over from her paltry welfare check, we would go to the zoo. She would treat me to all the ice cream I could eat, and we would visit the nearby park. But when the sun went down, my mother revealed her dark side.

I was a mischievous little boy, and my mother had little tolerance for my antics. I faintly recall whippings with electrical cords, but nothing as severe as the beatings that doctors described in my mother's psychiatric history at Mount Sinai. My grandmother did hear of some of those beatings and sternly warned my mother that she had to stop attacking and beating me. Because I was so light-skinned, bruises showed up prominently on my face and body. I was an abuse victim. My grandmother later threatened my mother and told her that every time she hit me, my grandmother would hit her back. On at least one occasion, Anna Pearl fulfilled her threat. But my mother didn't stop—or maybe she couldn't.

Between 1970 and 1974, my mother continued visiting mental hospitals, mostly as an outpatient. She was still heavily medicated on Thorazine. I would like to think that she was in a drug-induced state when the worst happened. I was about seven years old. That year, my world grew to consist mostly of Saturday morning cartoons and comic books, as well as a sick introduction to sex abuse.

One night when I was in bed, nearly asleep, my mother called my name in a singsong tone: "Do-mi-nic." The way she said my name, I knew better than to answer, "What?" Her tone clearly meant "Come here."

The one gift time has given me is that I don't remember exactly what happened, but what I do recall has scarred me for life. I remember being ordered to climb into my mother's full-sized bed. This request was odd because I had my own bed on the living room couch. The lights were out, and she whispered for me to take my clothes off. She usually told me to take them off when it was time to get dressed for school. But this was still bedtime, so I didn't understand what I was getting undressed for.

One by one, I took off my pajama pants, then the top. I looked at her when I got to my underwear. She nodded. I pulled off my underwear, too. How could I *not* obey my mother? She motioned for me to come closer to her. She had never really invited me into her bed. I slid over to her, and she lifted the sheets high so I could see her body. I got under the sheets and learned that she was naked, too. The smell was different, a little musky, unlike my sheets. She whispered, "Touch it," as she groped her breasts.

Mommy never told me that she loved me, so maybe this was her way of showing me. To think of this today makes me want to throw up. I rubbed her breasts and nuzzled my face deep inside her cleavage like she told me to do. I knew I had to do what Mommy said, but my instincts told me that something wasn't right. I have tried to erase this scene from my mind many times, but our genitals touched. My mother seemed aroused, and I remember seeing by the dim glow of the streetlights that her eyes were slightly rolled back in her head. I was terrified. She cut her eyes left to right as if she knew she'd be in big trouble if she got caught. But the door was locked and I was her captive—period.

Was this my initiation in the big world—into the big bed? The feel of coarse hair in her vaginal area perplexed me. Hair grows down there? I thought. Was I finally ready to do the things Mommy did with her boyfriends while I watched television? Was I doing it right? Mommy's breath was hot when she kissed me. My mother had never kissed me on my cheek, and now she was kissing me on my mouth. Was she finally making up for lost time? My little yellow body fit on top of hers like a tiny lifeboat on a huge cruise ship. But I was drowning in her sick world, though I didn't know it at the time.

Mommy turned me on my side, and I touched her everywhere: her hips, her thighs, her back, and that thick coarse hair between her legs. She touched my undeveloped penis. She rubbed it until I feared it was going to fall off. Nobody had ever touched me there before, not like that, to be sure. Mommy didn't look me directly in the eye, but she made strange noises and kept moving her hands. She lifted my whole body, all seventy pounds of me, and she kept moaning and mumbling and caressing. It didn't hurt, so I figured it couldn't be all that bad.

My mommy had never showed me this much attention. Whenever she picked me up from school, she barely said a word. Sometimes she just said, "Hey." When she gave me food, she would say, "You'd better not make a mess." I wouldn't get an "I love you" or a "You're such a good boy" ever. I was starved for her affection, and I was too young to discern when it crossed the line. I stayed in the bed with my mother for the remainder of the night.

I don't remember what I did when I awakened. Most likely, I went into the living room and watched cartoons. But like a cancer, this sick encounter began to fester in my young mind. Slowly but surely, over the days, weeks, months, and years that followed, I started to realize what she did had been wrong. Nobody told me. I figured it out from the ways other mothers and sons treated one another. My first memorable lesson in life was distinguishing the difference between my mother and the mothers of my classmates. My mother never participated in class trips, she never checked my homework, and she never talked to my teachers about how I was doing. When I developed friendships with other kids my age, I gathered that their mothers never did the things to them that my mother did to me. I knew better than to ask my friends—I could just tell. Over the years I often worried, asking myself, "Will I be a freak of nature? Will I ever even want a woman? Who can I tell about this awful stuff?"

I was years away from puberty, yet to this point, life had handed me one bad card after another. I was conceived in a closet, reared in the ghetto, humbled by poverty, abandoned by my father, and neglected, beaten, and sexually abused by my mother—the one person who was supposed to be my biggest protector. When I should have been learning my ABCs, I was instead learning how not to make my mother mad and how to tiptoe around her temper.

I've heard it said that children are free spirited, but I don't remember ever being free when I was young. My mind and my heart carried a heavy burden as far back as I can remember. As a child, I carried the pain of an adult. As an adult, I carried the pain of a child.

2

I kept our sick time together to myself. I did not obsess or cry about it. My mother acted as though nothing happened, and so did I. I honestly didn't know at the time how to interpret what had happened. For all I knew, as a child, all mothers did this to their sons. I knew it happened, but I instinctively knew it was something to be ashamed of, so I blocked it out. My soul slowly turned cold to the abuse and to my mother. I wasn't really even angry, just indifferent.

My grandmother and my aunts would never guess what happened, and I knew better than to tell them. I certainly knew better, when I was a child, than to confront my mother. I had no rights in Laverne's world. I was not respected in any way. When I misbehaved, she handed down her judgments like a rogue judge, swiftly and harshly. She showed no sympathy whatsoever for me, and all I could do was take it.

Bedtime suddenly took on a new meaning. After that awful incident with my mother, I felt that life had handed me a secret envelope. And every night, as I laid my head on my pillow, I had to safely secure that secret envelope away in my heart, vowing to never reveal its contents. I began carrying a great burden that would follow me like a dismal shadow for the rest of my life.

My burden and the sick behavior were all very subtle. You would think that something as cataclysmic as "sex abuse" would come with a thunderous explosion, almost as if someone had appeared in the sky and screamed, "Dominic, your life will never be the same from here on!" But my life was rather quiet as I slept on the living room couch in our squalid apartment. No bells or whistles of sex abuse rang out, nor were there tears or shrieks in the middle of the night. Just silence. As I quietly lay down to sleep night after night, an unspeakable bitterness engulfed my soul. My mind gave birth to many troubling thoughts. The birth of confusion was among the most damaging. Something inside would whisper, "Why did this happen to me? What did it mean? Will it happen again?" Those inner fears went on for years and years.

Like most children, I was inquisitive, but these were questions no child should have to ask. My confusion then met its close cousin, blame. I gradually turned on myself and asked, "Is my mommy dirty?" And the dreaded questions followed: "Was I dirty? Was I bad?" Truthfully, I knew the answers before I even asked the questions. And the answers essentially marked the death of my childhood innocence. I didn't shout my new self-truth from the rooftops, but I began to view myself as dirty and bad, and it wouldn't be long before my actions followed my thoughts.

The first person I turned on was my mother. With every birthday that passed, my instincts told me there was something terribly wrong with what she did. I was too young to express my disgust, but that perfect love that a boy typically has for his mother dissipated from inside me. Until my mother made this tragic assault, I had felt faultless, blameless, and free. Afterward I felt guilty, shamed, and bound. And it was my mother who was responsible for my prepubescent entry into what I now viewed as an unsettling world.

My biggest dilemma was that I didn't have a stable home. As I continued grade school, I split my time between our apartment on Vice Avenue and my grandmother's new residence on Topping Avenue in the Bronx, which was only about eight blocks from Carter Avenue, also adjacent to the Cross Bronx Expressway. I didn't know it at the time, but I lived with my grandmother at times when my mother's condition worsened or when my mother needed to be institutionalized. When she was locked up, I felt free, but, when she was released, I felt bound.

Sometimes I slept on my grandmother's couch, and other times I slept on my mother's couch. I just went back and forth from couch to couch, never having a space to call my own. The instability made my life that much more puzzling. My only connection with stability was television, and I realized early that the children on television who were my age didn't live the way I did. Kids in families like the one I saw on *The Brady Bunch* had two parents, their own bedrooms, and a perfect home. Television told me that something was wrong with my life because mine was nothing—and I mean *nothing*—like that. Even as I noted the stark contrasts between my life and the lives of television characters, I never let the disparity depress me. I didn't grow up reading books, either, so I didn't escape into a world of poetry or fantasy. Television gave me all my information. If the details weren't produced for film, I didn't see them.

Despite all the confusion that went on in my young life, I developed a sense of power and a sense of hope. I had a hunch that I was not a hopeless case. Though despair unfolded all around me, I never lost hope. It must have been an inborn, gut feeling because I certainly had every reason not to have hope. I had been handed a virtual round-trip ticket to the victim train, yet I refused to climb on board.

All hell was breaking loose around me, but my grandmother and my aunt did their best to bring a piece of heaven into my life by loving me unconditionally. They purposefully constructed my environment so I would be out of touch with my mother's reality. I wasn't allowed to play outside too often, and I was sheltered from many other kids in the neighborhood. No one discussed my mother's mental illness in my presence, and, as a result, I didn't know exactly what was going on in my mother's life. In retrospect, my relatives made the right decision. Other than the sexual abuse I experienced firsthand, I didn't have a clue that I was disadvantaged. I didn't even realize that I was illegitimate. There was so much love around me that I didn't even miss my mother when she disappeared for months on end, nor did I miss my father. Dominic Carter, for all intents and purposes, was living like a boy in a bubble.

My grandmother must have been a brokenhearted woman, but she never shed a tear around me. She lived through great heartache because she was separated from her husband as one of her daughters fought mental illness. In the twilight of her life, she became a mother again, this time to me, while she was battling heart disease and diabetes. She never complained or appeared burdened. I was showered with so much love and praise that I firmly believed the world was my oyster. I was still happy and still had a song in my heart. Like many children, I was confused and embarrassed at times, but I could still smile.

When my mother returned home from mental hospitals, she would sometimes smile, too. I tried to be happy to see her, but I was afraid to be left alone with her. She seemed scary and intimidating. Whenever we went to the park in the neighborhood, I felt that I was walking her, rather than her walking me. She was often in a drug-induced state, and she walked and talked very slowly. As though she was staring through me, she often slurred my name so that it sounded like "Do … mi … nic."

It was becoming increasingly clear that my mother was incapable of handling me, especially when she had to pick me up at school. She was supposed to come get me at elementary school at 3:00 every school day, but she failed miserably. I have vivid memories of walking home from school alone and waiting in front of our building on Vice Avenue. She wore a bright red coat, and, at every red coat I saw, I would anxiously stand up, only to sit back down on the stoop and wait some more. Sometimes other mothers in the building would feel sorry for me and take me to their apartments. They didn't realize I felt sorry too—I felt sorry that my mother couldn't care for me the way the other mothers did. But even as a child, I tried to stay positive.

But, when my grandmother was around, I didn't feel sorry for myself. She was my most ardent protector. My mother answered to no one except my grandmother. Whenever my grandmother found out I had been left alone, she would scold my mother severely. I can recall my grandmother telling off my mother, and my mother offering excuse after excuse. However, I knew that I should stay very still when my mother went on her rampages because, if I made one wrong move, my mother would beat the hell out of me in private. I tuned everything out by watching television, which was my great escape.

Sometimes my mother was late picking me up after school because of her boyfriends. I recall one in particular, a tall, hairy man with a beard. His name was Luther. Instead of helping me with my homework, my mother would tell me to watch television, so she could "talk" to Luther. She would close the shutters and the door of her bedroom, and I would hear Luther and her making strange noises. Even as a youngster, I found it easy to figure out they were having sex in her bedroom. Those noises were eerily familiar and sounded passionate and intense. I would turn the television down and listen very carefully to these men my mother gave her attention and her body to. I was especially intrigued because of what had occurred between my mother and me. Some of the sounds were reminiscent of our fateful night together.

After the sex act was over, Luther wouldn't stick around. None of my mother's men did. When Luther or one of the other men left, my mother would suddenly be twenty dollars richer, after having no money at all. She wasn't a prostitute, but most of the boyfriends my mother had somehow paid for her services. How could I possibly know the men were paying my mother? Before they arrived, she would tell me that we had just a little money for food or anything else. But after the man left, my mother always mysteriously had cash in her wallet. By my definition, Laverne wasn't a call girl because she took money only from men whom she was sexually involved with.

My father was not one of the male visitors who paid money for sex with my mother. I saw him just a handful of times in my life. Sometimes my mother would grab me and take me to see my "no-good daddy," as she called him. Whenever she got word of which Harlem street corner he was hanging out on, she would take me to see him so she could get some money. He didn't pay child support, and he was never held financially or even morally responsible for being my father. He was just chased down every now and then so Laverne could get a few dollars from him.

I remember my few conversations with my dad being short and to the point. In his thick Jamaican accent, he would ask, "Hey, boy, how are you, and how is school?" I would reply, "I'm okay." Sometimes he would ask, "What grade are you in?" but never much more than that. I received no hug, not even a pat on the back. He would exchange a few terse words with my mother while she tightly gripped my hand, and then he'd reach into his pocket and pull out a few dollars. That was his child support—eight dollars here, five dollars there. I suppose that's all I was worth to him.

But for almost every gap in my young life, my grandmother was there to fill it. Aunt Joann reminded me of an especially brutal incident that prompted me to run away from my mother for good. Apparently, when I was eleven and suffered another vicious beating delivered by my mother, I bolted out of my mother's house and got on the Number 41 bus along Webster Avenue. When my aunt reminded me of this incident, which I had long forgotten, I suddenly recalled sitting on a bus that was headed to my grandmother's house. Where I got the money to ride the bus I do not know. Perhaps I pleaded with the bus driver to let me get to my grandmother's house. But I took that long, bumpy ride from the southern part of the borough to the East Side and got off the bus at 184th Street, knowing I would never go back to Laverne.

When I arrived at my grandmother's door, she welcomed me with open arms and remarked to Aunt Joann, "That's it! He's staying here now." I was fighting for a safe place to live, and I was only in the fifth grade. My grandmother, Aunt Joann, and I lived together at 365 East 184th Street in the East Bronx. My grandmother did not file for legal custody of me because she didn't like dealing with the court system, especially after going through hell to get me out of foster care. But my grandmother would later regret not registering as my lawful guardian.

For the first time in my life, I felt completely safe. Grandmother, Aunt Joann, and I lived together on the third floor in a fairly decent, nine-story building located just off Webster Avenue in the East Bronx. We had a two-bedroom apartment (Aunt Inez was living on her own). Another first was that I had my own room and a twin-sized bed. On my wall, I taped a poster of football great Walter Payton of the Chicago Bears.

Grandma always picked me up from school on time. Sometimes she was there before the other mommies, and she kissed me on sight.

I began to call my grandmother "Ma" and to call my mother "Laverne." The older I got, the more I felt she was unworthy of the title "mommy." I figured that "mommy" was a term of endearment and affection—neither of which Laverne fulfilled for me. Revoking that title was my first act of defiance. Whenever my mother visited my grandmother's apartment, I would say "Hey, Laverne." From that day until the day she died, I would never call Laverne "Mom." With what little power I had, I blessed my grandmother with that title. Anna Pearl had become my surrogate mother.

But I was to have no surrogate father. My grandfather, Johnny, was long gone. The streets of New York had claimed his heart and soul, too. The family did not speak ill of Johnny, but I would later figure out that he had become hooked on using heroin, a habit he picked up after arriving in Harlem. In the 1970s, he became a full-fledged junkie. As sad as his situation was, I respect my grandfather because he always tried to fight his drug dependency, and ultimately he won. But he would never get back together with Grandma. My grandfather lived with a woman in Harlem; her name was Minnie. Sometimes Aunt Inez would take me to see him. Even though the civil rights movement had promised a bright future for blacks, many black men like my grandfather would never reap the benefits of those social changes. Johnny Carter, once a proud man who had hustled seafood to make a living for his family in the Deep South, now numbed himself with a white, odorless narcotic to avoid the harsh reality of the inner city.

My grandfather was not unlike millions of blacks from the South who migrated to the North for a better life, only to find that their lives were worse in a big city—indeed, much worse. Tragically, many found solace in heroin and alcohol. When life became more than they could bear, they may have viewed drugs as their only escape. Life was hard for these men. Unless a man had a job with the city government, money did not come easily. Education was not considered a priority in the segregated South, so many people, like my grandparents, struggled with the little education they had, and often it wasn't enough to bring their dreams to reality.

In spite of Grandpa's heroin addiction, my family allowed me to hang out with him from time to time. He took me to see the New York Mets play baseball at Shea Stadium, and once he took me on a trip I will never forget. I was about eight years old when he and I walked into an abandoned Harlem building. Inside were the living dead. The place was called a shooting gallery or a drug den. I can't imagine hell being any worse then this place, except these people wanted to be there. No one looked us square in the eye because everyone's eyes rolled back and forth in their heads. We stepped over the brown and white bodies of people slumped over. I recall one woman laid out with both arms and legs stretched out wide as if to be crucified. My grandfather grasped my hand as we carefully walked over people, needles, and trash until we reached the man whom Grandpa was looking for.

"Wait here, boy," Grandpa said before he walked away, and I was truly too intrigued to be scared. My mouth hung open as I watched a young man, about twenty-five years old, tie a rubber tourniquet around his right arm. He pulled it tight with his teeth and his left hand. As sunlight from a shattered window illuminated his desperate, drawn face, he injected heroin into his arm. His eyes began to roll back in his head. Then he leaned forward in a broken chair and rocked back and forth. I kept waiting for him to fall off the chair. I remember thinking, "Okay, this time he's going to hit the floor." Somehow, the man didn't. How that man, who appeared to lose consciousness, kept his balance on that rickety old chair amazes me to this day.

My grandfather soon returned, and we left the building. I remained in denial about Grandpa's drug use for a long time, but I have to assume that Grandpa bought some of his own "white lady" that day. In hindsight, I have mixed feelings about our field trip. On one hand, Grandpa was grossly irresponsible to escort a minor into an illegal, highly volatile environment where people were likely to do anything—and I do mean anything. On the other hand, my grandfather may have been trying to teach his young, impressionable grandson about the dangers of drugs by giving me a front-row seat in Hell's Kitchen. I would prefer to think that my grandfather was teaching me to just say no to drugs. But who am I kidding? Obviously, no child should have been exposed to this underworld.

Without my grandfather, my grandmother struggled financially, but she didn't bother him for help. We were poor, but I didn't quite realize our poverty because my grandmother always managed to take care of me, no matter our financial situation. I remember us not having enough food to eat until the first of the month when her Social Security check arrived in the mail. I always knew what part of the month it was by the meals I ate. If I had steak and pork chops, it was the first two weeks of the month. If I had bologna sandwiches and chicken backs, it was the last two weeks of the month. If times were really tough, I ate a mayonnaise or butter sandwich.

We made many trips to the local supermarket, where Grandma would buy three packs of chicken backs for less than two dollars. Many people fed chicken backs and necks to animals. The back and neck of the chicken are the least desirable part of the chicken to eat, but in the ghetto these cuts were plentiful. The meat was cheap, and my grandmother did her best to make it taste good. She treated the chicken backs just as she would a high-priced steak, even though the back of the chicken was full of fat and knobby spine bones. My grandmother would sprinkle salt, pepper, and paprika on the chicken parts before she stuffed them into the oven to bake.

There was a real art to eating chicken backs and necks. I learned to eat the chicken neck as if it were corn on the cob. I couldn't bite it through as I would a thigh or breast; I had to nibble it because there were tiny bones everywhere. And to eat a chicken back, I had to use my teeth to literally find the meat. There was a lot of fat at the bottom of the chicken back that I could chew like a wad of gum before spitting it out. I didn't realize at the time I was eating the least desirable part of the chicken; as far as I was concerned, it was good eating.

Cube steak was also a staple in our house. That cut is one of the least desirable parts of a cow. Grandmother would make it look almost like a hamburger, except she would dip it in flour, fry it, and smother it with gravy. The strong aroma would fill the kitchen and drift out into the hallway of our apartment building. Indeed, when cube steak was on the stove, all of my childhood friends knew what we were having for dinner. In these cramped quarters, dinner was an olfactory announcement.

By the end of my grade school years, I found myself being victimized again, but this time not by my mother. The bad boys in the neighborhood attacked me, and I found myself in one fight after another for the silliest reasons. These roughneck kids usually dressed in fashion brands designed specifically for ghetto life. Aunt Inez and my grandmother would not let me wear those clothes, no matter how I protested. And I wanted to wear them badly.

Inez bought expensive clothing for me from stores like Macy's and Bloomingdale's. I wore tailored slacks and buttoned shirts, which made me an easy target for boys who claimed I dressed like "white kids." I looked very different from my peers. They wore British Walker shoes, and I wore leather loafers. They wore baggy t-shirts, and I wore polo shirts.

Those kids made my life a living hell. They waylaid me in the hallway of my building and beat me up. I was a pretty even-tempered kid, considering my past, but the only time I consistently threw tantrums was when Aunt Inez visited our apartment with a department store bag. At those time, I cried like a baby. Inez said the same thing to me every time: "If you don't look like the ghetto, then you won't be treated that way."

Sadly, she was right. One by one, those boys who dressed ghetto-style, those who had beaten me senseless, were rounded up by police for petty crimes and were taken to the notorious Spofford Juvenile Detention Center. For many of those boys, the only graduation they would ever know would be within New York's penal system. First, the detention center. Next, Riker's Island. Final stop, Attica Correctional Facility upstate, or somewhere like it. Thanks to my grandmother and my aunt, I avoided trouble with the law because I didn't look like I was from the streets.

But I did have a big mouth and would sometimes provoke the boys who teased me about the way I dressed. I became their regular punching bag. When I was alone, I always had a sense of impending danger from those boys. Two boys who lived in the building and saw what was happening befriended me: Randy Codrington, nicknamed "Scoobie," and Ty Caldwell, whose friendships I enjoy to this very day. Whenever the rough kids would start trouble with me, Randy and Ty would step in. They weren't rough kids, but they knew how to talk the bullies out of beating me up. They used their street credibility to tell the bullies that I was all right, that I was a regular kid who just dressed differently. In turn, the bullies often backed off just because Randy and Ty had said I was all right.

One thing all of us kids in that building had in common was that almost nobody had a father. In fact, I remember just one or two traditional fathers in the whole building. But one advantage everybody had over me, no matter how poor they were, was that they lived with their own mothers. They would say to me, "My mother said this," or "My mother said that." I would say, "My grandmother said ..." Being fatherless was common in my neighborhood, but being motherless was not. My friends did not treat me differently because of my absent mother, but I felt like a motherless child. I kept my feelings to myself and tried to be a normal kid, though I had been robbed of my childhood long ago.

Fortunately, my grandmother knew the importance of keeping me involved in extracurricular activities. Getting involved in sports marked a turning point in my life. Grandma signed me up for a community program called the Police Athletic League, also known as PAL. The program involves a large group of police officers and staff members who go beyond the call of duty by essentially being father figures to fatherless kids. They took us on trips, taught us how to play stick ball, and even took us to some television shows.

Through PAL, I got my first fifteen minutes of fame by appearing on a popular, New York City—based children's television show called *Wonderama*. I was eleven years old, and all PAL kids were invited to appear on the show. The host, Bob McAllister, seemed to love the kids both on and off the camera. From him, I caught the celebrity bug, and I wanted to be a star. I still remember the opening jingle from the show:

> Well, well, that's really good news,
> I'm happy to say, I got good news today ...

I was part of a relay race on the show. Whichever team pushed the peanut to the finish line first would win. But there was a catch: you had to push the peanut with your nose. We didn't win, but I loved seeing myself on television. I was the talk of the building for a couple of weeks. My grandmother would brag, "Did you see my baby on TV?" I would beam with pride. The way Grandma told it, you'd have thought I was on the show every week.

In PAL, I learned how to compete and how to set goals. Soon I wanted to win and to be the best at whatever I tried. I wanted to stand out. I wanted people to know my name. Years later, when I became a journalist, PAL called me to host some of their fundraising events, and I gladly accepted their requests. I feel indebted to them for life.

I saw very little of my mother during my preteen years, which was fine with me. My family didn't see or hear much from her, either. We didn't miss her because, whenever she came around, trouble wasn't far behind. But one day, out of no where, Laverne issued an ultimatum to my grandmother.

"Give me Dominic back," she snapped at my grandmother on the telephone.

We were all in a state of shock. My mother was now living in the Patterson Housing Projects in the South Bronx where she would remain until her death many years later. She lived on the tenth floor in apartment 10E at 143rd Street and Morris Avenue, a filthy, crime-ridden neighborhood. The building always reeked of urine in both the stairwell and the elevator.

My grandmother was dumbfounded that my mother had the audacity to claim someone she had never truly wanted in the first place. I have never seen an old woman curse like my grandmother did on the phone with my mother that day.

"You stupid woman, bring it on!" she told my mother. "You come and try to take this boy! I dare you. Wherever the hell you are, you better stay there 'cause you ain't gonna ruin this boy's life. Bring it on!"

I knew from the conversation that my mother was trying to get me back. When my grandmother hung up the phone, she nearly collapsed. She grabbed her chest and kept mumbling, "Over my dead body will she take you! Over my dead body."

At eleven years of age, I had long made up my mind that I would never live with my mother again. I had matured to the point that I could connect enough of the dots to create a picture of my mother's neglect and abuse. At this point, I knew my mother should not have touched me sexually and that she shouldn't have beaten me. I also knew she was banking on my keeping quiet, but I had a plan to remain with my grandmother. My mother's single act of sexually abusing me was my trump card. I didn't want to tell the revolting tale of a mother and son naked in the bed, but I would tell it if I had to. I didn't know it at the time, but, in the immediate future, using that trump card was exactly what I'd have to do. I'd have to tell a total stranger what Laverne did to me.

I don't know if my mother was completely out of her mind or just a spiteful, evil witch, but she had her latest boyfriend, Bernard, serve my grandmother with a petition for my custody. In later years, I wanted to see that petition, so I wrote the New York City Family Court System to get a copy of the transcript. They sent me a copy of Docket Number 348675. The court document was called a Petition for Custody and/or Visitation. The top part of it read: "In the matter of a proceeding for the custody and/or visitation of Minors under article 6 of the Family Court Act." The petitioner was my mother, Laverne Carter, and the respondent was my grandmother, Anna P. Carter. Translation: the person arguing against my own interest was my mom.

As I flipped through the pages, item number 7 stated that "petitioner left child with respondent on and off because petitioner had to go into the hospital several times. On above date (June 7, 1975), the respondent told petitioner she doesn't trust petitioner with the child any more."

I thought the next paragraph was particularly remarkable. Item number 8 stated, "Petitioner is the mother of the child and is well capable of taking care of her own child." Another family court document under the same docket stated it was an "order to show cause pursuant to section 651 of the family court act" and that the hearing was held before the Honorable Judge Reginald S. Matthews. Next to the word *ordered* was the word *Dominic,* and my name was underscored. The document went on to state that I was to be physically produced in court on August 19, 1975.

I didn't know it at the time, but, after reviewing the document as an adult, I see that meant the judge could decide my fate. I would either go back to my grandmother or—my worst nightmare—be turned over to my mother. Another form stated that the hearing was before Judge William Rigler.

Even the mid-1970s, New York City's fiscal crisis affected me directly. It is indeed ironic that in my adult job, I still report on the devastation of the city's current fiscal crisis where children just like me suffer unnoticed. A document I later discovered from a lawyer named Stephen Latimer with Bronx Legal Services Corporation Counsel stated the following: "Mrs. Anna Carter came to this office on Thursday November 13, 1975, seeking representation in a pending custody matter. Unfortunately, because of budgetary and manpower cutbacks, we are unable to represent her at this time." My poor grandmother, who didn't have much of a formal education, had to defend herself in court against her own daughter on my behalf. But my grandmother was sincere, and she had the truth on her side.

Laverne didn't even have the nerve to face her own mother or the son she claimed to want so badly. We hadn't seen or heard from Laverne in at least two years. We believed she only wanted to hurt my grandmother yet again and she probably wanted more money from welfare, but she needed me to get it. It's my belief that she went to court because she needed another body—mine—to justify an increase in benefits from public assistance.

When Bernard handed my grandmother the court papers and abruptly left, I sat down next to my grandmother and told her a story that I knew she was not prepared to hear. "Ma," I said, my voice trembling, "Laverne did things to me that she shouldn't have done in bed and I—"

My grandmother put up her hand to cut me off. "Stop. That's all right. You don't have to say no more." Apparently, she'd heard enough. She looked at me through those round glasses that sat at the tip of her nose and tried to hide her disgust. Anna Pearl wanted to protect me from my mother's illness, though the poor old lady had no idea that I had already lived through the worst of it.

It turned out we were both protecting each other from Laverne's stormy life. I hated telling my grandmother about my mother's sexual abuse, but I had no choice. I knew she would believe me and not blame me for what happened. However, she couldn't bear to hear all of it. Head bowed, she stumbled into the bathroom and closed the door behind her. Sometimes I wonder if my telling my beloved grandmother such sordid news nearly killed her. Within months, she suffered a massive heart attack and had to have a triple bypass performed. Her open heart surgery caused her to miss several court dates, so she lay in a hospital with her chest sewn up and had to provide evidence to the Bronx court that she was hospitalized at Albert Einstein Hospital. Apparently, my cold-hearted mother could not have cared less about my grandmother's poor health, because my mother wouldn't drop the case.

The custody battle over me was more than my grandmother's heart could take. Grandma was the first person I ever told about the sexual abuse, but she wouldn't be the last. Months later, I told a judge. When Grandma and I went to family court, I remember telling myself not to even look in the direction of where my mother might be sitting. Honestly, I have no recollection of seeing her in the courtroom, though I know she must have been there.

A court officer escorted me to the judge's chambers, and, for a brief moment, I felt terrified. A big door swung opened, and I walked inside. The judge, who was about a foot taller than I, wore a black robe and smiled at me as he shook my hand. He may have been short in stature, but he had big, strong hands that somehow caused my trembling to cease. I wasted no time. I spilled my guts to this silver-haired judge—about how my mother ordered me into her bed and made me take my clothes off and rubbed my private parts and then beat me all the time and frequently forgot to pick me up from school. I told him how much I loved my grandmother and what good care she took of me.

I could see the judge's intense interest as I spoke. When I was finished, he put his big arm around my narrow shoulders and told me not to worry.

"Do you even want to visit your mother at any time, son?" he softly asked.

"No, I don't want to see her no more," I replied. The judge nodded and patted my back. I guess it was an open and shut case.

In a court document dated February 11, 1977, the judge found that I should remain in my grandmother's legal custody. The judge also said that I should not be forced to visit my mother and that I could decide whether to visit her. Apparently the judge saw that I had been well cared for by Anna Pearl since my early years.

Looking back, I can only imagine how the judge had felt as I told him that detestable story. I was only a naïve boy, but I instinctively knew that telling my story would silence my mother for good. And it did. The judge ruled completely in my grandmother's favor, granting her full legal custody of me. People had always said that I was a bright-eyed, handsome, articulate kid with a million-dollar smile. The judge must have noticed some of these qualities because he also told the court, "This child will go on to do great things." His prediction was accurate, but in the words of poet Langston Hughes, "Life for me ain't been no crystal stair."

Grandmother and I now had the law on our side, and I could finally exhale. When I was younger, I was fairly aloof to my mother and her strange ways. I kept all of the complex feelings that flowed through me inside. After our courtroom drama, I hated her, especially for trying to hurt me and Grandma and for making me the only kid among my friends who didn't live with their mother. I never let my true feelings show, but the contempt was festering in my heart. In my mind, Laverne no longer existed. She was out of the picture as far as I was concerned. By the time I was thirteen, she became pregnant again and gave birth to a girl, whom she named Malika.

When I graduated from the sixth grade, the class song was "Do You Know Where You're Going To?" by Diana Ross. I didn't know how, but I had a feeling I wasn't going to end up like most of the boys in our decadent neighborhood, and I surely did not want to end up a dead alcoholic like my father. I hardly flinched when my relatives told me my father was dead. He had always been dead to me. At age thirteen, I was coming into my own and living exclusively with my grandmother and my aunt Joann. I had a sunset curfew, and I would always push it to the limit. I was still making good use of my free time, aside from a game of dice craps every now and then. Grandma didn't have an extra dime to spend on other activities, but she kept up on what was free and dignified for her boy to do. I joined a karate class and the Boy Scouts, and I enrolled in nearby Fordham University's sports camp, which was free to poor kids in the neighborhood.

My favorite pastime was the cadet program; our branch was through the navy. Once a week, I would get decked out in a crisp blue sailor uniform with white spats covering my shoes. Although I'm not one to follow the leader, I enjoyed marching military style. "Forward to the right flank. March," the chief officer would bark. We would get to show off our skills during parades along the Grand Concourse in the Bronx. My grandmother was always there, cheering me on. There could be thousands of people, and I could always spot my grandmother. She'd be leaning on the barricade, her curly Afro glistening in the sun, wildly waving a handkerchief and dabbing the sweat on her brown forehead with the tears in her eyes. She was so proud of me, and I was, in turn, proud of her for never giving up on me as my parents had done.

Even though Anna Pearl was my mother's mother, she had never looked her age. She had lots of energy and was full of life in spite of the circumstances. But the misery in her life was getting the best of her. Slowly but surely, she started walking and talking more softly. She was in her fifties, and she was showing her age. She never complained, but I knew something was wrong. One day, while I was at Aunt Inez's apartment, my grandmother was rushed to the hospital with chest pains. She suffered a massive heart attack and had triple bypass surgery. My aunts tried to cover up the truth and just told me Grandma was sick. They did their best not to worry a puberty-stricken thirteen-year-old whose life depended on his ailing grandmother. We couldn't have known then that she would only have five years to live.

When Grandma returned home from the hospital, she had to take nitroglycerine to prevent another heart attack. She would place the small little white pills under her tongue. Sometimes I got Grandma something to eat as she lay on the couch. I remember telling her that everything would be all right. She agreed, but she suspected that her end was near.

In retrospect, I wonder if Grandma ever regretted moving to New York City. I never thought to ask her. She always seemed that spry young woman whom everyone called "Honey," who single-handedly brought her husband and her three daughters to a famous town that never seemed to live up to its reputation. Could that sassy woman have predicted that she would end up on a worn couch in a nondescript building with the former love of her life hooked on heroin, sometimes reduced to eating butter sandwiches?

My grandmother may not have been well educated and her dreams of a grand life in the big city may not have been realized, but what she did for me is worth more than silver and gold. She could easily have left me in foster care, or she could have let me go back to my deranged mother. But she took a stand for me. As long as I live, I will honor my true mother who believed in me when nobody else did.

When Grandma's health worsened, I moved in with Aunt Inez on Burnside Avenue in the Bronx. It broke my heart to leave Grandma, but I knew my leaving was for the best. My mother and I spoke on occasion, but under no circumstances did I want to live with her again. I would go see her and my new baby sister, Malika, but none of us pretended we could start all over and become one big, happy family. My mother was not showing noticeable signs of mental illness, but she still showed the same recklessness with Malika, except for the sex abuse.

With Grandma ailing and Aunt Inez taking care of me, Malika was on her own. Unless Malika cried out for help, the "don't ask, don't tell" policy would be in effect for another generation. I was concerned about my baby sister, but I was genuinely happy living with Inez. I didn't have my own room any more, but now I had lots of freedom. Inez worked from nine to five at the city's Department for Social Services, a good job for blacks in those days. I had a whole new group of friends. Aunt Inez was a good-looking young woman, and she loved to socialize. When I was left home alone at night, I would sometimes imagine a flash of my mother's sexual abuse, but I would quickly put it out of my mind.

Aunt Inez took over Grandma's role as my defender, especially in school. She always told me, "I may be growing up in the ghetto, but the ghetto won't grow up in me." She would babble about college for me, but, when I was in the sixth grade, going to college seemed light-years away. In school, I took a test for the gifted class, but my scores were a few points lower than the minimum required for the program. Those scores were good enough for Inez, though. She literally walked me out of my regular class into the gifted class. I was embarrassed, but I knew that my aunt wanted the best for me, so a gifted student I became!

As I grew older, I started to lose interest in my studies, but Inez was a constant thorn in my side, reminding me of the importance of studying and doing well. Whenever I got into trouble, she would march right down to my school, prepared to confront anyone who questioned my intelligence. She was well aware of how administrators during the 1970s treated the poverty-stricken children in neglected school districts, and she firmly let them know that Dominic Carter was going to be somebody.

Inez was right. Some of the teachers gave up on the kids before the first day of school. There was no passion for teaching and helping students to learn, just an attitude of "Let's keep these kids from killing each other until 3:00." The administrators and teachers didn't expect much of us, and the students and parents didn't expect much of the teachers. You could easily see the disdain on the teachers' faces. In fact, when a teacher showed a genuine interest in a class, it was shocking, and all the parents wanted their child in that teacher's class.

The summer before I entered junior high school, I made my first trip out of the inner city. I was thirteen years old and, like most kids in my area, had never left the Big Apple. Inez's best friend, Ruby, had lived in the same Bronx neighborhood as my aunt and had moved to the state of Washington. Inez sent me to stay with Ruby for the summer. Ruby wasn't blood-related, but she was just like family to all of us.

I took my first plane trip all alone on American Airlines. I was the only unescorted kid on the plane, so the flight attendant looked out for me. When I got off the plane, Ruby, her husband, Lowell, and her two daughters, Fatima and Halima, were waiting for me at the gate. I was so happy to see Fatima and Halima because they had been like sisters to me when they had lived in the Bronx. Ruby gave me a big bear hug, and her husband, who was white, said, "Gimme five!" I slapped his hand and knew that I would have a good time that summer.

We drove to their spacious home in Lynnwood, a suburb of Seattle. The house sat on several acres. I was so used to living in New York City that I honestly didn't know a big world existed outside the Bronx. I was awestruck by the well-manicured lawns, two-car garages, and the peaceful atmosphere. My entire life had been spent in neighborhoods filled with squalor. To me, the Bronx was ugly and dirty. Lynwood was clean and pretty. I couldn't get over the environmental contrast. Overnight I went from living in a tenement to living in a house surrounded by trees and grass.

Ruby's family traveled everywhere by car, not by subway and bus as I was used to. The trip got off to a bad start. I was so excited that I took the wrong set of luggage at SeaTac airport. I got the right bags the next day thanks to Uncle Lowell's forty-minute trip back to the airport. The hardest thing to adjust to was the time difference. Seven o'clock PM in Washington State was 10 o'clock PM in New York—that difference tripped me out, especially when I wanted to call Grandma and Inez.

Besides my grandfather, Lowell was the first man I developed a relationship with. It didn't bother me at all that he was white. I called him "Uncle Lowell." Lowell was tall, calm, and soft-spoken. He had a master's degree from the University of Washington, but he was not a show-off. He was the first man to teach me how to be industrious. I had to mow the lawn every Saturday, both acres of it. The work was backbreaking in the blazing sun, but I learned how to work until I got the job done. "Uncle Lowell" was one of the rebels in his family and also painted houses for a living. He taught me the tricks of the painter's trade, and I often painted along with him. He and Aunt Ruby also taught me how to drive. Seattle was a little eerie, but enjoyable, and I spent the best summer of my childhood there.

All that hard work paid off for me physically. Before my Washington trip, I had been slightly chubby and soft. I returned to my Bronx neighborhood with nicely developed muscles and a lean, toned body. At long last, I was a contender for the football games that were played for fun in the neighborhood. I quickly developed the ability to catch a football better than anyone else in the community. As a little kid, I had been picked dead last for games. Now, I became the first pick in the street draft—and that was a big deal. To be selected first meant you were the best player.

For the first time in my life, I knew I was exceptionally good at something, and I wanted to parlay that skill into success. When I'd played football years before, I'd just gone through the motions. Like many kids, I had lived without a clearly defined goal in mind. But suddenly I had dreams of playing professional football and buying big houses like Uncle Lowell and Aunt

Ruby's. Essentially, I had a vision that would prove to be the dominant force preventing me from living beneath my potential.

Years later, as a journalist, I would go on assignments that took me to Japan, Somalia, Israel, and the Persian Gulf, but it was this trip to Washington that confirmed to me that there was a world to be explored. That trip also planted the seeds of my desire for homeownership. I came back to the city much different than I had left it.

The following fall, I was back in New York City. I joined an organized football unit called the Pop Warner League, and our team was the Roadrunners. One coach who had a tremendous influence on me was a white man named Bill, a New York City police officer. He ultimately became a role model for me and about thirty other kids on the team. He was living proof of how to improve police-community relations. Bill pushed us to go the extra mile, but he never browbeat us if we fell short. He showed us how to play various positions, but more importantly he also taught us self-esteem and team spirit. At the end of the year, Bill presented all of the players with a trophy at the awards dinner.

I cannot recall his last name, but I credit much of my success to him. As a journalist, when I speak to young people about the pathways to success, I think of Bill. When I talk to my own son or toss him a football, I think of Bill. I don't know what financial rewards he received from giving so much of his time to some rowdy teenagers, but its dividends have paid off handsomely for me. I don't know if Bill is alive today, but I have often thought about being reunited with him. I want to in some small way return the favor. I just want to thank him. He made a big difference in at least one person's life. One of the young black boys he coached, a nobody in the eyes of society, went on to become a somebody.

By the time I reached high school, I had lived in six different residences over the course of about fifteen years. I had shuttled for the first half of my life between my grandmother and my mother and for the second half between my grandmother and my aunt. I longed for stability. While I was away in Washington, Aunt Inez moved into a two-bedroom apartment in the Throgs Neck Housing Projects, which is just a stone's throw from the Throgs Neck Bridge, connecting Queens to the northern part of the Bronx. I was home at last. I had my own room again, and Inez was my full-time protector and guardian. Unfortunately, I went to five different schools before I finally earned a high school diploma.

The first high school I attended in 1979 was Cardinal Hayes, a Catholic all-boys school in the Bronx. Although sending me there was tough financially for Inez, she managed to pay my tuition at the school, which was located at 153rd Street and the Grand Concourse. Since I had never dressed in fashionable street attire, I didn't mind putting on the uniform for school every day. I had to wear slacks, a pressed shirt, a tie, and dress shoes. I felt very nice when I dressed like a businessman, and I adjusted quickly to my new school's environment.

Parochial high school and public high school were like night and day. The priests who ran the school were no-nonsense, though from time to time I would try their patience. I still had a big mouth, and sometimes my mouth got me into trouble. Once, when I talked back to a priest, I got paddled in a private room. When the priest finished paddling me, I looked at him as if to say, "Is that all you got?" I was cocky but deadly serious. I realized that I had survived a lot of turmoil that would've sent most kids my age reeling. The priest could do nothing to hurt me. The only power that kept me in check was my desire to play football. I knew that if I got too far out of line, I would not be allowed to play.

I was a star on the freshman team. I was a middle linebacker on defense and a wingback on offense. I played the best I could so that I could move up and make the varsity team. I have fond memories of my days playing for Cardinal Hayes, where I felt like a big shot. I was one of the freshmen everybody was talking about. I would hear other priests say, "That Carter is going to be a big deal when he's on the varsity team." I loved the attention.

The only thing missing was the girls. Like most fifteen-year-old boys, I was as horny as a toad. I didn't have a steady girlfriend yet. My only problem was that I was a little shy and terrified of rejection. Gently testing out my lines on girls in the neighborhood, I would tell them how fine they were and hint how they should be with me. I did try my best lines on one girl in the community. Her name was Yvette, and she became my girlfriend for a short time.

I remember only one woman in the entire all-male school: the librarian. And talk about raging hormones—we even thought she was cute. But the girls our age would come around during our school dances, which were just like in the movies. The boys would line up along one wall, and the girls would line up along the other wall. And, slowly but surely, we would meet in the middle under the watchful eye of the Jesuit priests. There would be no hanky panky, but I have vivid memories of slow dancing with girls and getting excited and being so embarrassed. It was good, clean fun, but it didn't last long for me.

When my freshman year of high school was done, so was I. I was very serious about becoming a football star, and scouts were not as interested in kids from Hayes Cardinal High School as they were about athletes at DeWitt Clinton High School. So I transferred to Clinton for my sophomore year. Clinton, a public school, had a nationally known football team with a popular coach who had given some NFL players their start.

Aunt Inez was not thrilled with this transfer. She was well aware that many of the boys at Clinton High School were tough, but at least she wouldn't have to pay for me to go to school any more. So she didn't put up much of a fight.

Clinton, in those days, was also an all-boys school, and I joined the varsity team; but, make no mistake, this was no parochial school. In my opinion, besides their football program, all they did was breed future prison inmates. I had thought I was a tough guy. I had survived a lot of turmoil, but the guys who walked the halls in this school scared me half to death. The only thing that kept me from getting beaten within an inch of my life was football. These guys didn't bother athletes too much, but we did go to class in a hostile environment. Most of the guys were close to six feet tall, and what they learned best in school was the art of intimidation. Many of the boys were much older than typical high school student and were being warehoused by the educational system at the expense of kids who wanted to learn. If you acted smart and showed the least bit of interest in your schoolwork, you were a target for them, and you could be tackled in a staircase at knifepoint and robbed.

Dewitt Clinton High School had the feel of a prison camp. The hallways echoed with students cursing and threatening each other, and, when a fight broke out, it produced complete pandemonium. You would think that growing up in Harlem and the South Bronx would have prepared me for this violence, but it didn't. Only a juvenile detention center could have prepared me for this school. For my own safety, after the football season was over, I got the hell out of there. I had lost interest in academics and was failing miserably.

Aunt Inez demanded I be transferred to another school, John F. Kennedy, that was not in my zone, because it was a much better school. She was fed up with Clinton and wanted me out. Kennedy, which was nearby, had a much better reputation. This transfer was not supposed to be an easy task, but Inez made it happen. A lot of involved paperwork was intended to block parents from moving students from one school to another on a whim. But after Inez finished complaining to school officials at Dewitt Clinton, the principal simply picked up the phone and called the principal at John F. Kennedy to ask for a favor. And just like that, I had been transferred without much formality or paperwork.

The worst thing I carried from DeWitt Clinton High School was a sense of recklessness, resulting in one incident that could have easily cost my life. My aunt's boyfriend, Marvin Dixon, had known me as a child and was a cab driver. He owned an unlicensed gun that he used for protection and kept in our apartment. Marvin had moved in with us about two months after I got there. Having a gun in the house turned out to be a recipe for disaster with a daring teenage boy also in the house.

One day, a friend of mine was arguing with another guy over his girlfriend. I wanted to put an end to the debate, so I snuck the gun out of the apartment in a paper bag. As I held it, I remember feeling a tremendous sense of power. My misguided plan was to threaten the guy. I wanted him to back away from my buddy's girl. I walked up to the guy, who was taller than I was, pulled the gun out of the paper bag, and flashed a cocky smile. I didn't even have a getaway plan because we had ridden the bus to school. I had never considered the consequences of my actions: What would have happened if he had pulled out a gun as well? What if a police officer had happened upon us and shot me for wielding a weapon? I had no intention of firing the gun, and fortunately the guy backed off. I left without fighting or pulling the trigger. But I was still scared to death because I had to travel back to Aunt Inez's apartment with a concealed weapon on a city bus.

When I returned home, Inez was a complete wreck, screaming and crying. Her boyfriend knew the gun was missing and realized I was the only one who could've taken it out of the apartment. I handed it over, but not before getting told off by both of them. My aunt said she was disappointed in me. Like many teenage boys, I was rebelling, and I felt invincible. I started cutting class and failing, and I also talked back to teachers. I never got into drugs or crime like many of my friends, but I was still headed down the wrong path. In part I was just like many teens, but my behavior was also a result of all the hell I'd lived through as a child.

Kennedy High School was more integrated than Clinton and there was more order, but that order came too late. I was falling behind in school. Instead of filling my notebook with class lessons, I filled it with musical lyrics. Rap music was born in my hometown, the Bronx. Although I was born in Harlem, I was raised in the Bronx, where you had to be a survivor. Rap was the first music that spoke to the hearts of young people in the ghetto, and we couldn't get enough of it. The first big rap stars in the mid-1970s—the Sugar Hill Gang, Grandmaster Flash, and the Furious Five—inspired me to become a rapper as well.

All the guys had stage names, and I crowned myself "Master D." My friend Wayne Wood, who went by the name Master Rock, was my partner.

I spent many days dreaming in class about becoming a rap star and writing rhymes. Most of the boys had the same ambition. Rap took the Bronx and most of urban America by storm, just as doo-wop had some twenty years before. In the 1950s, a group of four or five guys snapped their fingers and crooned to an a capella beat. In the late 1970s, two or three guys shouted lyrics into microphones, and a DJ spun and scratched records from a turntable as background for the rapping.

Wayne and I expanded our act to include other people. Darryl Dyer, an old friend of mine from Cardinal Hayes, was really good at scratching records—that is, mixing one record with another and still maintaining the same beat and rhythm. Another friend, Sean Johnson, owned a lot of expensive equipment like turntables, a mixer, microphones, and speakers. Another pal, Willie Hutch, was also a member of our group. We did battle with other rappers in the community, and it was great fun.

One summer we performed our rap act at a community center. Backstage, I was very nervous. There were many young faces in the crowd, and I recognized some of the people from the neighborhood. And these kids would be brutal if we weren't any good. They would boo us off the stage just like the audience at the Apollo Theater during amateur hour. Even though Wayne and I were the rappers, the DJ had all the power. If he missed a beat while scratching records, it would ruin the entire song. Our DJ, Darryl, looked at us as we took the stage. I nodded and kicked off the song.

"He's Master Rock," I said. Wayne replied, "He's Master D." Then, together we said, "And we're the two MCs from the school Kennedy." Then I said, "I'm gonna say these rhymes—yes, one at a time—tell you party people—we can blow your mind!"

The crowd went wild, even though we had butterflies in our stomachs. But we didn't take our show on the road. Perhaps we could have, but we didn't really know how. Besides, every boy in the neighborhood had the same idea. I seesawed between rap music and football, and eventually football won. I knew there was a stage waiting for me, but I just didn't know which stage it would be.

My first love was sports, and my second love was girls. For all the hell I had been through with Laverne, I had a tender spot for females, as we boys called them. I was very tender with girls, and they seemed to like me very much. If a girl liked me, I liked her back, but, if I liked a girl who didn't like me back, I could hardly take it. In essence, I could not handle rejection. Whenever a girl dumped me, I took it personally. I was the great pretender on the outside, though.

I tried so hard to pretend that the trauma of the sexual abuse and abandonment didn't affect me, but it most certainly did. I had put it in the back of my mind, but it hadn't disappeared; it had just festered there, waiting for the right opportunity to explode. One girlfriend presented such an opportunity for my weary heart. I could not accept this rejection from the latest love of my life. I was a lovesick sixteen-year-old who had finally reached the end of his rope. I went into my aunt's medicine cabinet and swallowed every pill I could find, washing them down with a pitcher of water. Somehow I walked eight blocks to my girlfriend's apartment and rang the bell, but no one was home. I broke in, determined to wait there so she could see what she "made" me do. By the time I was discovered, I had passed out on the living room floor.

I taught myself at a young age how to control my emotions. Or at least I thought I had. I had controlled myself when my mother had viciously beaten me with extension cords. I had controlled myself when my father had clearly shown he didn't care whether I was dead or alive. I had controlled myself when my mother had left me alone with a group of complete strangers for months. I had controlled myself when my mother had forced me into bed with her naked. I had controlled myself when she had tried to take me back, sending my grandmother into hysterics. I had controlled myself when my beloved grandmother had had a massive heart attack and could no longer take care of me. But enough was enough.

When the ambulance came, I half-awoke to find the paramedics carrying me down several flights of stairs to nearby Lincoln Hospital. There in the emergency room was Aunt Inez, whom doctors had asked to wait outside. The doctors pumped my stomach, and it felt like I had vomited for days. I was admitted overnight, and hours later a hospital staff member brought me to a room to see a doctor. The doctor was a psychiatrist, and he tried to get me to talk about why I had swallowed the pills. I felt that he was treating me like a nut case, and I would have none of it. Irritated and belligerent, I said, "Don't run this crazy crap on me."

One thing led to another, and the doctors grew so shocked at my belligerence that they had me thrown out of the city hospital. In fact, the orderlies hadn't just thrown me out—they had sent me packing without my shoes and socks, even though I was a minor. At about five o'clock in the morning, I had to walk barefoot on the glass-strewn streets of the South Bronx, nauseated, angry, and lovesick. Of all the people in the world, my mother was the one who lived closest, just around the corner from Lincoln Hospital. So, without money or shoes, I chose to go to my mother's place. I told her what had happened, and she seemed to feel sorry for me. But I didn't view her as a compassionate person, and she didn't view me as an endearing son. She felt sort of like a distant cousin. I don't remember her embracing me or trying to intervene on my behalf. She just half listened and shook her head. My half sister, Malika, didn't know who I was, for she was just three years old at the time.

Suddenly I was holding a one-way ticket to Seattle, Washington. I never returned to Kennedy High School. Aunt Inez had insisted I get away from New York. I enrolled in high school in Aunt Ruby and Uncle Lowell's town. I knew Inez wasn't trying to get rid of me; she had realized she could no longer shield me from the harsh realities of life. I was a big boy, no longer a child whom she could order to another room to watch television. Aunt Inez knew I was falling behind in my studies, and, now that I was obsessed with a girl, she couldn't see any other option.

It was a smart move. The Lowells had moved to another house in nearby Edmonds, Washington, and I was going into my senior year at Meadowdale High School. Of course, I joined the football team. It was like I had died and gone to heaven. This school was unlike anything I had ever seen in the Bronx. The football field looked like Giants Stadium. When we had games, trainers taped my ankles up, just as they did in the NFL. It was just great.

During the first practice, the coach looked stunned. I wasn't a fast runner, but the ball stuck to my hands like glue. Everybody was talking about the black kid from the Bronx. They called me "Carter" with great reverence. They liked my confidence. I was like Muhammad Ali with cleats. "I'm gonna break all the records in this school, trust me, baby!" I would shout to anyone in the locker room. The day before my first game, the school held a pep rally that blew my mind. I had never even heard the term *pep rally* before, yet here I was at the center of one. I stood behind the gym doors in line with all the players, though I didn't know where we were going.

Suddenly I heard a booming announcer's voice that echoed throughout the gym and its cheering crowds. The announcer cried, "And starting at safety from the Bronx, New York, number 29, Dominic Carter." My teammates pushed me through the door, and I saw cheerleaders and thousands of kids shouting and clapping. My dreams of becoming a star were being realized before my very eyes. I held my hands up and did a cocky little dance, and the crowd went wild. I was ready to win.

But it wouldn't be my life if there hadn't been a monkey wrench in the deal. Hours before the game, the coach told me I would not be allowed to play. I was devastated. My transcript had arrived from New York. He told me I was academically ineligible because I had failed two major classes back in the Bronx. "So what!" I barked. I just couldn't see the logic in his decision, because, when I played football at the schools in the Bronx, no one appeared to care about my academics. So there I was, warming the bench for the first four games of the season as a penalty. I wanted to quit, but football was the only dream I had, so I held on. I improved my grades, and in the fifth game I was finally allowed to play. I made sure that on the field I let the school know they had made a mistake by keeping me on the bench.

In that first game, I made an interception that stunned the crowd. That put me not only in the local newspaper in Edmonds but also into the starting lineup. I went from being a nobody to a somebody on the team, and I relished every moment of the transition. Most of these kids had minimal exposure to blacks, so I was sort of a celebrity; being a New Yorker didn't hurt, either. I started calling everybody "baby," and I always chewed gum.

"Yeah, baby, we gonna do this, no prob!" I would say. I talked a lot of trash on the field, and we did really well. I was a brash, good-looking athlete, and I was a hit with the girls, whom I probably should have stayed away from. But I never let any other girls into my heart in high school, for I'd learned it was too easily broken.

After the football season was over, the thrill of Washington was gone. I was bored in Edmonds, and I missed the Bronx. I even started to talk back to Uncle Lowell and Aunt Ruby. One day they ganged up on me during an argument at the dinner table, and I knew my days were numbered. I whined to Inez so bitterly that she secretly sent me a plane ticket to return to the Bronx. All my aunt cared about was pleasing me, and I assured her I had the maturity to return to New York. After the argument, I was so bitter that I didn't even tell Aunt Ruby and Uncle Lowell I was leaving. I quietly packed my belongings, and, when they thought I was going to school, I took a cab to the airport. I never even said good-bye. They didn't do anything so egregious as to warrant that mean treatment, but I was an arrogant city kid, and I felt I didn't have to answer to anybody. Though, to my credit, I did keep my word to Aunt Inez. I didn't see that girl any more when I returned to New York. My girlfriend was to remain a thing of the past.

My fifth and final high school was Theodore Roosevelt on Fordham Road across from Fordham University in the Bronx. I spent my final semester in high school there. The term was uneventful because Roosevelt did not have a sports program. Remarkably, I was still graduating on time, but I was one credit short for my diploma. A gym teacher, a really nice gentleman, gave me an assignment I will never forget. He told me to read a book of my choice and write a term paper for the final credit I needed to graduate on time. I chose a book about football great O.J. Simpson. I finished the paper and made it to graduation.

Having completed high school, I was at a crossroads. How was I going to attend college and become a football star? I honestly had no idea. I sought a black guidance counselor for help. He looked at my grades, which were just average, and he also saw that I had transferred every year of my high school career. He thought he had me figured out. "Don't waste your time applying to college," he said. "You'll either be dead or in jail."

I was so shocked that I didn't even question his motives. I just thanked him and walked out. In retrospect, I'm glad he said that because I was going to make sure I proved him wrong. I took his words as a dare. The nerve of this so-called guidance counselor to predict my epitaph during the prime of my life! But no one could destroy my vision.

Imagine what would have happened if I had believed him! It would have been so easy for me to work the streets and end up just that—dead or in jail. I doubt that I was the first or last student he predicted doom for. And how many other students believed him and acted accordingly? I knew better, but I'm sure that not all of my peers did.

The die had been cast, but the question was whether I would break the mold. Arrogance is often viewed as a vice, but it can be a real asset when society sees you as a failure. I had too much confidence to say I was anything less than I envisioned. I may have been aiming high, but, damn it, even if I missed the mark, I would still do better than what so many expected of me.

I didn't go to graduation because I wasn't the pomp and circumstance type. But I did get my high school diploma on time. Five high schools later, I still graduated with all of my peers. I *made* a way possible through sheer will. In my personal school of hard knocks, I learned that my human will was a powerful force, indeed, a force to be reckoned with. I was born with a dream, a hope, and a vision. I didn't have much in the way of resources, but if I thought about something long and hard enough, I could usually figure out a way to make it crystallize. I was a budding visionary, though I didn't know it at the time. And I had my sights set on college.

3

After high school, the question became how I could turn my dream, my vision of becoming a professional football player, into reality. There was only one way to do it: to play football in college. Aunt Inez told me that I could probably get into a state school, so I checked to see which state college had football programs. While scanning the list alphabetically, I was intrigued when I got to the letter *C*. I had no idea what I was doing, but, from the looks of the pictures in the brochure, a college called Cortland seemed to have a pretty good athletic program. I didn't know or care about their academic program—hell, I didn't even know where Cortland was—but I filled out the State University of New York application and made Cortland my number-one choice.

I had attended five high schools in four years and had received an inferior public school education. But once again, my vision was becoming a reality anyway. I was accepted into Cortland's Educational Opportunity Program (EOP), which is designed for motivated students who are ineligible for admission by traditional standards because of their educational and economic disadvantages. Essentially, the program gave kids who could prove themselves a chance. I didn't care how I got in, as long as I was accepted.

Even more, as an EOP student, I qualified for a full financial aid package to cover the five-thousand-dollar tuition and housing cost, which I had no way of paying. But there was one catch. As part of EOP, I had to attend their six-week summer program created to prepare students for the academic challenges coming in the fall. Attending that program required me to ship out just days after high school graduation. After living on the West Coast for a season and getting a taste of suburban life, I was more than ready to leave the Bronx. However, more school right after graduating seemed a bit much. But what choice did I have?

Aunt Inez helped me pack my duffel bag and told me she was so proud of me. I didn't tell her, but I had no intention of ever living with her again. It was nothing personal; I just wanted out of the New York City projects. For the first time in my life, I was on my own.

I didn't hear anything from my mother. Her son was going to college, the first Carter ever to pursue an education higher than a high school diploma, and I didn't get so much as a phone call. Truthfully, I didn't expect one. My mother missed pretty much my whole life. She never threw me a birthday party or, to my knowledge, ever bought me a Halloween costume. As I entered this new phase of my life, I felt that my mother had really dropped the ball. However, I had come this far without my mother, so I would just have to continue my life without her. She was not part of my vision.

I boarded a Greyhound bus. Four hours and two hundred miles later, I was in another world. My mind was spinning. I thought to myself, "What did I just do? Where the hell am I? Did I make a mistake? Could I cut out? Would I fail and end up back in the ghetto?"

I never let those thoughts get the best of me as I explored my new community. The first thing that piqued my interest was the lack of noise in Cortland. I didn't realize how noisy New York City was until I set foot in Cortland. Crickets and squirrels made noise in the grass; but no city buses roared and no ambulance sirens screamed, at least not all the time. There was no subway system, nor were there towering buildings brimming with people. The campus sat high atop a hill surrounded by homes. Oddly, there was a tiny cemetery on campus. There were eerie-looking tombstones, some tipped onto their sides. I'll never know why this neatly maintained cemetery was set in the middle of a college campus. It seemed like death in the center of an area full of young people with a zest for life. I felt that I'd moved into the Twilight Zone.

One of the first rumors I heard fellow freshmen share about the tiny town was that it had a disproportionately high rate of incest, purportedly the highest rate in New York. I thought that was just my luck to begin the program in a negative atmosphere that reminded me of my sick past.

My first stop was my new dormitory, where I would stay for the six-week program. The building seemed sterile, but I had a magnificent view of the mountains of upstate New York and acre after acre of farmland. The room contained two beds, two desks, and two closets, nothing more. I met my roommate, a tall, skinny guy named Michael Bivens from Westchester County, New York. He was a smart-alecky but likable dude. His energy was contagious, and he was always up to something.

Having to share a room with a stranger creates a tricky situation for most freshmen in college. Sometimes it works, and at other times it can be a total disaster. Fortunately, Bivens and I got along fine. What did take a little getting used to was that we could barely walk three steps in any direction in the room without bumping into a wall. We had access to one community bathroom in the center of our floor. Using it took some adjusting because there was very little privacy. Most of the young men were embarrassed to walk around the shower area naked, but football had prepared me for that openness.

Only hours after stepping off the Greyhound bus, my first EOP gathering was held in the recreation room of the dormitory. All the underprivileged students from around the state—whites, Latinos, and African Americans—gathered in the center of the room, shoulder to shoulder. During our introduction to the school, a supervisor told the fifty or so of us newcomers, "Look to your left, and now look to your right. In one year, two of you won't be here." I looked to my left and my right and truly felt sorry for my neighbors because I knew the supervisor hadn't been referring to me. His statement proved to be prophetic. The guy standing to my left that day, Michael, my first roommate, flunked out after his freshman year.

During the meeting, we were greeted by a black man with a big, bald, shiny head. His name was Tom Newkirk, and he was the director of EOP, but I was more interested in his assistant. She was a light-skinned black woman with light eyes. She was absolutely stunning. She wore crisp red pants and a white sailor's top. She was about my height, five feet eight inches, and, when she walked up to me, our eyes locked. Without any notes in her hand, she said, "Tell me your last name, and I'll tell you your first name." She looked me in the eye as if she were challenging me.

"Carter," I replied with a smirk.

"Dominic," she said quickly.

I was impressed, and, better yet, I was smitten. Still cocky, I told myself that this beautiful woman, who was seven years my senior and brimming with confidence and professionalism, this woman would be my wife someday. I truly fell in love with her at first sight.

Her name was Marilyn Stevens, and that was all I knew on that hot summer day in June when I nominated her the future Mrs. Dominic Carter. I didn't know her interests, I didn't know if we were compatible, and I didn't even know if she was married. I was a college freshman, and she was already a college graduate who was working at a real job. Just a week before, I'd been in high school. None of that mattered to me. I wanted her ... badly.

It turned out we had a lot in common. She was from Harlem and had grown up poor, too. She had nine brothers and one sister. Her mother, Ruby Stevens, had showered her children with love, despite the fact that she had basically raised them alone. Marilyn could relate to me like no other woman I'd met in my life. But in her previous relationships, she had called all the shots. Marilyn was intrigued by the fact that, while I might be young, I did not lack confidence.

It did not start out as a whirlwind courtship. Whenever I flirted with Marilyn, she repeatedly turned me down flat. She thought I was a cute, little kid.

"Go date some of the girls your own age," she would tell me.

I'd reply, "But I want you! Age is just a number!"

I thought I was so smooth. She tried to hide her attraction to me, but I thought it was obvious she liked me. I could see it in her eyes. She looked at me as if I were crazy, but I turned around her "We can't date" statements and made her ask herself, "Why not?"

After class, I would hunt her down for "counseling." She was supposed to counsel me, after all. She instantly became part of my vision. I couldn't see my life without her. I believed she would one day love me, even as she rebuffed my early offers. She was a warmhearted and decent young lady—very neat and very proper. I would touch her hand, and she would calmly back away. But she was weakening. By the end of the summer institute program, she was mine. It would prove to be the best catch of my life.

After the six-week program, I went back to the Bronx. It was mid-August, and I was going to stay with Aunt Inez for a few weeks until the fall semester began in September. But I could barely stand being in the Bronx, which didn't feel like home any more. These days, it felt like a ghetto—a noisy, cramped ghetto. In a matter of six weeks, I had grown to love the simple life of Cortland and its smell of freshly cut grass, and I wanted to stay there. The Bronx also reminded me of the ugliness of my past life. It reminded me of my mother. I wanted out.

I returned to Cortland shortly before the fall semester of my freshman year just to be around Marilyn. For three weeks, I rented a shabby room in a old, dilapidated house. It was awful. I was alone, and, when it rained, the water would seep into the house. I didn't have anything to do. I decided to go to Marilyn's house for home-cooked meals. Aunt Inez was two hundred miles away, Grandma was dying, and sometimes I didn't have food. The bad thing about living alone is that it gave me too much time to think. I didn't have anything to study yet because class was not in session, so I spent my time thinking.

I thought of how far I had come. I thought about my mother. I was so far from her, and I wondered if she even cared. Was Laverne rooting for me to succeed in college? I didn't know how Laverne felt about me because we didn't speak often. We would just say, "How are you doing?" in three or four different ways, like "What's going on?" "What's doin'?" or

"What's up?" And before we knew it, we were both saying, "All right, gotta go." There was so much ahead of me and so much behind me, and I had difficulty feeling secure when I talked to her.

Living alone before school began, I didn't have anything good to think about. Just two months before, I had turned eighteen. I had spent a lot of time looking into a cracked, full-length mirror. I was a man. I had a broad chest and rounded shoulders. My waistline was thick, but I was still in shape. I kept my hair cut short, especially in the summer when the blazing sun cooked it a reddish-brown hue. I could do anything with my life, and no one had the power to stop me. At last, I was the captain of my own ship, but I had just one problem: I didn't know in which direction to steer.

This was where I always had wanted to be, but it was also where I had never wanted to be. I always wanted to be in charge, and I also believed I was my best advisor. But I never wanted to be alone. Fortunately, my loneliness was short-lived. When the fall semester started, Marilyn became my support system. She never looked down on me, and she rooted for me and kept me motivated. For the first time in my life, I was forced to buckle down and make good grades—and it was not easy at first. English 101 was difficult, but I was in love—even though Marilyn and I had to keep our relationship a secret. Marilyn had warned all the EOP students in advance how difficult English 101 would be, and now she had made that difficulty very simple for me. If I were to be a part of her life and if I was focused on earning a degree, this English class would be the first real hurdle. Marilyn helped me develop good study habits.

My freshman year, I majored in physical education and signed up for the football team. I tried out and practiced with the other students who had similar ambitions. I just knew the coach would take one look at me and sign me up on the spot. He had already seen game film of me from my high school football days. I hoped to become the star player at Cortland, just as I had been at Meadowdale. One day after practice, I walked into the gym and checked the list posted on the bulletin board for students who had made the team. My name wasn't there. I examined the list again, not believing my eyes. Dominic Carter was not among the dozens of names. I was numb with shock and very embarrassed.

Guys were celebrating and giving each other high fives for making the college team. The rest of us were left standing off to the side, looking like rejects. The one thing in the world I thought I was good at, the one thing that had kept me motivated through school had failed me. I was not part of the team.

I took that failure hard, especially considering the school had a division three team, which was a far cry from a division one school like Penn State, Notre Dame, or the University of Washington. What the hell was going to motivate me now? Didn't these coaches know that football was my sole reason for going to college? It turned out that the coach was looking for players with speed, and I never ran a good time in the forty-yard dash.

My life with my mother had not prepared me well for rejection, and I couldn't deal with being left out. I always went to extreme lengths to avoid feeling like a failure or a loser, so this was a major letdown. I had to be a winner—I just had to be. It wasn't in me to walk with my head down; my DNA just wouldn't allow me to do that. Luckily, Marilyn was in my corner. Had it not been for her encouragement, I would've dropped out of college that very semester. She helped me focus and see that life offers much, much more than football. She helped me turn a negative into a positive. I did turn around my thinking and vowed right then that I would never fail at anything else in my life.

Other events were about to happen that I could not my control. Aunt Inez called to tell me to get down to the Bronx to visit my grandmother. I didn't have a car, so Marilyn said she'd drive me. My aunt's tone wasn't urgent, but somehow I felt this might be my last chance to see my grandmother alive. I could tell from my aunt's voice that she was trying not to cry; she was trying to be strong.

The four-hour drive to New York Hospital on the Upper East Side of Manhattan seemed to take forever. Marilyn could sense my impatience as we drove. I promised myself I wouldn't cry, especially in front of my new girlfriend. When I walked into the hospital room, I took one look at my grandmother, and the blood rushed up to my head and down to my feet. I held onto the railing of her bed with both hands to calm my trembling. My beloved grandmother was most certainly at the end of her life.

I hadn't seen her since I had left for college. She was just fifty-six but looked much older and she was two shades darker than her normal complexion. Her stomach was bloated and disfigured. I suppose she was nearly blind because her glasses were so thick and heavy that they kept sliding down her nose. She had suffered kidney failure, and numerous tubes were wired to her frail body. Death was in the air. I looked directly into her eyes, realizing that she was ready to give up.

"Hi, Ma," I said, and my voice cracked.

"Hey, Bobby," she said, with complete enthusiasm.

I was stunned that she didn't recognize me, but dementia was taking over. Bobby was her nephew who had died years ago.

I wasn't mad, but I felt broken and helpless. It took everything I had to fight back the tears.

"It's me, Dominic," I finally could say, "and this is my girl-friend, Marilyn."

My grandmother evidently couldn't place who I was. My pride wouldn't allow me to pass out, but I wanted to. I wanted to lie down on the floor, with arms stretched wide, and just wail for the injustice of it all. What kind of ending was this for a woman who had sacrificed so much? What kind of final chapter was this for a woman who gave so much of herself and asked for nothing in return? Simply put, this was the most unfair, unjust, and downright despicable ending I had ever seen in my young life.

I had to do *something.* I went to the nurse and demanded to see the doctor in charge. In my mind, I was somebody special who warranted such attention, but in reality I was nothing more than an eighteen-year-old kid who loved his grandmother. An intern came in the hospital room. I demanded to see the chief, but he told me "the chief" wasn't available. I pleaded with the intern to do something, anything, to make her better. He listened to me with a blank look on his face. I felt the need to do or say something to try to help save the woman who had saved me.

"I'm sorry, Mr. Carter," the intern finally said. "There is nothing we can do."

I gave up then, but I vowed that one day I would be some-body, so that neither I nor my family would ever be treated that way again. In my view, the nurses treated her as just another dying body, a second-class citizen with no rights. They didn't see her humanity, her struggles, her specialness. In their eyes,

Anna Pearl was just another soon-to-be corpse to cover with a sheet.

My grandmother lay in the hospital bed, and I kissed her on the forehead and said good-bye. I tried to act as though it wasn't a big deal even though it felt like an earth-shattering moment. Marilyn and I left, and we took the long drive back to Cortland. I didn't want to talk about my grandmother's impending death, so there was an awkward silence in the car. As I had always done during painful times in my life, I tried to block out the situation. College had just started. I was staying at Marilyn's house almost every day now, as we were beginning a relationship.

The next morning, Marilyn and I were studying when the phone rang. It was my aunt, crying hysterically. She told me that my grandmother had died. I didn't react on the phone. I just acknowledged the news and hung up. Then I sat quietly on the couch in the living room. I didn't want to know too much because I was sure I couldn't handle even the image of my grandmother's death.

Anna Pearl was cremated because our family really didn't have any money. There was no memorial or funeral, so there was no reason for me to go back to the Bronx. I abruptly stood up and told Marilyn the news. I tried to be cool, for I was too ashamed to cry. Again she tried to get me to express my emotions. She knew how much I loved my grandmother, but, at that time, she didn't know the hell I had been through and why I viewed my grandmother as a saint. I looked straight ahead at the television, but I couldn't stop a few tears from trickling down my face. I quickly wiped them away and changed the subject. I think I started talking about football. Just that quickly, I forced myself to shut Anna Pearl's death out of my mind.

I didn't like losing control because if I allowed myself to cry, I might not stop. I can thank my mother for that ability. If I had ever dwelled on the awful way Laverne had treated me, my tears would never cease. It seemed that life was very cruel at times, but I refused to drown in my sorrows. Life would not stop me. The first time I could be alone, though, I couldn't hold back. I hunched over the edge of the bed and let my tears stain my gray crewneck Cortland sweatshirt. I cried almost out of obligation to my heart, which felt heavy with unexpressed grief. For the first time, I understood what it meant to have a heavy heart. I cried for a few minutes, got up, and continued my day. Marilyn's reaction was one of profound sadness. She tried to comfort me the best way she could by putting her arms around me. It was the embrace that I needed, but nothing could really make the situation better. My protector was gone.

My grandmother's ashes were never sprinkled over Seventh Avenue, as she had once wished. Anna Pearl loved New York City with all of her heart, but New York did not show love to her. The Big Apple had broken that country girl's heart. Anna Pearl was a visionary, too. She had packed up what little belongings she had and sought the Promised Land because she was determined to find a better life for herself and her family. A black woman, who society viewed as powerless, took what little power she had and ran with it. But the sassy woman had found bitter fruit in the North. And for that, I am so sorry. She did so much for me, but her time ran out before I could return the favor. My grandmother did not live to see me make it big, but she did know that I had started college. This much I knew. And from heaven, I'm sure she saw everything else.

It was time for a change with my life. I owed it to my grand-mother to stay strong and get my degree. With my football career washed up and with the realization that physical education majors had to take difficult math and science courses—the same classes doctors are required to enroll in—I changed my major to theater. Maybe I could be an actor. I had the confidence and the mouth, and I was pretty good on stage. I performed in a few campus plays, but all those rehearsals got on my nerves.

One incident did involve some off-stage drama. I had a small part in the Shakespearean play *A Midsummer Night's Dream*, and my buddy Jimmy Davis played the character of Puck. We were scheduled to attend another dress rehearsal, but we decided instead to grab a bite to eat with Marilyn. We were late returning to the theater, and our colorful director, Dr. James Palmer, who was also the head of the theater department at Cortland, went berserk. He sent out campus police to search for us, and fortunately, we arrived at the rehearsal before the campus security located us.

Another play I was in was directed by the Dean of the college, Dr. John Stockwell. The play was *Steambath*, and the backdrop was a bathhouse. The lead female character was top-less, and my only costume was a towel around my waist. One scene called for me to kiss a male friend of mine named David Potter on the lips. Some of my college buddies teased me, but it didn't bother me. Hey, that's showbiz, as they say.

But life can be so fragile. Potter was one of the first white guys I met on campus. A few years later, he left school and was the manager of a gas station in his hometown, Albany, New York. One day during a robbery, somebody shot and killed

David Potter. He could not have been more than twenty-five years old.

During college, I even joined the school newspaper and tried writing articles about the football team, but newspaper writing bored me to death. I wasn't interested in covering athletes because in my mind I was still one of them. Covering the games as a journalist only made me miss the sport even more. I also spent a lot of time in Cory Union, which was the center of student activity. Cory Union was the place where students could kick back and shoot the breeze. It had a very social atmosphere where I talked to people from many different walks of life.

Weeks later, I crossed paths with an Italian guy with a booming yet raspy voice. His name was Bill Salvatore. It seemed that overnight, he had become one of the big men on campus. I wanted to be popular like him and told him so. He urged me to join the campus radio station, WSUC. All the students and even the Cortland residents listened to it. Some time later, I was on the air as a volunteer DJ and found that I loved every minute of my on-air time.

"You're listening to WSUC 90.5 on your FM dial," I said. "This is Dominic Carter."

I had grown up listening to the top urban contemporary radio station in the nation, WBLS in Manhattan, so it was easy for me to copy the broadcasters' style. Rap was just beginning to explode in the early 1980s, and I spun records on WSUC that kept the whole campus dancing. I remember playing lots of Madonna because her music was just starting to take off in the dance clubs, and it had the hottest beats around. As expected, I became the next big man on campus. I switched my major again, this time to radio-TV.

Even though my dorm room was paid for the entire academic year, I lived in it for maybe a week. I moved in with Marilyn as soon as possible, even though living together was a risk because we were supposed to keep everything a secret. Living with her wasn't really a formal arrangement; I just never left her apartment. She became my rock. She was a great cook, and I ate like a king. Her only weakness was that she was not sentimental. She wouldn't say, "I love you," but she expressed it to me, loud and clear, through her actions. I wanted to get married right away, and she wanted to wait until I had graduated. So now I had two new motivators to stay in school: to make Marilyn my wife and to become a famous radio DJ.

My first summer after completing freshman year, I didn't go back to the Bronx for long. Instead, I stayed with Marilyn and took summer classes. I also got my first real paying job as a peer counselor. My supervisor was my girlfriend, Marilyn. Technically it was unethical for us to be working together, but we never abused the supervisor-worker roles. We had never confirmed our relationship with anybody, but I'm sure some students on campus could put two and two together. When we started dating hot and heavy, which had already passed by September of my freshman year, a lot of people knew.

Marilyn had a former boyfriend whom she would see every so often. His name was Calvin.

One day Calvin called her apartment, and I answered, "Who is this?" I almost snapped when I heard another man's voice. "Listen," I growled back at him, "Marilyn is *my* woman, so don't call my house any more."

Calvin backed off and even apologized. This grown man had no idea he was talking to an eighteen-year-old. I even surprised myself. I took it as a sign that Marilyn and I were meant to be.

My sophomore year in college was awesome. I still couldn't get football out of my system, so I auditioned for a football announcer job on the college station. Another student, Ted Demme, nephew of the famous film director Jonathan Demme, was the program director. He hired me on the spot. Every Saturday, we called the games. Ted taught me the ropes about sports casting, and I taught him how to loosen up. He had been raised in the suburbs and hadn't had much exposure to blacks, and he really embraced me.

Ted never bragged about being the nephew of the famous director; he acted just like all of the other students. In fact, he didn't reveal who his uncle was until after college. Ted would go on to have a huge impact on the music industry and on society. After graduation, he joined MTV and helped develop the show *Yo! MTV Raps*. It's funny how life works. This guy with whom I would call football games brought rap music to all of America. When I met him at college, he had little knowledge of black culture, much less its music. But he was obviously a quick learner. He also went on to follow in his uncle's footsteps and become a director. One of Ted's big films was *Blow*, a movie about cocaine, starring Johnny Depp and Penelope Cruz.

I have seen Ted once since college. We bumped into each other in a Miami airport when I was on assignment as a journalist. Ted and his uncle were part of a group who visited Haitian refugees at the U.S. Naval Base at Guantanamo Bay in Cuba. We talked about our past times together. Ted was a good-natured person. Sadly, he died at the young age of thirty-eight.

When I was a junior in college, I felt it was time to branch out from the books and start heading down the road in the industry that I wanted to be part of. I was in a rush to get my degree, and I set a personal goal to graduate in three years instead of four. One professor noticed my haste. Her name was Dr. Roseanne Brooks, and she was the head of the sociology department. I ran into her in a campus elevator on a cold winter day. Dr. Brooks, a heavyset chain-smoker, talked to me in an exasperated tone in between puffs on her cigarette.

"Mister Carter." She blew smoke. "Why are you in such a rush to graduate?"

I said, "Dr. Brooks, you don't understand. I'm from New York City, and I don't have any money. I'm the first one in my family to go to college."

She took a deep drag and cut me off. "Mister Carter, don't you know that these are the best times of your life?" Puff, puff. "Once you graduate, you'll only work to pay bills for the rest of your life. Slow down."

I looked at her and smiled, and Dr. Brooks walked off the elevator. I never forgot how she said it—it was almost comical—but experience has proved that she was 100 percent correct. At the time, though, she didn't change my mind. I was hell-bent on finishing school ahead of time and entering the workplace.

My college radio gig made me interested to work in radio, so I wanted to see what life was like in a professional radio environment. I went back to the Bronx for an entire semester for one reason: to intern at the famed WBLS radio station. I was very serious about my radio career, and I had finally gotten a chance to work at the station that I had listened to almost my whole life. I stayed with Aunt Inez, who still lived in the projects at the Throgs Neck Houses. Here I was, moving up in the world as a college student, still going in and out of the projects. Life was not easy, yet I have found that nothing worth pursuing is easy. More determined than ever, I would wake up at two o'clock in the morning and catch a city bus to Westchester Avenue. That bus ran only once an hour at that time of the morning. I would then enter the subway and take the Number 6 train all the way to midtown Manhattan. Inner City Broadcasting, the parent company of WBLS, was located on the corner of 43rd Street and Second Avenue.

Waking up at that ungodly hour every morning was sheer hell for me. New York is known as the city that never sleeps, but, trust me, just about everything and everybody is asleep at two and three o'clock in the morning. Even though my body screamed no, my will screamed yes as I made my way to the shower. My body would tremble at the notion of being awakened so early. I often needed about fifteen minutes to awaken fully, but I would usually be awake by the time I entered the subway in the Bronx at three o'clock in the morning.

Only a few people were around at that hour, so I got a personal look at the homeless population as I'd never been able to before. The homeless could be found at practically every turn. Many nestled into corners or slept on the subway benches where people normally waited for the train later in the day. The homeless people asleep aboard the train intrigued me the most. They usually commandeered an entire bench, their bodies stretched out with one arm and one leg dangling off the edge of the seat. Sometimes I would sit directly across from them and focus on their faces. Brown faces, white faces, men, women, and sometimes teenagers hooked on drugs found themselves in the homeless underworld. Often their mouths hung open as they slept and revealed rotten or missing teeth. Their skin was ashen and dirty with body fluids, which left dry stains on their legs. Their clothing was soiled and tattered, and they wore rundown shoes. A strong sense of compassion swept over me for these struggling New Yorkers.

The condition of the homeless people broke my heart day in and day out. Coming from a broken home myself, I knew the dynamics that could cause someone to lose hope and give up. Were it not for the grace of God, I believe that they could've been me. If the winds of fate had blown me just a bit further to the edge, I, too, could have given up. Instead, I was at the dawn of my career, a college student with grand ambitions, and I was headed to an internship at a broadcasting company. Still, these broken souls greeted me every morning. Sometimes I would find one of them awake, and I would always offer some loose change if I had any. (My internship did not pay me.)

When I stepped foot in Inner City Broadcasting's offices, which is home to WBLS and WLIB, I felt that I was in another world brimming with professionals who were totally energized, though the sun hadn't come up yet. It was an exciting atmosphere. The smell of coffee was in the air, and I was surrounded by people who also had dreams and visions. I was floored when I met Frankie Crocker, who was the undisputed father of urban contemporary radio, a real pioneer. He had a smooth, baritone voice. A tall, handsome, dark-skinned man with a broad nose, he would sit in a tiny studio, often wearing a cowboy hat as he serenaded millions of listeners. He was a singer's DJ. He could literally make a singer or break one.

Frankie Crocker did two things that I especially liked. He was the consummate bragger; he called himself "the Chief Rocker, Frankie Crocker," and all the big stars courted him, knowing he could single-handedly turn almost any song into solid gold. The other thing I really admired was his daily closing theme song. I don't know of any other DJ in New York City at that time that had a theme song, but Mr. Crocker did, and New Yorkers grew to love the song as well. It was a slow, jazzy, love song called "Moody's Mood for Love" by King Pleasure. I was not into jazz, but the chief rocker made me love this song, which he played every night before he signed off at 7:58 PM.

> "There I go, there I go, there I go …
> Pretty baby, you are the soul who snaps my control …"

The song also reminded me of Marilyn, who was some two hundred miles away. I would sing it to her on the phone when I was away from her. I missed her very much. My internship was a valuable experience. Sometimes I was a gopher, getting Mr. Crocker coffee or lunch, and I was the best damn gopher in the newsroom. He seemed to like me, and I really respected him.

I spent most of my time in the newsroom shared by both WBLS and her AM sister station, WLIB. Being exposed to those stations prepared me to work in news. I had to rip wire copy from United Press International, record audio feeds that came in every hour from reporters all around the world, and clip newspaper articles. I worked about ten hours a day. I didn't have any political or social connections, but I knew a good internship would get my foot in the door. I can still remember employees getting their paychecks on Friday, and there was never one for me. It didn't bother me, but I worked harder than most of the workers there. Yet I wasn't discouraged, because I knew my day was coming.

A true gentleman named Carl Ferguson was the newsman for the AM station. I remember telling him about my plans to be the next Frankie Crocker. He gave me a lesson that would change my career path. He told me that DJs did not have much job security because stations could fire them according to the latest ratings book. Ferguson was right. Even the chief rocker would come and go from time to time. Ferguson told me the news business was a much more stable job. I didn't take much convincing. I liked working in the newsroom, and I was developing the love of reading newspapers. I thought journalists wielded tremendous influence and power. Ferguson was a dedicated journalist who taught me the importance of maintaining contacts with newsmakers, and I learned a lot by watching him.

When I returned to Cortland in the spring, my life was quite different. Just as I was working hard, Marilyn was also struggling to excel in her field of higher education. One of the interviews I drove her to was in Alfred, New York, a farming community. Neither of us had ever heard of Alfred. And, of course, Marilyn was hired as an administrator at Alfred College. Don't get me wrong—it was a solid job—but it was even further upstate from Cortland, where I had to finish my undergraduate degree. We were about three hours away from each other, and we talked to each other on the phone late into the night. We weren't married yet, but it felt just like a commuter marriage.

Every weekend we would get together. We would take turns traveling 120 miles up and down the highways, taking in the scenic views of Elmira and Corning along the way. Mondays were the worst because we had to wait five days to see each other again. Sometimes Marilyn would call in sick on Monday, or I would leave class early on Friday. While traveling on the road to see her, I would literally count the hours: two hours to Alfred, one hour to Alfred, and so on. There is nothing as intoxicating as rushing to see the one you love.

In the summer of 1985, I was about to reach a major milestone in my life. I graduated from Cortland in three years instead of four, thanks to my hard work during three consecutive summer classes with a solid 3.0 grade point average. It was my first time wearing a cap and gown and walking to the graduation march. Finally, my whole family acknowledged that I had done something significant. A whole group from the Bronx came up to Cortland for my graduation, even my mother.

I was proud to be the first Carter to graduate from college. I was only sorry that my grandmother couldn't see me. My mother seemed proud, even though she had done absolutely nothing to get me there or to support my stay. I did not show any animosity toward her; being with Marilyn had somewhat mellowed me, so I just enjoyed the fact that we were all together in peace. Marilyn tried to bridge the gap between my mother and me, and I tried to oblige Marilyn. My anger toward my mother would ebb and flow over the years. It was a feeling I tried desperately to forget, but I just couldn't.

During graduation, I thought about that guidance counselor who had predicted death or jail for me. I thought that I should go back to Roosevelt High School and tell him off, but doing so wasn't worth my time. His underestimating me had been a great motivator.

I was young, but I was ready to commit to marriage. Two months after graduation, on July 12, Marilyn and I were married. Finally, the sun was shining on me. Not only was I a college graduate, but now I was a husband. These were happy times. Marilyn and I didn't have much money, and we had left our families in the city. I thought we were going to have a big wedding, but Marilyn had different plans. Somehow her position ended up the final one. Being independent, but, perhaps more importantly, private and shy, Marilyn wanted to pass on a big ceremony. She didn't understand the logic of spending thousands of dollars. So the mayor of Cortland married us in a small, informal ceremony at the tiny government building in Cortland, New York. Marilyn's family was not present or pleased. They wanted Marilyn, the youngest girl of the family, to have a traditional wedding, and they had put aside money for years, waiting for her special day.

Marilyn's best friend, Sheila Fripp-DeLeon, was also disappointed that she would not be planning a big wedding for her girlfriend. Sheila and Marilyn had known each other since they were six years old and had lived in the same building in Harlem. I had liked Sheila from the moment I met her because, like me, she was a straight shooter who didn't hold back her feelings. I was a big fan of her husband, Ray, a quiet hardworking man whom I considered a personal role model. Ray worked two full-time jobs and never complained. His wife, Sheila certainly made her feelings known about our marriage plans. There are only two girls in the Stevens family, and Marilyn was the one everyone expected to have a big wedding. Marilyn's college pal, Ron Johnson, who remains a dear friend to this day, served as one of the witnesses. One of Marilyn's colleagues from her years at Cortland, Debbie Pointer, held a small reception at her home.

Debbie, the assistant financial aid director at Cortland, always joked with me that if I didn't treat her girlfriend right, she would accidentally lose my financial aid papers. I don't think she was joking, yet we always got a good laugh out of that. I never had any intention of leaving Marilyn.

As a new husband, I wanted to take care of my wife. We still had a commuter situation, but not for long. It was time to get a real job, and I starting interviewing for news reporting positions in the tiny television markets in upstate New York. One gig in Watertown, New York, which is home to a sprawling military base, paid $18,000 a year. That hadn't been bad money, but the station had wanted me to be in their sports department, in which I had no interest. Another possible job in Utica, New York, paid only $10,000 a year, which I found unacceptable. I knew I couldn't live or pay back my student loans on that income.

With the job market looking bleak, my wife encouraged me to get a graduate degree. I hadn't even thought about doing that. I was happy to have my bachelor's degree, but a master's degree, and one from one of the best communication schools in the country? Syracuse was only thirty miles away from Cortland. Ultimately, the idea grew on me. I applied to Syracuse University's SI Newhouse School of Public Communications, which has a renowned broadcast journalism program and distinguished alumni. I wanted to be a part of that group.

I had come a long way since high school. My three years at Cortland had taught me to pursue excellence, and I would no longer settle for second best. I don't know where this sudden ambition had come from, but it was part of my new outlook on life. I didn't believe in laziness or just getting by. My whole attitude changed for the better, and I was always on the go. In college, I had often traveled to distant cities to build up my resume and my experience on the air. From Cortland, I frequently drove down Route thirteen to Ithaca's Cornell University to make the minimum wage as DJ for a nightly program, *Nightsounds*. The show was on from 10:00 PM to 2:00 AM. At other times, I would drive those lonely, dark roads upstate and work at Syracuse University's radio station. I worked hard because I knew I was headed for something big.

I knew that Newhouse had been among the preeminent communication schools to emerge during the explosion of the mass media during the 1960s. I thought my acceptance at Newhouse would be a given. Even though I had a letter of recommendation from the president of my undergraduate institution, SUNY Cortland, and a solid grade point average, Syracuse University roundly rejected me for their graduate studies program. I was devastated but still determined to get in.

At about the same time that I was rejected from Syracuse University, my wife wanted me to move with her to Alfred. That was the last thing I wanted to do. Instead, Marilyn decided to move closer to me. She went to a job interview at SUNY Morrisville, a small, two-year school about twenty-five miles outside Syracuse. The school catered to its population with farming majors like horse husbandry. The campus was literally filled with farmland and farm animals. During her interview, I waited in the hallway. Marilyn was offered the job on the spot. When she walked out with the president, Donald Butcher, he instantly took a liking to me. We spoke for a few minutes, and he said, "So what do you do?"

I replied, "I'm looking for work now."

Dr. Butcher said, "Well, I have a job opening for a dorm director and graduate assistant. Do you want it?"

I couldn't believe what I had just heard. Who knew I could get a job so easily? So Marilyn and I moved to Morrisville.

But I wasn't giving up on my newfound dream of becoming a Syracuse University graduate student. I made only $6,000 a year, but we didn't have to pay any rent because we lived in an apartment in the dorm. Our immediate neighbors in the building were eighteen- and nineteen-year-old students. Marilyn was twenty-eight, and I was twenty-one, so we were like senior citizens compared to the freshmen and sophomores who were just starting out.

Though Marilyn and I were both from the largest metropolitan area in the country, we adjusted easily to living in a community where you could drive right through on the main road in about sixty seconds. Morrisville didn't have its own police force; the state police covered the area. At the time, there was just one convenience store for the whole town. But it was a great place to live. At least it was convenient for Marilyn, because she could walk three blocks to work. Even though Syracuse had rejected me, I decided to enroll as a non-matriculated student at Syracuse and to begin taking one class at a time.

In the fall of 1985, I enrolled in a graduate class at Syracuse in TV production management. The course was intimidating at first because I was not enrolled in the school full-time, and I was the only minority in the class. I had to drive to Syracuse two or three times a week. But what a beautiful drive it was, especially during the summer. I vividly remember traveling up and down the hills of Route 20 through scenic Cazenovia, New York. The university itself was like a shining light on a hill. Like Cortland, the university sits high atop the city of Syracuse as a beacon of hope.

Newhouse was a two-building complex with a commanding presence. Students felt that they were part of something special. I was a model student at Syracuse and aced the TV production management course. Greatly encouraged, I reapplied for admission to Newhouse, believing that I had proved I could succeed in this prestigious institution. I believed wrong. They rejected me again. That denial hurt worse than the football team cut at Cortland because I couldn't understand why I'd been rejected.

Syracuse also had a law school, and I decided to take the standardized examination for law school admission. Surprisingly, I was accepted conditionally into the law program—but then why wasn't I good enough for their communications school? For football, I couldn't run fast, so that had been a fair rejection. But I had proved my academic ability by taking a class on my own time with my own money and getting a solid grade. To demonstrate my ability further, that spring semester I took television programming and nonfiction broadcast writing, and I received a B in each class.

Determined to gain entry to the university's program, I marched straight to the dean's office for an explanation. It was a brazen move, but I refused to take no for an answer. Trembling, and with the rejection letter in hand, I asked the dean, "Why am I denied admission?"

The dean said, "I'm sorry, but there's nothing I can do."

I wasn't finished. I stormed over to the office—of the president of Syracuse University. He wasn't in his office. I was so angry that I'm surprised the administration didn't call the police.

When I returned to the third floor of the Newhouse School, I got surprising news. A secretary said, "Mr. Carter, this is for you," and handed me a letter.

"Congratulations," the letter began. "You have been accepted to the SI Newhouse School of Public Communications. A center of excellence ..."

I wiped the tears from the eyes and read the fine print. It was a conditional acceptance. I had to maintain a 3.0 average to maintain my matriculation. I had to work twice as hard to get in, but that was fine with me because I knew I would succeed now that I had been given the opportunity. Marilyn and I celebrated with a big dinner at a local restaurant. She is a stickler for education, and she was thrilled to tell her family that, yes, her husband was young, but he was also ambitious. She never said she was embarrassed by the fact that she was seven years older than I am, but I knew that my success made her proud.

My work experience as a dorm director at Morrisville was about to be put to good use. In higher education, administrators serve at the discretion of the president of the college. And our protector at Morrisville, Dr. Donald Butcher, was leaving for a better opportunity. The next administrator in line decided not to renew Marilyn's contract. Just like that, we were out of jobs. Never wanting to repeat the hell of a commuter relationship, Marilyn enrolled in the PhD program at Syracuse University and also obtained a teaching position at a small Catholic high school in the city of Syracuse. With one year remaining of graduate school, I got a new job as the housing director for the Summer Institute Program at Syracuse University. It was similar to EOP for about fifty incoming students. My experience in residence life at Morrisville was a big plus in getting the job.

The following fall, I became a dorm director for the South
Campus at Syracuse University, which is where most of the athletes lived. The football players especially liked me, and I could
relate to them. Marilyn and I lived in a two-bedroom duplex
apartment free of charge, and it was truly the happiest time of
our lives, even though our combined salaries were about
$20,000 a year. We went to the movies and football games at
the Carrier Dome, and we held hands as we walked throughout
Syracuse's lush campus. We were newlyweds in every sense of
the word. We were not making a lot of money, but we were rich
in love and were looking forward to a bright future. We would
later marvel at how we, two underprivileged kids, excelled in
education and exceeded our family's expectations.

As a graduate student at Syracuse, I was 100 percent business. Since I had to maintain a B average like every graduate student, I couldn't take any chances. I worked at the radio station,
WAER, and practically lived in the library. I formed close alli-
ances with some of my professors, one who told me, "If you
want to succeed, stop talking like a black man, and act and
sound white." Ouch. And how in the hell was I supposed to do
that? I'm not saying the professor was wrong, but where was I
going to put my Bronx accent, and what was I going to replace
it with? I hadn't the foggiest idea.

His comment was my first clue that I would have to work
twice as hard to succeed in broadcasting. I had to learn a new
vocabulary and tone if I were going to be successful in radio and
television. But the challenge didn't stop me at all. I forged
ahead, accent and all, holding fast to my vision. I tried to get
comfortable with my voice and its cadence. I listened closely to
the intonation of other broadcasters and compared the way they

sounded to the way I sounded. I studied the rhythm of their voices. I had a throaty, resonant voice, but it was clear as a bell. It was a rich voice that bellowed from the cavern of my chest, and you knew when I was on the air.

In the fall of 1986, which was my first semester as a matriculated student, I took a class for what was called "experience credit." That meant an internship at a local television station, WTVH, a CBS affiliate. I worked the assignment desk, ripped wire copy, and assisted reporters on assignments. The managers even offered to hire me as a production assistant, but I turned them down. I had nothing personal against the city of Syracuse, but I didn't want to live there for a long period of time. I was confident that I was good enough to work in the big time—New York City.

That internship class stayed with me my entire career. When I turned in my final paper on the internship one hour late, I learned a lesson that I would never forget. My professor, Dwight Jensen, gave me a final grade of C even though I had earned an A. Even the news director agreed that I had deserved the top grade. In spite of my protests—and I could protest—Professor Jensen didn't budge. I felt that race played a role in his decision, but I could not prove it. He simply said, "Now, Dominic, you will learn always to respect your deadline." To this day, I have rarely missed a deadline.

Newhouse certainly lived up to its excellent reputation. Its staff was second to none, and I learned how to write broadcast copy and how to conduct interviews. I had been transformed from a kid who couldn't have cared less about school to an adult who could study communications law, journalism ethics, and research methods. I was successful because I worked hard and I believed I could succeed.

In the Carter family, I was the first full beneficiary of the civil rights movement. Thanks to an affirmative action program, I had been able to attend college and to dream bigger than the confines of my apartment in the projects. Life wasn't easy for me, but it was workable. Had I been born in another time—say, in my grandfather's day—my fate might have been quite different. But the 1980s held a new promise for ambitious young black men. The playing field wasn't level, but we still had a chance to knock the ball out of the park.

One of the best lessons I learned in school was the power of the human will. But the way I had to damn near beg to get into Syracuse University always left a sour taste in my mouth. I had a B+ average, and I only had four months left of graduate school. I would soon have my master's degree. Then I was about to face another serious challenge.

The New York Times

New York City Edition
Section 12

Television

S E P T E M B E R   8 - 14

Eyes on New York

NY 1: An All-News Station
With Home-Grown Talent

BY ROBIN POOREBIN

Chester Higgins Jr./The New York Times

From his humble beginnings Dominic could have never
imagined his future included an appearance on the cover of
the NY Times TV Guide.

A future Journalist in the making.

Young Dominic during happier Times.

From the NYC Housing Projects to the White House with
President Bill Clinton.

A humbling experience. Dominic's father never signed his birth certificate.

A shocking document Dominic would not see until he was almost 40 years old.

Dominic's crowning glory as a Journalist, interviewing Nelson Mandela. During Mandela's historic 1990's trip to the United States, only two Journalist in New York City out of thousands would sit down with him. Dominic and Ted Koppell of Nightline.

A rare happy moment for Mother and Son. Laverne Carter travels to upstate New York to attend Dominic's college graduation. The first in the family to receive a college degree.

Broadcasting live from democratic national convention in Boston.

1960's. Quality time for Dominic with his maternal figure and protector, His Aunt Inez.

An Easter Sunday on 125th Street in Harlem, NY. Top left, Laverne Carter, Dominic's aunt, Inez Carter. Dominic center, surrounded by two friends.

Grounds of Rockland State Psychiatric Center where mother's Dominic would spend months at a time locked up.

Daily reminder to and from work every day for Dominic of his mother's past.

Chip off the old block. Dominic's daughter, Courtney, at
the mayor's residence practicing the news.

Courtney as a high school student and Entertainer Michael
Jackson following Dominic interviewing him.

1983. College Days in the Dorm.

Grandma Ruby. Dominic's beloved mother-in-law. January 1999. Before she became ill. Doing what she did best, entertain family and take care of others.

A weekend home from college. Dominic, and his fiancee Marilyn visitng his eldest sister Malika. A todler here in this photo, Malika will soon be 30 years old.

A rare Vacation moment. Dominic with his kids in Hawaii.
Dominic Jr, (left) Courtney (right)

4

All of my life, I've had to fight. Even as an infant, I had to fight pneumonia and heart defects, and, as the years went on, I struggled with a mentally ill mother. Life threw me one curve ball after another, and somehow, someway, I always stepped up to the plate. I didn't realize it as soon as I left graduate school, but I was on the fast track to journalistic success. Four months before I finished my graduate studies, however, another curve ball was headed my way.

The news director for Inner City Broadcasting, headquartered in New York City, called my apartment in Syracuse at the beginning of my final semester of graduate school. The company, Inner City Broadcasting, was the owner of the same stations where I had interned, WBLS and WLIB. The news director's name was David Lampel. I thought he was calling for me to fill in for vacation relief, but his request was quite unexpected.

"Dominic," he said, "we have a position for a field reporter here, but it's available now, and, if it doesn't work out, we're going to cut you loose." Lampel spoke matter-of-factly.

Without missing a beat, I told Lampel that I'd be down in New York right away, though I had noticed his not-so-subtle disclaimer of "cutting me loose." But I knew in my heart that I would be successful as long as I could control my own destiny. Life has taught me that success was about timing and, more importantly, about hard work. I have never really believed in luck. I firmly believe one has to create his own opportunity. Unlike many of my colleagues, I did not have a political hook to get a job anywhere. What I did have was an indomitable spirit that would not take no for an answer. As an intern, I had worked twelve to eighteen hours a day without getting one thin dime. I had proved myself, and I had known it would only be a matter of time before I would get a break. And Lampel's news was a big break, indeed. I was honored to begin my career with those stations.

There was only one huge problem. I had worked so hard to get into Syracuse, and the job required that I begin before graduation. But job openings, especially at WBLS/WLIB, did not come frequently. I might have to wait several years before I could get another such opportunity. The man I would be replacing, Joe Bragg, had gone over to a rival station, WRKS, also known as KISS-FM. Bragg had always been a mentor to me, and I was suddenly given the opportunity to fill his shoes. His were big shoes, because he was a very good reporter and had quite a loyal following. Yet I detested the thought of giving up my master's degree to pursue a job that wasn't even guaranteed, especially considering I already paid several thousand dollars for that last semester of classes and could not obtain a refund.

But it was money that helped move my decision along. My proposed annual salary at the radio stations was $37,500 plus overtime and an expense account, complete with benefits. This was a lot of money for most college students, but for me—a poor kid from the Bronx—this was a virtual pot of gold. No one in my family had made this much money before. All through college, I had lived on stipends, student loans, and financial aid, and my campus jobs usually paid for my room and board. I had big plans for the future, and big money was at the center of those dreams. Sure, I wanted my master's degree, but I also wanted the stability of a full-time job with great benefits and salary.

After much deliberation with Marilyn, we decided I should go for it. Quickly, I submitted the withdrawal papers for my classes, packed my bags, and headed downstate—though I didn't have a home to move to. Marilyn remained in Syracuse to finish a class toward her PhD. She had impressive academic credentials, including a master's degree in reading education. So I wasn't worried about her future. But moving was somewhat bittersweet for me because I had become accustomed to living in small-town America, and now I was headed back to big-city America—and the same city where my mother lived.

This time, there was no way I was going to stay with Aunt Inez. I deeply appreciated all she had done for me, particularly spending thousands of hard-earned city employee dollars on my development. She was more like a mother to me than an aunt, but I did not want to return to a life in the projects. I stayed instead with my new mother-in-law, Ruby Stevens, whom I adored. I called her Ms. Stevens until the day she died. She was a short, soft-spoken woman who, like my family, had migrated from Georgia. I immediately adopted her as my mother, and she embraced me as she did her own sons. She lived at 50 Morningside Avenue on 119th Street in Harlem. The building sat directly across from Morningside Park, which separates Harlem and Morningside Heights. Columbia University sits on the other side of the park; years later I would be asked to speak at Columbia's renowned school of journalism.

Ruby Stevens was a modern-day warrior. She had raised eleven children in the tough community of Harlem, essentially by herself. I could never imagine how this woman had done it. She lived in a three-bedroom apartment and, just like my grandmother, she knew how to make ends meet. By the time I came into the picture, Ms. Stevens was living alone, as all of her grown children lived on their own. Ruby had a rough time, as the city had claimed most of the men in her life. It's said that parents are not supposed to bury their children, but Ruby Stevens had buried more than half of her brood.

Her son Jackie was brutally murdered over a woman. Her son Jimmy was an IV drug user who died of AIDS. Her son Henry, also a drug user, died of AIDS on what would be my daughter Courtney's first birthday. Ms. Stevens's son Lenny, another drug addict, died of a brain aneurysm. Her son Junior, another addict, died of a drug overdose. Her son Lewis died of lung cancer. And her baby son, Kenneth, woke up one morning when he was thirteen and found that he couldn't get out of bed. He would never walk again, and, several years later, part of his leg had to be amputated below the knee. Kenneth spent the rest of his life paralyzed and in a wheelchair. His condition, known as an AV malformation, resulted from veins that did not function properly. The condition claimed his life shortly before his thirtieth birthday.

But four of Ruby Stevens' children did quite well. My wife, Marilyn, was the star of the family, having earned the most college degrees. Judy Buckery, another daughter, is an administrative assistant for the New York City Police Department. Ruby's son Larry was an officer in the U.S. Army and, years later, retired as a sergeant in the New York City Police Department. And Ruby Stevens's son Tony completed an MBA from New

York University and works with the New York Human Resources Administration. For all of her heartache, Ruby Stevens never dwelled on the past but chose to focus on the present and the future. She showered her children with love and affection. She may have lived through a lot of family heartache, but she was never crestfallen.

As for my new career, I came out of the gate running. I had an edge because I was already familiar with my work environment, thanks to my previous internship. But I still had some butterflies in my stomach because I knew that if I didn't do well, I would be history. My work shift, from 5:00 AM to 1:00 PM, took some getting used to. My body rebelled every time the alarm clock went off at three o'clock in the morning. But my mother-in-law got me moving every morning. The sound of her pink bedroom slippers scuffed down the hall in the stillness of the night, letting me know it was time to get up. Her help in awakening me was just one of many examples of how special Ruby was to me. Half awake herself, Ruby would lean over the hot stove just to make breakfast for me. The vapors of coffee brewing on the stove helped me get out of bed. After a hot shower, I scarfed down scrambled eggs and sausage and bolted out of our Harlem building into the night air.

I took a bus that traveled across Harlem from the west side to the east side and then down Second Avenue to the offices of WBLS and WLIB. WBLS was 107.5 on the FM dial, and WLIB was 1190 on the AM dial. WBLS, a legendary urban contemporary station since the late 1960s, was a dominant 50,000 watt station with legendary talent like Frankie Crocker and Hal Jackson. I had met both these men during my internship days. WLIB was the smaller station, and its format at the time was black talk. The stations shared the same newsroom on the second floor of a high-rise office building on Manhattan's East Side. My eight-hour shift rarely lasted only eight hours—it was more like before sunup to after sundown. But because there was always so much going on at the station, the days sped by quickly.

Every morning I grabbed my bag and filled it with a professional broadcast tape recorder, headphones, cassette tapes, extra batteries, a notebook, and two microphones in case one failed to work. I wore my press pass around my neck and reported breaking news in the morning. A city teeming with eight million people always had news of some sort. Whether the news focused on a water main break or a shooting, there was rarely a dull moment.

I quickly learned how to write for the ear of listeners. A good radio reporter must be able to make listeners imagine a scene. I proved to be a natural interviewer. I asked tough questions and got all the sides to a story, no matter how long it took. The secret of my success in journalism is centered on fairness. I firmly believe that people should be treated the way I would want to be treated. That meant no cheap shots or unethical behavior. No professor or mentor taught me that philosophy, which was an approach I developed for myself.

Some reporters would forget their manners during an assignment, especially following a tragic death. During some of my assignments, I saw reporters who banged relentlessly on the front doors of families who had recently lost loved ones. These reporters kept their cameras rolling just to get a broadcast-worthy comment. The reporters never considered that such families might not want to be disturbed in the midst of grief. I never behaved that way. I always showed compassion and respect and tried to tread carefully. If I had to knock at the door of a grieving family, I offered my condolences and politely asked for a comment. If that approach failed, I might call a politician associated with the case for a comment. Getting a story does not mean sacrificing one's dignity. I've looked into the faces of grieving families many times and can easily see the pain in their eyes. These families usually don't understand that everything they say can and usually will be included in a reporter's story, and they often blurt out whatever comes to mind without giving their words much thought. I must admit that sometimes I let my interview subjects know that they should be careful what they choose to tell me, especially the subjects who are wracked with grief or pain, I have a big heart for people in misery, so I typically walk a fine line between listening and empathizing with people.

In the early years of my career, my actual on-air performance caused me to develop a love/hate relationship with my voice. I sounded raspy, and I had a thick, New York accent. I tried to change my voice but had little success. I sounded like a black man who'd been born and raised in the Bronx. However, my distinctive accent was a blessing in disguise, for no one confused me with other reporters. Once you heard my voice, you knew it belonged to Dominic Carter. My voice soon worked to my advantage and became my calling card. My sign-off was imitable: "Reporting live and direct from Manhattan, Dominic Carter, 1190 WLIB News," with an emphasis on the call letter "L." People loved to emulate me, but at least they knew who I was, and that's what really counted.

As for my appearance, I no longer had the lean, football-player build because I had filled out around the waist. Living the good life and eating in upscale restaurants in New York City started to show. I gained a little weight in my upper torso but maintained my skinny legs. I kept my beard cut very neatly to frame my jaw line and then to connect to a thin mustache. I considered myself a handsome character.

Many of my first assignments involved crime stories in some of the same impoverished neighborhoods that I had grown up in. I realized this awkward dichotomy. About seven years before, I had been on the inside of the poor neighborhoods looking out; now I was on the outside, looking in. As I covered stories of abuse, neglect, and death, no other reporter would imagine how familiar these problems were to me, and I surely didn't tell them. I just reported the facts and never allowed the stories to affect me personally, clearly showing how detached I had become from my troubled past. To look at my happy face during those assignments in my old neighborhood, one would never know how much I had in common with the people in my reports.

Even though my listeners were predominantly black, I never once considered myself an activist or a person who was empowering the community. I called the events just as I saw them and let the chips fall where they might. If people didn't like the way I reported an event, that was their problem. I thought I was little more than the messenger.

However one type of assignment would always charge my emotions. Those were stories that involved abused or murdered children. Perhaps I reacted that strongly because children are so vulnerable. Also, just ten years before, I had been one of those abused children. One such story occurred at a housing project in Brooklyn during the height of the crack cocaine crisis. A gunman knocked on the door of an apartment and opened fire right through the door. He was looking for an older brother who lived there and who sold drugs, but the brother wasn't home. Instead, a six-month-old baby, asleep in his crib, got caught in a hail of bullets. The child was rushed to Bellevue.

I arrived at the apartment at around 6:00 AM. The family let me in, and I sat and talked with the child's grandmother. Families often felt comfortable letting me into their homes. They told me they recognized my voice and liked my work. As we made small talk with the family of the baby who had been shot and waited for word of the baby's condition, the child's mother burst into the apartment and hysterically announced that her baby was dead. I was the only reporter in the apartment, and the family completely broke down. They screamed and leapt out of their seats. But the grandmother's face is the one I remember to this day. She froze when she heard the news and fell back into her chair with her mouth open wide, yet silent. Some call that look a silent scream. The situation was so frantic inside the apartment that I expressed my condolences and quietly left.

By the time I reached the elevator, tears were streaming down my face. Despite being choked up, I reported the story live, somehow able to maintain my composure. Normally I would stay and talk to the editor after filing the report, but this time I had to hang up as soon as the facts were in. With the phone booth as my shield, I shed tears for that troubled family and for that baby whose life had ended before he could even walk.

Another story was that of little Carlina Renae White. In 1987, Carlina had just been days old when she had mysteriously disappeared from Harlem Hospital in Manhattan. I was heartbroken as I interviewed the parents and the grandparents, who were themselves completely distraught. The baby had disappeared without a trace and was never found, dead or alive. No one appeared to know who took the cherubic, eight-pound infant. I would go on to cover many horrific news stories, but the ones involving murdered and abused children and tiny caskets were the ones I couldn't handle.

My new career sapped all of my energy, but I still made my way upstate to see my wife, though not every weekend. My newfound wealth allowed me to fly instead of taking the bus. In those days, People's Express Airlines offered a cheap flight to Syracuse for about thirty dollars. I would stash tapes of my work in my luggage so Marilyn could hear my reports. She was proud that I was slowly become a local celebrity; some of her friends even recognized my work. During one of my visits, Marilyn got pregnant. I had been pressuring her for years to start a family. In a couple of months, she would move back to Harlem from Syracuse to join me and her mother.

Aunt Inez was thrilled that I was a reporter for her favorite station, WBLS. She bragged about me to everyone she knew. My mother was proud, too, but she knew better than to brag about my position, at least in front of me. I gave Laverne Carter credit for that. She had done nothing to help me advance, and she didn't pretend she had. Laverne knew that I viewed her as an outsider. I knew better than to allow myself to get too close to her, so she did the next best thing: she got chummy with my mother-in-law, whom Laverne knew I adored.

Suddenly, Laverne began making frequent trips to visit my mother-in-law. I didn't block their meetings, but I knew Laverne was up to something—I just didn't know what. In those days, Laverne's mental illness was not easy to detect. She didn't slur her words, and she easily communicated with people. From my vantage point, she had stabilized. I talked to her just like I talked to anyone else. My mother-in-law, Ruby, was a peacemaker, and she enjoyed entertaining my mother. But Ruby had no idea what my mother and I had been through. And I sometimes wondered what was going on with my sister, Malika. I wouldn't dare prejudice my sister against my mother by telling her about my horrific background with our mother, but I would look deeply into my sister's eyes to look for those telltale signs, like not making eye contact with me or sending a visual plea for help that only a sibling could detect. I never saw those signs in Malika, so I prayed that she was coping just fine.

Once Marilyn moved back to Harlem, I drove our car to work instead of taking public transportation. During the wee hours of the morning, I would enter Central Park from the north at 110th Street and cut through the park, a route that shaved about fifteen minutes off my commute. As I drove, I passed ambulances, police cars, and other emergency service vehicles that had pulled over and parked off the main roads. Looking inside, I could see that the civil servants were fast asleep. I could've exposed them in a news story because they were on the clock, sleeping on the city's dime. I thought to myself, so much for the city that never sleeps. Truthfully, I didn't want to rock the boat, at least not yet, because I knew that I had to pick my battles.

When I was twenty-five years old, I found myself on the front lines in a racially divided city. My name was recognizable, my paychecks were getting larger, and my wife was about to deliver our first child. The pressure on me was enormous. I worked long hours every day and tried to remain objective about the volatile stories in the black communities. The founder of Inner City Broadcasting, Percy Sutton, was one of the most powerful and influential African Americans in New York City. At times, I had to do unflattering stories about Sutton's cronies. I played those stories straight, and I must admit that he never pressured me to give any story a particular slant. But I was still on edge. I needed a release.

My base annual salary of $37,000 quickly ballooned with overtime to more than $80,000. I had a pocket full of money and very few expenses, yet who was I kidding? I still wasn't happy, and I didn't know anyone who could make me happy. No one in particular made me unhappy. I just felt empty deep inside. Before I knew it, I was on another path, not a career path, but a path of self-destruction. Perhaps I went along that path because of the pressure from work, or perhaps my weakness resulted from my immaturity.

Whatever the reason, I sought release inside nightclubs and partied all night long. Sometimes I would not come home for an entire weekend. I would party all night and crash on one of my buddies' couches before starting the cycle all over again. One minute it would be Friday night, and the next minute it would be Sunday afternoon. My behavior caused tremendous tension in my marriage, but it didn't matter to me at the time. In my career, I was excelling rapidly, but in my personal life, I was headed downhill—just as fast. I started living in a fool's paradise, believing that Dominic was the life of the party, though, in reality, there was little to celebrate. I needed to show the world that I'd made it, but I did it the wrong way for all the wrong reasons. I hung out with high school buddies from the Bronx. I was the big spender, and the drinks were always on me. I was on the radio, I knew the politicians, I had influence, yet I had nothing. I had gained the world but lost my footing, though I didn't want to admit it at the time.

I despised being a nobody, from the days when my grandmother had been treated like just another dying black woman in the hospital. I despised the days when I had been poor, especially having nothing to eat except butter sandwiches for dinner. Finally, I had fame, money to burn, and freedom. I tried to explain to my wife that I had too much pressure on me. In reality, many people didn't know my face, but they knew my name, and when they found out that Dominic Carter was in the club, I got royal treatment, just as I had always imagined. My behavior was reckless, but it was also a dream come true. Everybody wanted to be my friend, everybody told me they knew who I was, and I loved being in the limelight.

After my social activities, I would make up with Marilyn by taking her on expensive trips to Mexico and Puerto Rico, but, when I got back to New York, I would work Monday through Friday, party all weekend, and throw away thousands of dollars in the process. Marilyn and I had been married for about five years, but the grass looked greener elsewhere. With a new baby on the way and added responsibilities, I could feel the heat, and it was not pleasant. Marilyn and I had been carefree in the past, but, when she got pregnant, our freewheeling times ended. Because of my past, I could not fully appreciate love, yet I was hell-bent on hiding my emotions. But covering my emotions didn't work well with my family. As my wife prepared to become the mother hen, I played in the lion's den. During her ninth month of pregnancy, Marilyn called me and told me to come home because she could deliver our child at any time. What did I do? I stayed out of the house for the next two days.

In days past, I might have been confused about being a husband, but I was not confused about being a new father. No matter how much my wife thought I might miss seeing our child when it was born, I was determined not to miss the birth. I was there when Courtney Ann Carter was born January 28, 1988, at Metropolitan Hospital in Upper Manhattan. I named her, and I was amazed that I had created another human being. That was the most powerful feeling in the world. As Marilyn and I filled out Courtney's birth certificate, I thought back to how my father hadn't filled out mine. I was so overcome with emotion that I could hardly speak. I had helped usher in a new generation of Carters, and I felt a strong need to protect and defend my new bundle of joy.

I was prepared to do anything to keep her from the evils of the world, especially the evils that I had seen early in my life. I knew I couldn't create a perfect world for Courtney, but I vowed to come as close as I could. In my view, I had suffered enough to cover all future generations, starting with my firstborn. I felt that she should never shed a tear because I had shed them all. Never would a disappointment come my child's way because I had already faced the worst disappointments a child could face. I had paid the price, and I bore the emotional scars to prove it. Courtney's birth was a cleansing of a generation's sins for me. Tears spilled from my eyes when I held Courtney for the first time. She squinted her little eyes and peered at me and, from that moment on, stole my heart.

Laverne showed up at the hospital to help celebrate Court-ney's arrival. Surprisingly, my mother's presence didn't bother me one bit. In fact, it was the closest I would allow myself to let-ting bygones be bygones. I had no fear that Laverne would ever harm my daughter because I knew that Courtney would never be alone with my mother. My mother was fine in public, but when she was behind closed doors alone with a child, that was the time to be afraid—very afraid.

Now that I was a husband and a father, my wife and my mother-in-law pressured me to develop a closer relationship with my mother so that we could be a big, happy family. Laverne came by on the weekends to see Courtney, and I wasn't rude, but I didn't act like she was a beloved mother and grand-mother. It was time to end this phony family reunion stuff. After countless times of my wife and my mother-in-law pushing my mother on me, I would hear no more of it.

"You don't know Laverne like I do!" I said sternly to Mari-lyn, who continued to pressure me. At last I sat down with Marilyn to explain what my mother had done to me. I took a deep breath, and let it out. "Laverne sexually abused me when I was a little boy," I said. "She's crazy."

My wife looked back me at me in disbelief. I didn't want to go into specifics. Marilyn looked entirely embarrassed. The con-versation concluded with my wife gently trying to ask follow-up questions, but, for the time being, I had said enough. One might think my silence would have stopped Marilyn from inter-fering, but it didn't. Her intentions were good, but I suspected that my mother's intentions were not. The only result of my wife's interference was that I felt angry again over my child-hood. I had done well when my mother had been out of sight, but now that she was visiting the apartment all the time, the past experiences were more than I cared to deal with. So again I went out to party my troubles away.

In 1988, I went on the road for my first big national assignment and to escape the immediate issues at home. After having lost in 1984, Jesse Jackson was running again to be the Democrats' nominee for president, and this time the radio station was sending me to cover the story. The news director, Lampel, casually mentioned my new assignment. "Dominic, I want you to go on the road with Jesse for two weeks," he said.

I was excited to travel, even though Courtney was an infant. Jackson was an electrifying person and a natural charmer. He was good-looking with wavy hair, and the women loved him. Judging by the way the women fawned over him, at times he resembled a rock star more than a preacher. Later I was a little saddened to hear of his love-child imbroglio in 2001, but I was not entirely surprised. The temptation from women must have been overwhelming. They acted like groupies, and it was quite a spectacle.

This was the first time I would leave home for several weeks. Traveling with Jackson meant I would miss my baby girl's milestones. I just knew I would miss her first tooth, her first laugh, and the first time she would sit up alone. And, sure enough, I didn't hear Courtney's first words in person, I didn't see her teeth come in, and I didn't see her take her first steps. Yet my wife was patient because she knew how hard I was working. When I called home, Marilyn would put Courtney on the phone, and she would babble into the receiver. I can still hear those gurgled words to this day.

I had a lot to gain by covering Jackson. If I didn't go, I would lose out on covering a major national story, and I would possibly lose my job. If I did go, I would ensure a bright future for little Courtney, who would never have to live in the impoverished conditions that her father had endured. It was an easy decision to make, and I hoped that Courtney would understand one day.

One major reason that Inner City Broadcasting paid for this assignment was that Jackson, though a prominent fixture during the civil rights movement, was not regularly covered by the mainstream press. Percy Sutton, a good friend of Jackson and a former local politician himself, wanted to make sure Jackson got fair treatment in the press. So I boarded a plane and joined Jackson's entourage. The two-week assignment turned into almost a full year of following Jackson from city to city. It was the assignment of a lifetime for me. As a youngster, I had watched Jesse Jackson pick up where Dr. Martin Luther King had left off. Jackson was always on television or on the radio because he was the "keeper of the dream." I had gone from sitting in front of a television watching Jackson to standing next to him and putting him on the air. I had to pinch myself to make sure I wasn't dreaming.

Throughout the campaign, Jesse Jackson turned to me to reach thousands of potential voters in New York City. He was being outspent by his rival Democrats, including frontrunner Massachusetts Governor Michael Dukakis, but Jackson would make up for his lack of funds by campaigning non-stop. Jackson had his own plane, complete with Secret Service agents, about fifteen reporters, and a handful of campaign staff workers. He hop scotched the nation, city by city, so often that I never bothered changing the time on my watch. Los Angeles, Denver,

Atlanta, Seattle, Connecticut—the race was breathtaking. I was with Jackson every day, often for sixteen hours or more, and I was fascinated by his oratorical skills. He could truly work a crowd. When he visited high schools, he would tell the students not to "commit the sin of doing less than your best," and the students ate it up.

On March 22, 1988, at the Frauenthal Center in Muskegon, Michigan, Jackson told a compelling story about the working poor before he outlined his agenda for universal health care. The crowd of several thousand people stood up and roared—and I mean *roared*—in approval. The Jackson campaign and the press entourage remained in Michigan for quite some time. After Detroit, we hit Ann Arbor, Kalamazoo, Lansing, and Flint, and we even stayed several nights in Ypsilanti. Jackson's intense campaigning paid off, for he won the Michigan state primary in March, to most people's surprise. One Michigan newspaper, apparently on deadline, made the wrong call and declared Dukakis the winner. Jackson did his best "Dewey defeats Truman" pose for the cameras while holding up the inaccurate Michigan newspaper headline.

Meanwhile, I was making headlines of my own back home. A local popular newspaper, *Newsday*, did a story on my career with WLIB and included my coverage of Jackson. I was overjoyed. The story was not just a mention; it was an exhaustive article complete with pictures of my wife and baby daughter. On April 13, 1988, I was the subject of "Blacks in New York: Reporter Tuned In to Listeners." The article began with my work on the Howard Beach case.

> Carter, bearded and barrel-chested, is using the [pay] phone
> to report the story live for WLIB ... already soaked with
> sweat, Carter quickly barks out the story's basics.

I loved how the paper described me as a "buoyant, aggressive
twenty-six-year-old." Although I had been with WLIB for only
a year, the paper noted how I handled the tense chain of events
with ease.

> With an explosion of racially charged stories in the city dur-
> ing the past year, Carter has landed on a journalistic hot
> seat, a challenge he's accepted with enthusiasm.

Reporter Barry Meier added,

> The [Jackson] assignment, however, is an important step
> for the young journalist. For one thing, it's the first major
> national story he has handled ... Fellow reporters have
> already nicknamed him "sleepy" because he has fallen back
> asleep after filing his initial 4:30 AM report for the station.

I didn't like the "sleepy" comment because I had literally
worked myself to tears at the station, and the comment implied
that I was lazy, which I most certainly am not and never have
been.

One day during the Jackson campaign, we left the East Coast
at 6:00 AM, hit another city by 10:00 AM, then crisscrossed the
country and ended on the West Coast at 1:00 AM, though it was
4:00 in the morning back in New York. This shift in time zones
meant that I had to keep going until 5:00 AM New York time to
file my report. When I finally checked in to my hotel room, I

lay down and cried like a baby. I wasn't mad at anybody in particular. I just cried from sheer exhaustion.

The "sleepy" comment in *Newsday* followed me throughout the campaign. During a layover in Dallas, I was so exhausted that I missed the Secret Service bag inspection for the flight to South Dakota. I felt tired and ornery and decided I wanted a day off. I intentionally missed the flight, but my move backfired. Within hours, Lampel called my hotel room and told me firmly, "Take the next available flight and get back here to New York." I hadn't been home in a month, so I had been happy to return. But when I got to the office, Lampel threatened to fire me, and I was scared to death. I apologized profusely, and, after two days, he sent me back on the Jackson campaign trail.

From a journalist's point of view, I was in good company. Some of the other reporters assigned to the campaign have gone on to have stellar careers. One is Gwen Ifill, who at the time was with the *Washington Post*. She went on to join the *New York Times* and to become a star correspondent at NBC News. Now she has her own national political show on the Public Broadcasting System. Another regular on the campaign was Michael Frisby, then with the *Boston Globe*, who moved on to the *Wall Street Journal* as a White House correspondent. It was Frisby who stood up in the middle of a White House news conference and asked President Clinton if he'd thought about resigning over the Monica Lewinsky scandal. Clinton looked directly at Frisby and responded in classic Clintonesque style: "It's never crossed my mind." Frisby's question and Clinton's response made headlines around the world.

Other very capable reporters following Jackson: Mike Duffy for *Time* magazine, Priscilla Painton for the *Atlanta Journal-Constitution*, David Maraniss for the *Washington Post*, Marianne

Keeley for ABC News, and Nancy Lane for CNN. Lane has gone on to become a top producer at CNN. Every now and then, legendary *Washington Post* political correspondent David S. Broder, who won the Pulitzer Prize for distinguished commentary in 1973 and also appears on the national Sunday morning political talk shows, would come on the campaign trail.

A highly interesting spectacle during the Jackson campaign was watching the Secret Service in action. Jackson was the first black man to make a serious bid for the presidential nomination, and the Secret Service took no chances with his safety. Jackson often wore some type of bulletproof clothing. Before we boarded the campaign plane, the Secret Service had what was termed a "bag call" hours before the flight. The bags had to be laid out so that bomb-sniffing dogs could go through them. This bag call could be a real inconvenience because it was a daily ritual, and we often had a short turnaround in every city we visited. As a shortcut, I learned to pack all of my belongings into one bag to make it easier for me to get around. Another trick I learned was that, the night before, I would take out my clothes for the next day and re-pack my bag to take downstairs for the Secret Service before bedtime. That action would buy me an extra hour and a half of sleep, an amount that may not seem like much, but it makes a world of difference when you work sixteen hours nonstop.

During one inspection, agents found a bullet on the plane. That discovery delayed us for close to two hours. I am not certain if anyone ever found out where the bullet came from. When we traveled through cities, the Secret Service usually shut down traffic and led us on a direct route to our location. It was amazing to see all the traffic on every street come to a standstill for us. Buses would also pick us up directly on the tarmac at the airport. Such special attention spoiled me, and from then on I would be very impatient waiting in traffic.

Jackson kept working his magic during his campaign stops, and I kept reporting what he did and said. I consider this campaign as the assignment where I truly proved myself. All of us reporters practiced our impressions of Jackson that would leave us howling in laughter: "Keep hope alive! Keep hope alive! I am—somebody!"

Heading for the Democratic National Convention, Jackson showed no signs of defeat. He would tell reporters, "If they had our money, they would surrender. If I had their money, they could not compete." Meantime, the mainstream press had all but written off any notion of a Jackson victory. There were headlines saying discouragingly, "Jackson Can't Win," and "What Does Jesse Really Want?"

While I was on the road with Jackson, my grandfather died. He hadn't been around when my grandmother had died several years before. He was estranged from the entire family. But he had won his battle over heroin addiction and had left this world clean and sober. I respected him, but his passing did not move me to tears. In fact, I was a little annoyed. I wasn't even in New York, which was thousands of miles away, and no one else in the family could handle the arrangements. I asked my wife to coordinate the plans with Johnny's girlfriend, Minnie, and a decision was made to have him cremated.

My mother continued reaching out to my mother-in-law and visiting our apartment during the holidays. Laverne joined Marilyn's family for a Thanksgiving feast of turkey, yams, and collard greens. I was a no-show because I had to make an unexpected trip with Jesse Jackson. For this trip, I needed an expedited passport for a fourteen-hour flight to the Middle East. Jackson had been trying to arrange delivery of 600 pounds of Christmas gifts to American troops in the Persian Gulf. In the end, under a new Pentagon policy, he would not be able to distribute the gifts because the Reagan administration had banned visits to military installations and ships in the Persian Gulf except by officials on government business. But Jackson decided to proceed with a fact-finding trip, anyway.

Not one for patience, I wondered how I would survive fourteen hours of flying. The flight left at ten o'clock at night, so I was able to sleep overnight. I closed my eyes, but before I could sleep, I spent a few minutes thinking about my accomplishments. In a matter of a few short years, I was traveling the world free of charge. In my work, I mingled with the rich and famous, some of people who a couple of years ago might have been afraid to get on an elevator alone with me.

I was the first in my family to travel the nation and the world. I guess I had a lot in common with my grandmother, Anna Pearl. Two generations before, she had taken the bold step of leaving the red hills of Georgia and traveling to New York City. Her daring to board a Greyhound bus for a far-distant place led to my boarding a plane to the Middle East. My dear grandmother had laid a foundation for me to take steps into the unknown and to branch out into new experiences. Anna Pearl went as far as she could go as a Negro woman born during the humiliating Jim Crow era, but, as her grandson, I had inherited her tenacity and was willing to circle the globe.

On this plane with Jesse Jackson, I dreamed of my grandmother, the woman I called Ma. When I wasn't asleep, I listened to the charismatic Jackson. Never wanting to waste time,

Jackson held chat sessions with all parties involved, from staffers to reporters. He spoke passionately about whatever issue was under discussion.

On that trip, our group stopped in countries like Bahrain, Saudi Arabia, and Kuwait. I was spellbound. Here I was, a poor kid from the Bronx, in a completely different world. I had made quite a name for myself. When other reporters asked "Why?" I asked "Why not?"

Jackson lost the democratic nomination, but the true highlight of my radio career was the visit of Nelson Mandela, who was the symbol of the struggle against apartheid in South Africa. Nelson Rolihlahla Mandela was born in July 1918, and joined the African National Congress in 1942. After two decades of fighting for the end of the racist apartheid system, he was given a life sentence and sent to a notorious maximum security prison near Cape Town. After twenty-seven years behind bars, Mandela continued his work and headed to the United States for a twelve-day, eight-city tour. His first stop was New York City. This visit was a triple-crown story because it had local, national, and international appeal. New Yorkers prepared to treat Mandela as an adopted son, and the newly crowned Dinkins administration gave him first-class treatment. Mandela was given a parade along the Canyon on heroes up lower Broadway in Manhattan. Major rallies for Mandela were planned in Harlem and Yankee Stadium.

The security was provided by more than twelve thousand officers along with helicopters, boats along the banks of the East River, insulated bomb trucks, and sharpshooters. There was a "Mandela-mobile," similar to the popemobile, complete with a flatbed truck and bulletproof glass. Mandela's security was far more involved than that provided for Jesse Jackson's detail.

Mandela was a big interview for any journalist. Every network wanted him and did their best to get him. I wanted to get an exclusive interview with Mandela, but I knew it would be hard to obtain permission. I began to doubt my ability to get the interview and allowed a defeatist attitude to stop me before I even tried. Fortunately, I quickly conquered my fears. If I had ever stayed in the defeatist frame of mind, I certainly would not have succeeded in the radio news business.

With Mandela's visit still about two weeks away, I needed the right person to help me schedule an interview. Every city government administration has a go-to person who has the mayor's ear. The go-to guy for Dinkins was Deputy Mayor Bill Lynch, Dinkins' former campaign manager, who accomplished the enormous feat of getting the first black mayor elected in New York. I pleaded with Bill Lynch to give me an exclusive interview with Mandela. He laughed at me.

"Every reporter and their mother wants that interview," Lynch said. "Besides, Dominic, Mandela's staff will have a say in who he wants to talk with. I can't make any promises to you or anyone."

I couldn't take no for an answer. I had to find a way. Mandela was widely viewed as the only surviving member of the Big Three in the black community, the others being Martin Luther King and Malcolm X. When Mandela later spoke at rallies, he invoked the memories of those two men. I called anyone who I thought could help me land this interview. On the surface, it probably seemed laughable that a small-time radio reporter with a predominantly black audience even dreamed of interviewing the most sought-after black man in the world. The idea was laughable to everyone but me. Again, I asked, "Why not me?" I never looked down on myself, and I had very healthy self-esteem, for which my colleagues respected me. The Dinkins administration respected me, apparently, because after weeks of hearing my pleas, they granted my request for an interview.

The only reporter who interviewed Mandela ahead of me was ABC's Ted Koppel. But I still beat Koppel to the punch because my interview aired first, while his aired later in the evening on a special edition of *Nightline*. I beat all the broadcast and cable networks, even the international media, because I believed in myself and put in a lot of hard work to get this international figure in an interview.

My preparations for the talk with Mandela were exhaustive. I asked my engineering team from the radio station to meet me at the mayor's official residence, Gracie Mansion, which overlooks the East River. Everyone at WLIB and WBLS were depending on me. If anything went wrong, I would be the one held responsible.

After passing through a metal detector and walking past bomb-sniffing dogs, my team and I set up our equipment in a side room of Gracie Mansion. I didn't hear from Dinkins or Lynch, but I knew about when Mandela was to arrive because armed security stood outside the door. After days of near panic, I told myself to focus. I reminded myself that Nelson Mandela was just another human being. But who was I kidding, this figure was an international icon.

Suddenly the doorknob turned and in walked a six-foot-tall, caramel-skinned man with a cherubic face. Mandela had opened the door and let himself in, just like that. I introduced myself and told him how honored I was to meet him. He was very gracious, calm, and soft-spoken. He sat down in a chair that I had set up for him. As I seated myself, I could hardly believe I was sitting across from the man who had almost single-handedly brought down the system of apartheid. Yet Mandela called me "Mister Carter."

A few months before, the entire world had watched as this man had been released from years in a maximum security prison, and now he was sitting in front of me. Unlike my colleagues who were vying for the same interview, I did not have the privilege of a private school education, nor had I come from a wealthy family, but I had one thing that pushed me to the front of the line: determination. From the outset, the interview with Mandela was a seemingly impossible feat to accomplish. I was successful because I remained persistent. I even made a series of phone calls to anyone who could help me get this interview.

I had a few minutes to spare before the interview officially began, so I made small talk. "Mr. Mandela," I said, "you have just finished twenty-seven years in prison, yet you don't seem to be angry."

Mandela smiled. "I could not be angry, young man, or it would have been giving in to those who jailed me," he said. "My anger would have destroyed me."

I was awed by his quiet confidence, which truly humbled me. During the interview, which was an enormous success, Mandela and I were live on the radio with WLIB host Gary Byrd for about fifteen minutes. Afterward, he posed for pictures with all of us, including me and the engineers from the radio station.

It was obvious during my radio days that I would have an even brighter future, one that I hoped would be in television. My appearances on television quickly multiplied. I was on the

Charlie Rose show on PBS to talk about local politics. During that show, I was impressed by how sharp Rose was mentally and by his ability to ad lib. I also appeared on the award-winning PBS documentary program *Frontline* with then-*New York Post* reporter Pamela Newkirk. The woman who introduced that Frontline segment was Judy Woodruff, who at that time was a star anchor on CNN.

I also did a local PBS show called *Thirteen Live.* The show's producers asked that I appear with a panel to discuss the administration of Mayor David Dinkins. The program was hosted by Marlene Sanders. Then I appeared on a panel with the late Andy Logan, who wrote the *Around City Hall* column for *New Yorker* magazine. The column, which first appeared in 1969, was considered legendary by many in the politically astute. Also joining us on the panel was Michael Tomasky, who worked at the *Village Voice* and went on to *New York Magazine,* and William Murphy of *Newsday.*

I made numerous featured appearances on a popular New York public affairs show tailored to the black community. The show was titled *Like It Is,* hosted by legendary journalist Gil Noble, and aired on the local ABC station. As a top city hall reporter, I was frequently asked to give my opinion about local politics. During one appearance I made on the show, the guest was none other than the governor of the state and an icon of the Democratic Party, Mario Cuomo. During the taping, I tried to grill Cuomo. He remained stoic, but I could tell he was not happy, and he made his displeasure known in the men's bathroom of the television station. I was already standing at a urinal when Cuomo walked in and stood by my side. He turned his head to look me squarely in the eye and said, "You know, Carter, you think you're hot shit." I smiled and took his remark as an indirect compliment. I knew it wasn't personal. I did note that the state police officers, part of the governor's security detail, were standing behind him, dressed in business suits to blend in with the crowd, but still heavily armed.

I also appeared on the popular show *Sunday Edition,* which aired on the local CBS affiliate and was hosted by Jim Jenson. I did a point/counterpoint with a man who went on to make national headlines himself, Joe Klein. Years later Klein would write the hugely popular book *Primary Colors* about a Clintonesque presidential candidate who is confronted by sex scandals and manages to distract the public into believing that he deeply cares about human problems. *Primary Colors* debuted to great fanfare; its author was originally anonymous, but Klein was exposed as its author after the book was published.

In a rare move, WCBS-TV sent me on an audition with a camera crew to report on a story and put it together. The station received hundreds of tapes a week from veteran television reporters nationwide. The news director at WCBS was Paul Sagan, a tall, no-nonsense news prodigy who had been promoted to the top job in local news in his mid-twenties. I had lunch with Sagan, and, a short time later, he told me that after viewing my tape, he concluded I wasn't ready for television. He assured me that one day I would be a big star, but not yet.

"How dare he!" I thought. I didn't want anything else to do with WCBS, and I rebuffed his offer to join their future roundtables with Jim Jenson. I had my pride, no matter how foolish it was to turn away from a paid weekly television appearance.

In 1992, I became disgruntled with the radio business. I was making fairly good money—up to $85,000 annually with overtime—but some reporters still made more money than I did, and that disparity infuriated me. Then and now, salaries are a serious matter to me. A person's pay shows how much a company values that individual. I had increased WLIB's number of listeners tremendously, and I didn't think I was being treated fairly. In May 1992, Paul Sagan left a message on my answering machine.

"Hey, Dominic, listen," his message said. "I'm starting a *new* news operation, and I'd like you to come on board. Please call me as soon as possible."

I used Sagan's offer first as an excuse to get more money from my bosses. I explained in detail why I would leave if they didn't increase my pay. First, I went to Hal Jackson, who was also vice president of Inner City Broadcasting and who treated me like a son. "We'd love for you to stay, Dominic," he told me. "Let's see if we can work things out."

Next I went to Pierre Sutton, son of Percy Sutton and the CEO of Inner City Broadcasting. Pierre's response was, "Dominic, we're gong to try to meet somewhere in the middle. You're part of our family."

Then I went to David Lampel, who had been promoted to senior vice president. He had given me my start, and when I walked into his second-floor office and explained that I was seriously thinking about leaving LIB, I began to cry. I had a deep sense of loyalty to Inner City Broadcasting, and I didn't want to appear ungrateful. I knew they had taken a chance on me when I had only been a kid from the Bronx and when no one else would. I cried harder in Lampel's office than I would at the death of my own mother. I could tell that Lampel felt a little awkward, seeing a brash, young reporter break down. He calmed me and said that everything would be all right.

My last stop was Percy Sutton, who said, "Mr. Carter, some-times a bird has to spread its wings, so go and make a success of yourself."

That was that. I submitted my letter of resignation, and my last day at WLIB/WBLS was June 12, 1992. I was twenty-six years old, I was about to embark on a whole new career in tele-vision news with a fledgling, twenty-four-hour cable network, and I had another baby on the way. My marriage was still on shaky ground, but Marilyn and I were still forging ahead with our plans to build a family. I loved my wife and my baby girl, but I had not yet come to terms with my past abuse and the impact it might have on my future.

Everyone in the family was excited about my foray into tele-vision news, especially my wife. She supported my move into television, and we knew that I had just been give access to a whole new level of success.

5

As I began an exciting new television career, I should probably have considered this time as one of the happiest in my life. It wasn't. Laverne Carter, who was incapable of being maternal when I was a child, had the nerve to morph into a loving mother for her grandchild. Her greatest role yet involved acting as if nothing had ever happened with me. She wanted to pretend that she had never tried to strangle me. She forgot about those threats to throw me out a window. And she definitely wanted to absolve herself of her despicable sex act with her own flesh and blood. She was still coming to my mother-in-law's house, and she was brazen enough to act like we were all a loving, stable family. I felt resentful when I would walk in from work and see her sitting in the kitchen or the living room.

Sometimes her face was the last thing I wanted to see, but I had to pretend that she and I didn't have a dirty little secret. Yet anyone who looked closely could see that something was wrong, though most people didn't know what. They probably thought I was holding a grudge because Laverne hadn't raised me herself. I tried not to show my bitterness, but it was impossible not to let some of my feelings slip. I constantly asked myself, "Why me?" She could have had sexual contact with almost any man—even the psychiatrists had noted her physical appeal. Then why had she chosen her little boy?

But I was no longer that vulnerable little boy. Now I was a man who still lived with a boyhood shame. I had worked in radio for six years, and my colleagues would never have guessed what I had lived through because of my mother's abuse.

At least my life was improving professionally. My hard work as a radio reporter had paid off bountifully, with my annual salary reaching nearly $90,000. One would think that a transition to television would surely translate into greater fortunes. Yet it didn't. The yet-unnamed twenty-four-hour cable news channel was a bare-bones operation with a very small staff. The cable news channel staff offered me $50,000 to be a reporter. I was dismayed because that salary was far below the industry standards for a New York television reporter (though that amount was at the high end for this startup operation). I had been trying to reach my personal goal of a six-figure salary, and I was being asked to take a pay cut of $40,000 a year. I was so incredulous that I sent my 1991 tax returns via Federal Express to my new bosses as a way to plead my case for higher compensation.

Paul Sagan, however, remained unmoved. He was in his early thirties, a bespectacled, six-foot-two man who was firm but fair. We had first met when he had run the news operation at WCBS-TV in New York City. As vice president of the cable channel, he was no-nonsense and had exceptional news management judgment. He had been handpicked by Time Warner Chief Dick Auriello to run the new television station that was quickly becoming the talk of the town. Even The *Daily News* featured a quick tidbit about my departure detailing my jump from radio to television.

All of my radio colleagues and my future television colleagues knew I was making a big career move. I was constantly fielding questions about my decision. People asked, "Are you nervous?"

"Are you ready for prime time?" I was getting sick of their obvious doubts—and perhaps their envy.

Other issues on my mind were personal. My second child was on the way, and my wife was pressuring me to buy a house. I felt very comfortable with our living arrangement in Harlem because the place was dirt cheap and was in a decent area, and we had a built-in caretaker, my mother-in-law, whom I absolutely adored. I recognized the irony: I could hardly stand my natural mother, but I genuinely loved my mother-in-law. Though my wife deeply cared for her mother, she wanted a home of her own. She believed I should have something concrete to show for all my hard work. Marilyn was looking out for my best interests and those of our daughter and our child-to-be. However, knowing about my pay cut, I knew I could not focus on thoughts of a new home.

I also felt concerned about the sentiment of my radio colleagues, who predicted doom, not just for me, but for any black reporter who made the foray into television. During my radio career, I had always heard people say that television was a vicious, cutthroat industry that was not particularly fond of black men. My colleagues strongly believed that black reporters would, at best, shine for a moment and then be shoved out of sight, out of mind, then out of a job.

My final concern was about my professional future. Who knew if the media behemoth, Time Warner, would stand by its first cable news channel for the long haul? If the channel wasn't profitable, would the company abruptly cut its losses?

I had many doubts and unanswered questions, but as I had learned from my childhood experiences, I put my fears behind me, though this time I had a lot to lose. By the time I started in June 1992, the new cable channel had a name, New York 1

News, and it would debut on Channel 1. The cable channel was staffed by a group of young, ambitious reporters who were set to take Gotham by storm. Our news team made news before we actually started reporting the news because our format and news delivery style were to be completely unorthodox. The most noticeable deviation was that the reporters from New York 1 worked alone in a news market that regularly used two- and three-man teams to report the news.

I had an edge in this one-man market because, as a radio reporter, I had worked solo. But I soon found out that carrying a tape recorder is entirely different from carrying a thirty-pound camera and tripod. In fact, contractually, we television reporters were not reporters; we were officially called video journalists, sometimes known as VJs. But the VJ moniker never stuck, and we were called reporters, even by managers.

There were persistent rumors that other news crews would not take kindly to our solo approach because if we proved that we could get the news without using an additional camera operator, then the fate of the teams that took along cameramen could be in jeopardy. I already knew many of the news crews from my radio days. With the exception of one of two snide comments from cameramen, apparently afraid that our approach would one day eliminate their jobs, most of my colleagues from other networks treated me with respect.

New York 1's format also deviated from the approach that other stations used. Instead of a live broadcast, our station devised a series of taped news segments called wheels. Essentially, the budget called for hiring only three full-time anchors, but the anchors could not read news copy live for eight hours nonstop. So the anchors taped each story separately and then put the stories into a sort of juke box that could be programmed to look like a live show, even though every story actually stood on its own. The jukebox format allowed producers, who functioned more like computer programmers, to change the order of stories when the news warranted.

The only time New York 1 resembled other news shows was when there was breaking news. Producers would ditch the wheel format and go live for an event, but, when the event was over, the producers would return to the wheel. New York 1's whole format was so radical that most of us reporters didn't understand it until we had been on the air for about a month.

New York 1's coverage focused strictly on New York City. Such specialized news became an emerging trend, as News 12 Long Island had begun the local cable news format, which was successful, and New York 1 wanted to capitalize on that concept. The area had five borough reporters—one each for Manhattan, Brooklyn, Queens, Staten Island, and the Bronx. There were also fifteen traditional beats like crime, entertainment, and health. But the crème de la crème of the reporters were the political reporters, who were then Andrew Kirtzman and me. Former Mayor Edward Koch had made New York City politics exciting because of his exuberance and his "how am I doin'?" shtick. As a result, the average voter had a better idea of the goings-on at city hall than during previous mayoral administrations.

David Dinkins inherited Koch's political fervor, and Andrew Kirtzman and I were anointed to help stir the political world even more. New York 1 initially wanted to make me the Manhattan borough reporter, but they switched me to politics before I came on board. Paul Sagan was a visionary in this respect, and he decided to have a political team as opposed to just one reporter. The political unit devoted all its energies to

New York's colorful political landscape. This approach was considered radical at the time because all the local stations had just one political reporter, if any at all.

Sagan's move to put me in the political unit was also bold because placing me there reflected the diversity of New York City. It didn't hurt that I had extensive experience covering Jesse Jackson and other prominent politicians. But at first, I didn't see the brilliance of this move. I didn't want to be in the political unit because I thought politics was boring and that the public was cynical about elected officials and did not follow local politics except for a popular election. I feared that I'd fade into the background, just as my radio colleagues had predicted. I initially resisted the assignments and would complain, but the managers reassured me that I was a perfect fit. It turns out that they were right.

My counterpart, Andrew Kirtzman, also proved to be a good choice. Andrew was a fast-talking, clean-cut New Yorker; he was tall, thin and quite sophisticated. I had met him during a radio interview a few years before New York 1 was up and running. He and I had been part of a panel, and someone had made an anti-gay comment. Andrew had waited until a commercial break and then had cursed the guy out. I liked the fire in his belly; he was clearly no pushover. Before coming to television, Andrew had been a health reporter at the *Daily News,* and his claim to fame had been a major piece on how the New York City Department of Health had botched mammogram results. His exposé made the front page and proved that he was a tough investigative reporter.

Another member of the political unit was Melissa Russo. She had just completed a graduate degree in journalism studies and worked as our video producer and as an assistant to Andrew and me. Paul Sagan believed that the three of us could shake up the local political scene. He was right, but we had to learn a great deal about television before we shook anything up.

Bringing New York 1 to life took a lot of training for the entire staff of about a hundred people, most under the age of thirty. As I celebrated my twenty-eighth birthday on June 18, I was part of an extensive training class for reporters aptly called Boot Camp. The station hired a consultant who taught us how to shoot news stories. The challenge was daunting because we had to learn a lot in a short time. We learned how to white-balance the camera so our footage would not be blue on the air. We learned how to use the tripod so the footage would not be lopsided. My favorite part was practicing live shots. The whole group stood next to the live truck, while one reporter at a time did a mock live report and tossed back to the studio. Some of the reporters were very green and seemed very intimidated; I was not. I had reported live events for years on radio, and my experience worked in my favor. When I did my live shot, the news director, Steve Paulus, said, "Now that's a live shot!"

I liked Steve right from the start, and my instincts told me that he liked me, too. He had also been with Channel 2 as Paul Sagan's assistant news director, and he left the CBS flagship station to help create New York 1. Paul and Steve were quite a pair; they balanced each other out and made for a nearly perfect management team. Paul was a straight shooter, a pleasant man, but not personable. He wasn't easy to get close to. He strolled around the newsroom wearing the same uniform every day: a crisp white shirt, suspenders, tailored slacks, and a tie. He was married and had children, but that was all we knew about his personal life.

Steve was altogether different. He was very compassionate and personable, and everybody considered him a friend. He, too, had exceptional news judgment but was very patient. He was a good story teller and had met his wife, Laura, while he had worked at Channel 2. When he left Channel 2, he had been given one of the biggest farewell parties the news business had ever seen. Most importantly, Steve had an open-door policy; anyone could walk in at almost any time, and he would stop and listen. Though I had known him for only a few weeks, I felt comfortable talking to him about my concerns—and I had many. Steve would tell me to relax. "I have confidence that we're going to make a big splash," he'd say, though he didn't tell me I was the one who would be making the first waves.

The training period was rocky. For up to ten hours a day, we would listen to lectures in a small room, and I hated feeling confined. I had been reporting for years, and suddenly I was being lectured on how to be an effective journalist. I thought those lectures were a waste of my time, and I was bored out of my mind. I later found out that I was not alone. There was a lot of fine-tuning that needed to be done, but by September we would be live on air. I seriously wondered whether my colleague were ready for prime time in New York City. I still wondered if I had made a mistake, even as management was pushing me out front as one of their main reporters.

From day one, I didn't like using the camera because I felt awkward being a reporter and a cameraman at the same time, especially at city hall. I didn't pretend that I liked the double job. All of us complained in private, but in public we would compliment the station's management as though we all thought the dual responsibilities were a novel idea. Privately I wondered how I could hold a microphone, a note pad, *and* a camera at the same time. However, I was up for the challenge.

The station was just under ninety days away from the first newscast, and we didn't even have a fully constructed studio yet. New York 1's first home was at 460 West 42nd Street, the heart of an area in Manhattan known as Hell's Kitchen. The studio occupied the fourth and fifth floors of a five-story building that had been used primarily for television production from independent companies. Inside, the studio had been painted bright pink, white, and blue. The ceilings were well over thirty feet high.

New York 1's launch date was September 8, 1992, at 1:00 PM. About two weeks before the launch, several members of the staff were interviewed for the local newspapers, and I was pushed out front because I was already well known to the press and the public. On September 3, *Newsday* did an article on the greenhorn news channel, saying that "the city's first all-news channel features a controversial, cost-effective concept: the reporter and the camera operator are the same person." They went on to say the following:

> On an uncharacteristically sunny day in August, New York 1 News reporter Dominic Carter is moving fast. And he has to. A beefy, barrel-chested man who used to ply his trade for radio station WLIB, Carter bounds down the steps of the State Supreme Court on Centre Street with surprising nimbleness—surprising because he has to lug a camera that's as large as a small turkey and weighs about as much as one, too ... After he sets up the camera to interview Senate candidate Bob Abrams for a future piece, he checks the viewfinder, shuffles the tripod, focuses the lens, pushes some button and then ... jumps in front of the lens,

straightens his tie, clears his voice, stiffens his back and says,
"This is Dominic Carter, New York 1 News ..."

At this point, a member of the Bronx district attorney's
staff taps him on the shoulder and says, "What else can you
do, Dominic? Play right field?"

The station had twenty reporters and five anchors, and *Newsday* opened the piece with me. What was interesting was how
they seemed almost puzzled about the new cable news station's
way of doing business with television reporters. They went on
to describe our new, bare bones approach to news, and its possible repercussions.

When the *Newsday* story came out, I had mixed emotions
about it. On one hand, I felt emboldened because my picture
was splashed on the first page of the article. On the other hand,
part of the article reaffirmed my concerns because the reporter
had sought the opinion of WNBC's senior reporter, Gabe
Pressman, who was considered to be the dean of the New York
press corps. According to the article, when asked about our new
venture, Gabe had said:

> New York 1 represents a retrogression rather than progression. It's a disservice to the people of New York to give such
> short shrift to the photographic component of TV news ...
> I'm appalled at the thought they're going to try to delude
> the public, and the poor kids who are veejays, that this is
> the way to practice journalism.

That comment came from a journalist whom I had worked
with and deeply respected. But Gabe's reaction failed to discourage me. I couldn't understand what the industry was so
worried about. Perhaps the other stations were trying to protect

their turf. Gabe had been in the business before I was born. All I could do was hope to prove him and all the other skeptics wrong. New York 1 went on the air as scheduled on September 8, and our big story focused on Mayor David Dinkins. He was on the set live with our midday anchor, Leslie Devlin, and management considered that interview something of a coup. In its first hours on the air, the little news station had snagged the city's mayor live. Not bad.

I'm not sure that many people watched us in those early days. We had lots of calls from viewers about how different we looked; some viewers loved us, and others hated us. They picked our work apart from the graphics to the music to the appearance of the reporters. We suffered lots of technical glitches, which left some staffers extremely frustrated, but once we were on the air, we stayed on the air. One policy was that New York 1's newscasts would not simply be a rundown of the day's horrific events. Management would not allow us to show body bags or other graphic shots. The bad news was often balanced with good news that didn't make the local news channels. We would do three-minute stories on popular street festivals, marathons, and fundraisers for local charities.

I was plugging away at my political assignments and was still going to city hall every day. But now I was loaded down with camera equipment. I made my deadlines, only now the timing was more challenging. And I even had to wear makeup. I refused for a while, until I saw how uneven my skin tone looked on television compared to that of my colleagues. I had to teach myself how to dab on pressed power before I stood in front of the camera.

My first big television assignment outside New York City came less than three weeks after the new station went on the air. Nydia Valesquez, a local politician, won the Democratic primary in Brooklyn's Twelfth Congressional District, and Puerto Ricans in New York and on the Island were overjoyed. Dinkins was a big supporter of Valesquez and accompanied her back to Puerto Rico for a rousing homecoming. Steve Paulus sent me and another new reporter, Lynda Laverne, who was Puerto Rican and knew her way around San Juan.

Traveling on assignment may sound glamorous, but it is anything but. It is nonstop work on unfamiliar territory, with big money at stake on satellite time, airline tickets, hotel stays, and rental cars. If I missed my deadline, I would lose several thousand dollars for the company. I had to navigate in an unfamiliar city or country, learn how to communicate with gestures if I didn't speak the language, and figure out how to get to where I needed to be, all while playing *Beat the Clock.*

We left for the Puerto Rico assignment on September 25, 1992, and it was sheer hell. Not only was Puerto Rico sweltering, but we were still getting used to the bulky new equipment while we were trying to keep up with the mayor and soon-to-be congresswoman. The logistics proved to be a nightmare. We had trouble communicating with the New York station because cell phones were still a novelty, and we couldn't get to a phone without missing the walking tour.

Puerto Rico was gorgeous; its splendor completed by lush gardens and cobblestone streets. Thousands of Puerto Ricans were waving American and Puerto Rican flags, but I could not appreciate the beauty of it all because I was stuck doing the jobs of three people. Lynda and I eventually worked the kinks out and shot some decent tape, obtained interviews, and fed all of the tape back to New York 1. We were proud of ourselves. When we called the station, though, we received no compliments on our hard work. Instead we heard complaints that we hadn't held our shots long enough. Those ungrateful reactions were my first lesson in how television producers have one-track minds and don't care if we damn near killed ourselves in getting the story. We returned to Manhattan in the wee hours of the night. The trip had been like a one-day commute to Puerto Rico and back. We were so tired that Lynda fell completely asleep during the cab ride back to the station. Lynda went on to great success; she was named a lead anchor for the NBC affiliate in New York.

While I was in Puerto Rico, I knew there was a strong possibility that I might miss an event that a father never wants to miss: the birth of a child, but thankfully Marilyn did not give birth while I was there. Toward the end of her pregnancy, doctors couldn't get a reading on the baby's heartbeat, and Marilyn didn't feel any movement from the baby. Doctors were concerned and warned her that they might have to do a caesarean section. On September 28, her obstetrician told Marilyn to check in at the hospital as a precaution. I, of course, was at work. That evening while I was busy on assignment, my brother-in-law, Larry Stevens, had to fill my shoes and take my wife to Columbia Presbyterian Hospital in Upper Manhattan.

My wife called me, asking me to come to the hospital. I tried to reason with her, asking her to let me finish my work, and then I would rush over to the hospital. I figured I had plenty of time because she wasn't even in labor yet. My calm, soft-spoken wife was furious. I was torn between two worlds: family and business. But my wife would tolerate it no longer. Two months prior, we had argued about the family-work dilemma as we had driven down Broadway in our car. As the conversation grew heated, Marilyn had startled me by saying, "My God, what comes first, your family or your career?"

With a straight face, I had turned to her and said, "My career!" She had started to cry, and I really hadn't understood what I had said to upset her. For years, my family hadn't even been a close second. My career had been more important than anything else, except for the well-being of my kids. Perhaps remembering that conversation, Marilyn gave me an abrupt ultimatum from the hospital: "Get your butt to this hospital now, or don't ever come home."

Feeling guilty after my wife's rebuke, I walked over to the assignment desk, which was a few feet from the editing room, and told my coworkers I had to leave. Rushing over to the hospital, I prayed that my son wouldn't be born before I got there. The moment I walked through the door, Larry met me in the hallway and then abruptly left, relieved that he wouldn't have to be in the delivery room. Marilyn's labor was brief. Within two hours of my arrival, Dominic Terrell Carter Junior had been born, weighing ten pounds and eleven ounces. During the ninth month, he probably hadn't been moving because he had had no room to move.

Dominic's birth reminded me of the birth of my daughter, who was now four years old. When Courtney had been born, I had felt that a little angel had been presented to me, and I would coddle, pamper, and cherish her. I knew I would spoil her and give her everything that had not been given to me. By the time my son was born, Courtney had been a little lady in ruffled pink dresses and shiny Mary Jane shoes. She had my friendly eyes, but hers were a bit wider, and she had a cute, squeaky voice. I gave her the nickname "Munchkin." When she looked up at me, her eyes smiled in complete approval.

As special as Courtney was, I now had a son. But how was I going to protect him from the predators of the world? I had no doubt that my wife was an outstanding mother who would love and protect her child even at the expense of her own life. But how was I going to teach this boy to become a man? No one had taught me.

The best fathering comes from a father, who can teach lessons that are often never spoken. Fathers live a walking testimony; they may not talk as much as mothers, but children certainly watch them and take copious mental notes. Fathers set the standard as the leader of the family. My father had failed miserably, leaving me with a few scattered mental notes that I would not use on a pet, much less a child. I'm told by Aunt Joann that my father took me to Yankee Stadium to watch a baseball game when I was about three years old, but I have no memory of this event. My father made no impression on my life, and I find just about everything he did unmemorable.

As I cradled my son in that sterile hospital room, I hadn't the slight idea how I was going to mold this newborn boy who already had my name. I wanted him to be more than his father. In some respects, I had been a lost cause because I was born into a world of mental illness, sex abuse, shame, and poverty. Despite my accomplishments, those incidents were still part of my life's tapestry. Hard as I would try, there was no hiding the past, no erasing it from my memory. No matter how far I would go in life, all I needed to do was turn around to recall the pain.

By the late fall of 1992, I was a father times two, a husband, and a rising television reporter. I was amazed at how New Yorkers responded to me, screaming out my name from hot dog stands, taxi cabs, and apartment buildings. As my job carried me to various parts of the five boroughs, people from all walks of life recited my name and asked to shake my hand as if I were running for office. But the seduction of the nightlife kept calling me, and I kept answering. The attention at the city's hottest night clubs was tempting, to say the least. When I went into clubs, I was ushered into the VIP section and found that everyone wanted to talk to me, especially women—lots and lots of pretty women.

I wanted my wife to come out with me, but in my mind she was a homebody. Socialization was not her priority; raising her children, holding down her job, and working toward her PhD were more important. I thought I was a responsible father and, at the very least, a solid role model for my kids. But on a daily basis, my wife was starting to resent me for the life I was leading, and I was too wrapped up in my own world to notice. The path of destruction was one I could easily have avoided, but I flatly refused to move away from that path. I wanted to be a loving family man and enjoy the status that gorgeous women brought me. And I did just that. It's not right, but it's the truth.

I wanted a stable family with a lovely, responsible, and caring wife and beautiful children, but at the same time I wanted to be the life of the party. I would go to bars and buy drinks for all of my friends, pulling out a wad of money that impressed them. I was living like a fool, but, at the time, I thought I was on top of the world.

At the end of December 1992, I was sent on another international assignment, this time in Somalia. My station, New York 1, was less than six months old, and I couldn't have been more pleased. But the trip was no vacation, to be sure. Karim Hajee, the police reporter, accompanied me, as did a manager, Marc Hopmayer. We were assigned to follow U.S. military troops to Somalia for a mission called Operation Restore Hope. A tribal war had broken out in the east African country between two feuding warlords, and millions of innocent Somalis had been caught in the conflict. As a result of the vicious fighting, villagers in the area could not get food or fresh water, and images of starving, emaciated Somalis were being broadcast around the globe. In a deal brokered with the State Department, U.S. Army personnel were sent into the war-torn region to deliver food and clothing to civilians during a temporary but precarious cease-fire.

Going into this assignment, I knew there was a possibility I would not come back. I had seen footage of brutally murdered American soldiers whose bodies were held up by smiling Somali soldiers. I was scared, but the sense of danger was something of a turn-on. The station purchased bulletproof vests and, because of the risk, took out special life insurance policies on all their employees who were making the trip. I approved of the life insurance, thinking that, if I didn't return, at least my family would be rich. A small part of me figured that it would be better for everyone if I wasn't around, though I did not have the desire to take my life at my own hands. My wife was frustrated with my attitude about work, and I was frustrated with the pressure. Then I partied to try to relieve the stress, and that was not a good mix. Sometimes I was depressed for no apparent reason.

It took days for our news team to board a military plane from McGuire Air Force Base in New Jersey for the 7,000-mile trip to a country a little smaller than the state of Texas. As we waited at McGuire Air Force Base, everyone seemed fairly relaxed.

Another colleague, Israel Colon, whom everyone called Yogi, came to the base with us, and we ended up playing cards. He won almost half of our spending money. Yogi, a personable and popular guy, was the type of person who would give you the shirt of his back.

The police reporter traveling with me, Karim Hajee, was a handsome man with a thick Indian accent, and he was outgoing and vibrant. He was a young world traveler. Karim had grown up in Kenya, in East Africa, and had worked as a journalist in Canada. He had a hearty laugh and was a real ladies' man. Don't ask me why, but Karim always called me "Sweet Cheeks," perhaps because I had a wide smile and chubby cheeks. The other man I traveled with on that assignment, Marc Hopmayer, had a deep baritone voice and was the serious one of the bunch. He had been a professional cameraman at other stations around the country, and he was the one we all turned to when we needed help with the camera.

The military flight from McGuire Air Force Base did not have the luxury features of a commercial aircraft. We flew for nearly a full twenty-four hours on a C-141 cargo plane that has no seats, just nets to sit on. We were given ear plugs for the entire flight. The first stop was at a base in North Carolina. Then we flew directly to a secret air strip outside Cairo. En route, we had a midair re-fueling, which was frightening because another plane came close to the top of our plane and, with a gas cable, transferred fuel from its tanks to ours.

While in Cairo, we had a sixteen-hour layover, during which I witnessed my first sandstorm. It was as if sand was snowing everywhere—in my eyes, my ears, my mouth, and as far around as a person could see. When the sandstorm was over, I realized that the daily temperatures differed radically from those in New

York. The Cairo temperatures reached up to 100 degrees during the day and dipped down to around 60 degrees at night, and it was hard for my body to adjust to the temperature change. The weather literally made me sick.

When we finally arrived in Somalia's capitol, Mogadishu, the U.S. military officials warned us that if we left the base, we did so at our own risk because snipers were poised all along the countryside.

Marc got off the aircraft first to video Karim and me getting off the plane. We were wearing blue winter parkas with the New York 1 logo emblazoned on the right front pocket. We interviewed soldiers and townspeople and called the station to do telephone interviews.

During the entire trip, I was weak with chills and nausea; I felt like I had the flu. Visiting Africa was a personal milestone for me, but I didn't fully appreciate its significance because I was sick the whole time. In spite of my fever chills, this was the story I filed that aired on New York 1.

> After nearly a full day of flying on a C-141 cargo military airplane and a sixteen-hour desert stop in Egypt, we finally arrived in Somalia. It was about 6:00 AM, and already ninety-five degrees. We had been braced for bad conditions, but nothing could have prepared us for the harsh reality. No electricity, no drinking water, no food, nothing! There were no sleeping quarters at the Mogadishu airport. This run-down hangar is a home for military personnel. Each soldier has a cot with a net over it to keep the bugs away. Twenty-year-old U.S. Army Captain Jeffrey Hunts is with the Air Force. He hails from Queens. He says, "Their living conditions are deplorable. Sub-human, I would say. We do field deployment. So we train and practice sanitation and improvise comforts from nothing."

As I stood now in front of the camera, clutching a microphone and trying not to shiver from chills and sounding a little nasal from a stuffy nose, I said, "The airmen say in a few days they will have shower facilities and note that the best way to deal with the entire situation here in Somalia is to remain optimistic."

In the televised report, I asked another airman, twenty-eight-year-old Curtis Green from Arkansas, "Tell me what a day is like for you," and he replied, "Work twelve hours, sleep five or six hours, and just read the rest of the time."

I interviewed another soldier, a chaplain whose name is Steven Boorlin. He was dressed in Air Force fatigues, the uniform military personnel wear in the field. I asked him about his job, and he replied, "Help people deal with depression, loneliness, anxiety, fear."

I returned to Captain Hunt, who wrapped up my televised report by saying, "The military is making a difference. We are seeing some of the food shipments leave here. The food is slowly but surely getting out there."

We also interviewed other soldiers and townspeople who were eager to speak with us and talk about their experience. I concluded that the soldiers were doing an outstanding job and were risking their lives to help people in a foreign land. Seeing the crisis in person was much worse than viewing it on television. I instantly realized that the luxuries we Americans take for granted are not available to people in other parts of the world. One afternoon, I had a desire to run to the corner store to get water, and I realized there was neither a corner nor a store, and there were no bottles of water to buy because even fresh water was considered a luxury.

Our news team stayed in Somalia for several days and then returned to New York. The return flight was an adventure in itself. On the swing back, we were in a small military jet. This one had seats, and we were supposed to stop in Mombasa, Kenya, but were rerouted to Jeddah, Saudi Arabia. As we prepared to land in Jeddah, we were stunned when the commander announced that one of us could not leave the plane because it would cause an international uproar. He said Jews were not allowed to step foot on the soil. Marc Hopmayer was Jewish, and, even though we wanted to get off the plane, I decided that we had traveled together, so we would leave together. I was frankly offended by the anti-Semitic policy, so I stayed on the plane in protest, as did Karim. That anti-Semitic policy remains in effect to this day.

Leaving Jeddah, we flew to Djoubiti, Algeria, which is on the northern tip of Africa. I could barely pronounce Djoubiti, and it was here that the adage "what can go wrong will go wrong" came true. In the news business, reporters have to be able to get their stories out. We had been instructed to give phone interviews to coworkers in New York as often as possible. The bosses had even issued an e-mail to the staff to make sure we were given priority treatment and were not put on hold. During the layover in Djoubiti, we had time to do a phone interview, but first we had to reach the international telephone operator. To do so required paying fifty dollars for a telephone card to someone we didn't know. We then had to sneak out of the airport and take a cab to the nearest pay phone in Djoubiti. We called New York 1, and we were put on hold. Then we had to buy another phone card, and this time the phone interview went through.

From Djoubiti, we went to Frankfurt, Germany, where we stayed at the military hotel on base. We enjoyed our first hot showers and a full meal instead of military rations, which left us constipated. After leaving Frankfurt, we headed home. I was now confident that New York 1 would succeed.

Back in 1989, my childhood friend, now a police officer, Randy Codrington, and I had chipped in to buy real estate in Harlem. By now, I had already blown thousands of dollars partying, and I realized it was time to start making investments so I would have something to show for all the money I was making. Randy and I joined forces—one hundred thousand dollars in cash—to buy a five-story brownstone at 504 Manhattan Avenue in the heart of Harlem off 120th Street. I was reluctant to buy the property because I knew I wouldn't have time to be a landlord, but Randy assured me that he would take care of most of the legwork. I went ahead with the deal because there were ten units in the building, and it had great potential for income.

The building was, without question, a fixer-upper, but most of the work was minor, and there was no structural damage. Before we bought the building, the New York Buildings Department had cited the dwelling for 500 violations. That may sound like a lot, but they were mostly minor to medium violations. We thought we could handle the repairs, but we were wrong. Randy and I tried to do all the work, but we couldn't handle the load. We even hired some of my friends from my high school days—Sean Johnson, Steven Brandon and his brother, John Williams—along with the man who was serving as the superintendent of the building, Herman Hector, a real character. Herman was fifty years old, but he looked like he was thirty-five. He had a deep Caribbean accent. We paid the guys around fifty dollars a day, and we paid for lunch.

As I worked around the clock as a television reporter, I had to add a new list of responsibilities: repair sheetrock walls, make minor plumbing repairs, and take care of a boiler. I was absolutely overwhelmed. My work with New York 1 consumed my entire life, and there were not enough hours in a day to manage and maintain a building. But I was no quitter. Even though the tenants paid between $250 and $500 dollars in monthly rent for the one- and two-bedroom units, we still tried to make the place beautiful. We put art on the walls in the hallways and flowers in the lobby. We painted the walls and scrubbed the floors. We tried to make that building, surrounded by abandoned buildings and vacant lots, livable and even desirable. We did this work years before the restoration of what would become a famous area.

Yet, the stress of keeping the building up to code was hardly worth all of the effort. We'd fix one thing, and something else would break. Some tenants complained, and rightfully so, but they were not angry because they knew we were doing our best; they also knew their landlord was a television reporter who wouldn't let them down. But other tenants complained to avoid paying rent, a scam that has existed in large cities for years. I was ready to get out and I told Randy that I was ready to sell, but the property wasn't exactly a hot commodity.

It all came to a head when Randy rented an apartment to a woman who I'll call Anna. She was the girlfriend of a childhood friend of ours, Kevin Redd. Like the rest of us, Kevin grew up poor. He was determined to take the fast track to get money, and he started dealing drugs and engaging in other criminal activities. Anna was a seductive young woman who ran with a dangerous crowd. She had a young daughter and needed a place to live. Kevin, who was locked up on Riker's Island facing a murder charge, pressured Randy to rent apartment 4F to Anna. My instincts never failed me, and I was dead set against that rental, but Randy went against my wishes and allowed Anna to move in.

One Saturday night in January 1993, Anna traveled to the Bronx with her young daughter, and she was shot to death, apparently in cold blood, by the male companion in the car with her. It was a ghastly New York crime scene; the baby, who was unharmed, was left alone, crawling in her mother's blood. The following Sunday morning, the story was on the front page of the *Daily News*. When I woke up on Sunday morning and read the story and later when I heard it on television, I didn't panic. I calmly went about my day, but I knew the investigation of her murder would eventually end up at Anna's apartment, which was in the building that a prominent television reporter owned. And I was that prominent reporter.

I went to work on Monday and didn't say a word to anybody. Then Andrew Kirtzman, who sat directly across from me in a cubicle, hung up the phone and turned toward me. "Hey, Dominic," he said. "Bad news. The *Daily News* is doing a story on you, calling you a slum lord."

Kirtzman, who worked at the *Daily News*, kept in close contact with his colleagues, and I was grateful for his tip. Then the phone rang, and, when I answered, I heard the voice of a *Daily News* reporter, Jose Lambiet, a rookie trying to make a name for himself at my expense. I knew that I had gone into real estate in Harlem for the right reason—to give back to the community—but I also knew no one gave a rat's ass about my reasons. All anyone wanted to know was why a celebrated reporter would own a share in what they thought was a rat-infested building in Harlem.

Sure enough, on January 28, 1993, the *Daily News* ran a disparaging story titled "They Fought Slum, then Bought It."

> Dominic Carter, New York 1 News' self-described crusading reporter who once exposed the plight of Harlem residents at the mercy of their slumlord … now co-owns a squalid apartment building in Harlem that has been cited more than 220 times by several city agencies for safety and code violations, including lack of heat in winter. A reporter … saw a rat scurrying up the decrepit staircase. Exposed wiring stuck out from walls on the third floor …

But that wasn't the whole story. Reporter Lambiet greatly exaggerated the situation. There may have been some days where apartments had heating problems, but there certainly were not any wires sticking out of walls. That was a complete fabrication. But the damage had been done.

Before the article came out, my bosses, Steve Paulus and Paul Sagan, summoned me to Steve's office. They were not happy. The imbroglio was snowballing into an apparently bigger problem than it actually was.

Paul, looking disgusted, immediately snapped, "What the hell happened?"

I was nervous, but I stood my ground. "The whole thing blew up in my face," I said. "I wanted to get a loan to fix up the place, but no bank would give me one in that high risk area. I was just trying to give back to the community."

Paul did not reassure me or placate me. "Well, Dominic," he said, "if your story turns out to be accurate, you don't have anything to worry about."

I knew I'd told the truth and that I had no need to worry. A local television station, Channel 7, said its *Eyewitness News* program was going to pick up on the story as well, but the assigned reporter had talked them out of it.

Shortly after this event, Randy and I sold the money pit, and Paul never said anything else about it. But the jokes from my colleagues haunted me for days and weeks on end. They thought it was funny, but I nearly had a nervous breakdown trying to keep that building together.

Meantime, the New York political scene was heating up as Democrats and Republicans started jockeying for the mayoral election. A lot of New Yorkers, black and white, were unhappy with Dinkins, and the city's first black mayor was certainly under pressure. In January 1993, the election was eleven months away, and Rudolph Giuliani, who had lost to Dinkins by one of the slimmest margins in history, was again running for mayor on the Republican ticket. This time around, I was walking an even finer line because I had greater influence on television than I'd had on radio. But behind the scenes, Dinkins would tell me privately that he felt he was taking unfair shots from white reporters, and his only salvation was the black reporters who he felt could understand the awkward situation he was in. It was obvious to most political observers that David Dinkins couldn't be too black lest he turn off the white voters, and he couldn't be too white lest he turn off the black voters.

Though Dinkins had ridden into office on a wave of racial politics, he would soon learn that that the sword of racial solidarity cut both ways. It could heal the city, but it could also leave a nasty scar. Rudy Giuliani scrutinized Dinkins's every flaw. His campaign mantra was, "One standard, One city."

Rudy, of course, was implying that there were different societal standards for different racial groups. I still tried to broadcast the truth as I saw it, but I could clearly see that unless something major happened, Dinkins would, to his dismay, be a one-term mayor.

A major distraction from the mayoral race was about to affect New Yorkers strongly. In late February, I packed my bags again, this time for a trip to Japan. It was rare that top management officials went on assignment, but the news director, Steve Paulus and I, accompanied Mayor Dinkins to Japan for a business conference focused on developing business between New York and Tokyo. Steve was good company, and our time in Japan cemented our relationship. Though he was the news director, Steve carried the camera on that trip and learned how to shoot. I went in expecting to do all of the work, but he proved me wrong.

Steve's lineage was part Japanese, and he knew all about the culture and loved teaching me about Eastern customs. I didn't speak a word of Japanese, and I didn't understand the Japanese way of doing things. I didn't see any other black people in Tokyo, but no one made me feel out of place. The city was strange but beautiful. The women at the hotels were radiant in their kimonos, and some would bow to me. I returned the bow awkwardly, and I cracked Steve up.

Japan's subway system was immaculate, unlike the subways in New York City. In Japan, workers known as "subway pushers" crammed the commuters into the cars. When we left Tokyo to go to Osaka, we took the bullet train, which connects that country's capital with other major cities. The bullet train travels at speeds around 300 miles per hour. It was so fast and I was so scared that I had two immediate options: to scream with paralyzing fear or to sleep. I slept.

We had been in Japan for only a few days. On February 26, I fell asleep around 8:00 PM after a day of shooting interviews with translators and lugging equipment. At 2:00 AM, Steve banged on my hotel room door. The time was around noon in New York, and an explosion had occurred at the World Trade Center. I jumped into my clothes and ran with Steve to find the mayor. Details started trickling in. A blast produced a crater five floors deep in the parking garage basement. Windows had been blown out, and hundreds of people were injured. Six people had been killed. More than 50,000 people were evacuated from the World Trade Center complex in the hours immediately following the blast. New York 1 was the only TV station that decided to spend the money to cover Dinkins's trip to Japan, and the investment paid off a thousand times over. New York 1 had exclusive access to the mayor, a benefit that the other New York stations didn't have at the time of a citywide crisis.

This was the coup to end all coups for the rookie television station. We went to a nearby television station in Osaka and, with the help of a translator, rented the entire studio and did a live interview with the mayor that was beamed to Canada and back to New York. It was a chaotic time because local and federal officials confirmed that the blast had been no accident. That discovery left the whole city on edge, fearing what would be next. The people in New York City needed to hear from the mayor, and there I was, sitting right next to him in a studio on an island known as the City of Water. No one at the station spoke a word of English, and Steve was playing the role of technical director, gesturing and explaining directions to the technical crew who did not speak English.

Mayor Dinkins and I appeared on camera in a wide shot featuring the backdrop of the unfamiliar Japanese studio. Dinkins had on a silk windbreaker jacket and clutched note cards in his hands. He told me that he wanted to give a statement right at the beginning, and then I could lead the interview as I thought best. The floor director, not speaking a word of English, queued me by urgently pointing his finger at my head to tell me we were live. I proceeded as I always did, with a very calm demeanor. I said:

> Mayor Dinkins had another full schedule set for here in Osaka. But that has all changed with the incident that has occurred in New York City. Now Mayor David Dinkins is here with us. He has a statement that he's going to read to the people of New York City, and then we will have the opportunity to ask him some questions. Mr. Mayor!

I looked straight at the Mayor as he began his statement.

> Good evening, fellow New Yorkers. I thank New York 1 for permitting me to speak briefly to you tonight. As I'm on my way back to our city, I want to bring you up to date on the events that have transpired over the last nine and one half hours. At approximately 12:15 PM, there was a large explosion at the World Trade Center.

New York 1 leader Paul Sagan, ever the promoter, made sure the New York 1 logo was on the tape so that when other stations replayed our footage with the mayor's comments—and all the stations did—they saw Dinkins and a huge New York 1 logo in the upper left hand corner. If you hadn't known what New York 1 was, you learned that day.

After the mayor gave his prepared statement, I conducted a live interview, and I conducted it well. I was locked into a foreign studio thousands of miles away from New York, but I was told that the interview went over very well. When I checked my voicemail in Osaka, there were dozens of congratulatory messages on my voicemail regarding the Dinkins coup—and one message that signaled what would lie ahead. That message was from Rudy Giuliani's cutthroat media consultant, David Garth, who was clearly furious over New York 1's covering David Dinkins' trip to Japan. Garth's message said he was angry because I was not reporting the story objectively, that I was too partial to Mayor Dinkins. He didn't intimidate me, but he did let me know that the political mudslinging had officially begun. Garth and his team were prepared to use every intimidation tactic known to man to rile up the press and get Rudy elected. They were playing hardball, and New York 1 was at the top of their list.

I laughed at their tactics. They had no idea what I had seen in my life; they had no idea how tough I was. I had tried to play fair, but they had mistaken my kindness for weakness. Not everyone did, though. In September, my kindness would bring a prominent politician to tears.

New York 1 was celebrating its first anniversary, and I rang it in with a big-time exclusive story. City Comptroller Elizabeth Holtzman was known by the press as the Ice Queen for the hard line she usually took when dealing with the press. Behind her back, the press called her much worse. She had been elected to Congress in 1972 when I was just eight years old, and she had become a key player during the Watergate hearings. She had decided to take a more local approach to politics and had become the first female in a series of male-dominated job—notably as the first female Brooklyn district attorney. Later, she had been elected the first female city comptroller in 1989, and she was preparing for reelection to that post after failing in a bid for the United States Senate.

In that failed Senate bid, Holtzman had been involved in a nasty, three-way Democratic race with local politicians Geraldine Ferraro and Robert Abrams. Holtzman was roundly accused of running one of the most negative campaigns in New York City's history by repeating ugly, unsubstantiated rumors about Ferraro's alleged mob connections. Reporters commonly referred to the two women's barbs as a cat fight. The race was harrowing, and, though Holtzman won the Democrats' nod, she still lost the November election to long-time incumbent Senator Alfonse D'Amato.

The race left a bitter taste in mouths of many voters, and early polls reflected this attitude as Liz Holtzman ran for reelection for comptroller. About a week before the primary, I was doing a taped interview with her for a segment that profiled the candidates. She had never really given me a hard time, but she was sharp as a whip and played politics almost as though she were playing chess.

For the interview with Holtzman, I had an intern with me, Ashley Higher, who functioned as my camerawoman. Because conducting an interview and tinkering with a camera were both challenging parts of the job, we often taught interns how to shoot film, and then they could accompany us on interviews. At 8:00 AM, we set up in Liz's office. A few minutes later, she walked in with an air of great confidence. She had been under fire for a questionable campaign loan, and she knew I was going to ask her about it. But I didn't want her to be on the defensive.

My style was to treat people the way I wanted to be treated. I had interviewed Liz many times over the years, and I wanted to relax her before I got down to the tough questions. I was intrigued by her rise in politics and by her ability to survive in a pool of political sharks.

After softening her up for a while, I began the real interview with a question that she clearly did not expect. "Ms. Holtzman, how would you sum up your more than twenty years in politics?"

Her eyes widened and then filled with tears. I was just as shocked as she appeared to be. She finally replied, "It has been an effort to try to do good for the people."

Incredulous, I responded, "Why are you emotional? What's wrong?"

Holtzman appeared shaken, and tears spilled from her face. "Nothing's wrong. It's just, it's been a long period of service, and whether it was standing up for the Constitution or whether it was standing up for—"

She abruptly stood up and excused herself from the interview. She went to an adjacent room, and I looked at my intern, Ashley, in disbelief, and told her to turn off the camera.

Liz returned some twenty minutes later. "If I don't get my cereal in the morning," she said, "I get very emotional. You know, sometimes it's very tough when you have a long record of standing and fighting for people and trying to do what's good, and then the record is maligned or distorted." She seemed to be making light of her conspicuous reaction. I guessed that Liz was carrying a lot of stress. Her Democratic opponents, Alan Hevesi and Herman Badillo, were drilling her about the ethical issues surrounding the campaign loan. But that story was old news after she cried during my interview.

Once again, I had a hell of an exclusive. When the interview was over, I called Paul Sagan and told him that Liz had broken down during my interview. He couldn't believe it. His natural newsman instincts left him skeptical.

"Do you think the tears were real?" he asked.

"I believe so," I said. "I don't think she was trying to get sympathy from the public."

Paul told me to hustle the tape back to the station. Liz Holtzman's twenty-minute breakdown became a big story on every newscast that night, and it made every paper the next day. Much credit goes to Ashley Higher, the intern, who, in *60 Minutes* style, zoomed into Holtzman's red face and captured the tears of a woman who many considered the hardest-working female in politics. On page five of *Newsday,* the headline read, "All Choked Up; Liz Loses Composure During Taping for TV."

> With her integrity under constant attack in recent weeks, city Comptroller Elizabeth Holtzman halted a television interview yesterday when her eyes welled with tears and her voice cracked as she was asked to reflect on her long political career. The display of emotion was rare for Holtzman, who tough, steely demeanor has always been a key part of her public persona. But the breakdown offered a peek into Holtzman's anguish.
> *Newsday*

On page 1 of the B section of the *New York Times,* the headline read, "Holtzman Breaks Down at Interview."

> Six days before Primary Day, New York City Comptroller Elizabeth Holtzman broke down during the taping of a television interview yesterday morning, so upset when a

reporter asked her to sum up her career that she left her
office for 30 minutes to regain her composure.... The
reporter, Dominic Carter, asked, "Why are you emotional?
What's wrong?"

When Liz Holtzman wrote her book *Who Said It Would Be
Easy?*, she mentioned my interview with her. I was impressed
that of all the accomplishments in her life, she considered our
interview the best way to begin her life story.

Meanwhile, my own life story and its ever-spinning madness
involving my mother continued to haunt me. Laverne and I had
a hot and cold relationship. She appeared to be pleased with my
television fame, though not as excited as Aunt Inez, who made
sure that all her friends and family knew that her nephew was a
television reporter. Sometimes Inez even called me her son,
indicating how close we were. I could have purged my mother
from my life quite easily, but it just wasn't in me. I worried
about the fact that studies clearly show that many abused children often grow up to be abusers themselves or to be vicious,
cruel adults. Prisons and mental institutions are full of people
with backgrounds similar to mine.

But the abuse and neglect I suffered didn't destroy me. My
survival did not result merely as the luck of the draw but was
intentional on my part. I was determined to be a success, not
just professionally, but with my children as well. As my daughter entered school, I showed her where no one should ever
touch her and make her promise to tell me if someone violated
her private parts. I would point to various areas of my own body
through my clothing to illustrate my point. Of course, Court-

ney was just a child and sometimes believed we were playing some sort of game. I would get deadly serious.

"No, sweetie, pay attention to what Daddy is telling you," I would say. My wife believes I had an obsession because of my frequent warnings to my children over the years. There are very few people I trust with my children: my wife, my mother-in-law, and Aunt Inez. Everyone else, no matter who, is under suspicion. I doubt I would have been so untrusting if not for my own difficult childhood.

Even though my mother sexually abused me and had thoughts of killing me, the only action I could take was to prevent myself from getting too close to her. I called Laverne's apartment from time to time to check on my sister, Malika, who was now about ten years old. My mother always asked me for a couple of dollars, which I always gave to her, and sometimes I took food to her. My ego would sometimes tempt me to neglect Laverne the way she had neglected me, but I never did. I still didn't know the full extent of my mother's mental illness history, but she functioned normally and did whatever she had to do to survive. She appeared to have no dreams or goals, simply moving from one day to the next, going through life her own way.

But she made one move that angered me. She became a foster mother. Imagine that! She didn't want her own flesh and blood and had dumped him into foster care, and now she wanted to take care of someone else's child? What kind of screening process would allow a woman with a record of mental illness to take care of a young child? I didn't tell a soul about my history of abuse, but I realized that New York City's child welfare system is seriously flawed. I was so disturbed about my mother's possibly becoming a foster parent and harming another child that I wanted to report Laverne myself, but I didn't want to hurt her or Malika. So I just made sure I kept tabs on their daily lives because I knew that their living arrangement could have been potentially dangerous. Regardless of how I felt about the situation, I didn't have the courage to come forth with what I had on my mother.

The name of the foster child was Antoinette, and she was only a few months old when my mother took custody of her. Antoinette was from a troubled family, and her parents were heroin users. My mother nourished Antoinette as she went through withdrawal from the drug. No one could see that Antoinette had gone from a bad situation into a worse one.

Laverne had a new man in her life, Eddie; he was a few years younger than Laverne and regularly beat her. I was always called upon to come to her rescue. Suddenly, I had become my mother's keeper. One day when Eddie and Laverne were fighting, he bent her thumb all the way back, breaking it and sending her to the hospital. I was working on an assignment when I got the news, and fury came over me—not necessarily for Eddie's actions, but because the ghetto was pulling me back again into the middle of a senseless dispute. My first instinct was to kill Eddie, but I knew that a murder charge would end my career, and then I'd be left asking myself, "Was murder worth it?" I was also aware that Eddie could possibly stab me to death.

When I finished work that day, I said good-bye to my colleagues and drove over to the projects with makeup still on my face. I took off my suit jacket and tie and beat Eddie as he cowered in a corner with his head tucked between his knees. He was six feet two inches, and I was five feet eight inches, but my blind rage clearly frightened him. I kicked him in every part of his body that was exposed and cursed him like I had never cursed anyone before.

As bad as that beating was, Eddie was not fazed. He continued to beat my mother, and then the inevitable happened: he tried molesting the girls, my sister Malika and little Antoinette. Antoinette had been with the family for a few years. And now my mother had adopted her. Antoinette was officially a Carter.

Eddie often ordered Laverne to go to the store and, while she was away, according to what my sisters told the authorities, he would ask the girls to sit on his lap. Malika was still in grade school, and Antoinette was just about to enter kindergarten. I prefer to leave out the details because I respect the privacy of my sisters.

I was thankful that there was no intercourse. Eddie continued molesting the girls for several months, apparently, before Malika finally told my mother, who, according to Malika, did not believe her at first. At a time when Malika should have been giggling with her girlfriends and trying on new clothing and makeup, she was instead living in fear of a man who was not her father.

By the time I got to the apartment, my mother had called the police and they had already arrested Eddie. I went to the police station to find out what the charges were. While I was there, the police officers kept saying, "Dominic Carter, what are *you* doing in here?" I was embarrassed, but I just gave them a quick hello and kept moving.

I had been in the precinct many times before to cover stories just like the one I was living now. I had interviewed the Bronx District Attorney, Robert Johnson, whose office would be handling Eddie's case, and I could easily have phoned him to make him aware of the details, but I didn't. I was so embarrassed by what had occurred that I didn't even want him to know my connection to the case. So I waited my turn in one of the most crime-ridden precincts in the United States to protect my two sisters from the same type of madness that my grandmother had protected me from. Eddie ended up in jail, and Laverne obtained a restraining order to keep him away from the girls. Malika and Antoinette went back to live with Laverne.

When I first found out about Eddie's abuse, I didn't have the heart to tell Malika about my firsthand experience with sexual abuse. How could I find the words to say, "I know how you feel. Mommy did something bad to me, too." The young, confused girl would probably have gone into shock if I had told her the truth about Laverne's behavior toward me. Yet I had to summon the courage to protect the next generation from Laverne's maddening life. Years later in 2007, I told Malika what had happened between our mother and me. She'd had no clue about anything except that I was very distant with Laverne. Malika had never known why I was so cold to Laverne, and she seemed very sad when I told her.

After the nightmarish evening when I went to the police station to protect my sisters from Eddie, I woke up the next morning and went to work as if nothing unusual had happened. I flashed my million-dollar smile, made small talk with my colleagues, and went back to reporting on the hotly contested mayoral race. All the while, I felt like I had an electronic bracelet around my ankle that could call me back to the ghetto at a moment's notice.

Things at work were almost as chaotic as things at home. Dinkins versus Giuliani was the biggest mayoral race the city had seen in a long time; it even became national news. The election featured a white man and a black man, and the city was again divided along racial lines. This time around, apathy seemed to settle over the black community. African-Americans seemed dispassionate about the election and about Dinkins, who had received a lot of negative press during his four years in office and had clearly lost touch with his base in the black community. Whites started calling Dinkins a lame-duck mayor, and Giuliani was laughing all the way to the election booth.

Dinkins was forced to call in his top Democratic guns, and he went straight to the top. President Bill Clinton was in town to help bolster support for Dinkins, who was trailing in the polls. The newly-elected president was loved by New Yorkers, especially black New Yorkers, and Dinkins seized every photo opportunity with the commander in chief. I had met Bill Clinton when he was still governor of Arkansas and was visiting New York City. Even back then, I could sense that he was very comfortable around black people.

My assignment this particular day was to cover the Clinton and Dinkins event, which was at Cooper Union, a distinguished institution, in Lower Manhattan. I took the assignment one step further and assured my bosses that I would get an interview with the president. At this point, I had thoroughly proved myself, and my bosses gave me all the resources I needed. What I didn't tell my bosses was that I had no assurance the president would talk to me; I was taking a huge gamble.

When I arrived at Cooper Union, I saw a sea of reporters, who probably had the same ambition as I, and a bevy of Secret Service agents, who were surrounding the school. I firmly believe that the Secret Service view part of their job as making the lives of reporters more difficult. I was doing live shots near the school, and all I could do was hope that the president would come out of the entrance nearest me. At any point, the Secret Service could change the route, especially in a city that was still reeling from the February terrorist attack at the World Trade Center. I had everything in place to do the interview. I had a cameraman, a live truck, an assistant, and even a technical person who held a portable microwave to beam the signal back to the truck because we were too far away to run cables from the truck to our location. I had everything I needed—*except the interview.*

Suddenly, Clinton and Mayor Dinkins emerged from the door near me and began greeting New Yorkers along the street. Miraculously, Clinton was heading my way, and I signaled to the studio producers to go live. I had no idea whether Clinton would stop to speak with me, but I acted as if I was sure he would. At that point, I was literally doing two things live on the air at one time. I was talking about the event at Cooper Union and watching Clinton get closer to me. When he was within earshot, I turned away from the camera and said, "Mister President, Mister President, we're live on New York 1 News. May I ask you, sir, a few quick questions?"

Clinton stopped and Dinkins stopped, and we spoke for about four minutes, which is a long time for a live, impromptu interview with the president. I heard a cheer erupt in the newsroom through my earpiece, and I felt yet again on top of the world. I kept calm and asked Mr. Clinton questions, and he calmly answered every one of them. When the interview was over, I felt like kissing him because I was so grateful that he had stopped, but I knew not to make any sudden movements with the Secret Service watching my every move.

Weeks later, all of the New York 1 reporters were being interviewed for a TV campaign to promote the station. From nowhere, the interviewer asked me, "You interviewed the president of the United States live? How did you pull that off?"

I replied, "I just knew I could get him."

"You could get him, huh?" the interviewer said.

"Yeah, I could get him!" I said. I thought we were playing around and that the promotional materials would never include my remarks. But the producers did include my comments in a thirty-second promotional spot that ran for months, as I was heard over and over on television: "I can get him." My colleagues teased me again, but I preferred the "I can get him" jokes to the slumlord jokes.

By this time, my wife was fed up with my running around, and we were fighting more than ever. She wanted me to be accountable and to explain why everyone else seemed to be enjoying the fruits of my labor—at the expense of my wife and two children. Purchasing a house, she felt, meant doing something worthwhile with our money. Also, Malika was getting fed up with Laverne and wanted to move in with me. My friends were always calling, asking to borrow money or to go with me to a club. Everybody wanted something from me, and I felt that they were sapping nearly all my strength. By day, I was interviewing the most powerful people in the world, but by night I was interviewing my sisters, trying to find out the extent to which they had been molested and trying to counsel them as a big brother.

On October 6, 1993, I was walking to an assignment. Suddenly I felt tightness in my chest. That tightness was the scariest thing I had ever experienced, and I stopped moving. I put the camera down and told an intern that I had to leave immediately. I got into a cab and went to Beth Israel North Hospital, which was right across from the mayor's official residence, Gracie Mansion. I went to the emergency room, where the nurses and doctors immediately recognized me. When I told them I was having chest pains, they seemed as alarmed as I was. I was put into a room and immediately hooked up to monitors. My blood pressure was abnormally high.

Nurses were running in and out of my room. I feared I was about to have a massive heart attack as my grandmother had suffered several years before. I was admitted right away and diagnosed with hypertension, exhaustion, and diabetes. A diagnosis of diabetes was, of course, better than a diagnosis of a heart attack, but I remember thinking that life had finally slapped me down hard. The triple diagnosis meant I would have to take drugs to control both the blood pressure and the diabetes for the rest of my life.

I had been given yet another load to carry. I was disgusted that I had inherited diabetes from my mother and my grandmother. No amount of money, fame, or influence could ever make me healthy again. All I could be, at best, was stable. I could no longer eat what I wanted, whenever I wanted. Doctors were telling me about the importance of a strict diet, and I felt like telling them to kiss my butt. I had to admit to myself that I was no longer a superman.

My brief hospitalization was reported in some of the local newspapers, and Giuliani and Dinkins called to wish me well. And the only good thing that came out of this experience was meeting the chief of cardiology at Beth Israel North, Dr. Roy Pizzarello, who for years remained my personal cardiologist.

I was not suicidal, but during this time I started to predict my own demise. I told those closest to me, "I'll never live past forty-five." Why I picked forty-five, I do not know, but what I was essentially saying was that I was tired of running after success. I was tired of living in two worlds: one of privilege and one of poverty. I was tired of raising the bar for myself and clearing it, only to raise it again. I was tired of thinking about my past, and I was tired of trying not to think about my past. I was tired of taking two steps forward and feeling that my mother was pulling me one step back. I felt that if death knocked on my door, I would certainly let the Grim Reaper come in.

In spite of my pessimistic outlook, I took the blood pressure medication that would help prevent me from having a heart attack But taking pills was such a hassle that I often forgot to take them during the busy election period and ended up missing doses. By Election Day, the polls showed that Giuliani was favored to win. If, as some pundits say, Dinkins rode into office on the heels of the Yusef Hawkins racially charged murder in Bensonhurst, then he was riding out on the heels of the murder of Yankel Rosenbaum.

On August 19, 1991, a car filled with orthodox Jews spun out of control and onto a sidewalk in Crown Heights, Brooklyn, killing a seven-year-old black child named Gavin Cato. Angry black residents surrounded the car's driver, who was whisked away by ambulance ahead of little Gavin Cato, who was still pinned under the car that had hit and killed him. This treatment infuriated the growing crowd even more in the mixed neighborhood of blacks and Jews. As the night wore on, a mob of blacks roamed the streets seeking revenge and fatally stabbed twenty-nine-year-old Hasidic student Yankel Rosenbaum, an Australian researcher.

Days of rioting and looting followed in Crown Heights, and it took days for the police, clad in riot gear, to restore order. Many Jewish leaders laid the blame right at city hall, and Dinkins was yet again trying to heal a divided city. The task wasn't easy this time, for Giuliani was exploiting the Crown Heights riots as a personal failure for Dinkins.

Dinkins did the best he could to counter the attacks, but the damage had been done as the city marched toward the November election. This election was New York 1's first mayoral election, and my station and all the other broadcast media were putting all of their resources into the election night coverage. I was prepared to work late into the night; the polls closed at 9:00 PM in New York City, and elections typically were not called until around 11:00 PM or midnight.

Andrew was assigned to Giuliani's election night hotel, and I was assigned to Dinkins's hotel. Usually election parties are festive events where the party faithful gather and prepare for a big celebration. But at Dinkins's hotel, an ominous, black cloud hung over the large room, though everyone tried to act as if it were not there. At around 11:15 PM, Steve Paulus told me through my earpiece, softly and compassionately as if not to alarm me, "Dominic, listen, we're about to call the election, and Dinkins lost. We're coming to you in about one minute."

A chill went up my spine. I said, "Okay, thanks."

Mayor Dinkins had always treated me with tremendous respect. It was hard not to like the charismatic mayor. For almost every major story I had done, from Yusef Hawkins to Nelson Mandela, Dinkins had somehow been involved. When he invited the press to Gracie Mansion, he would hold my daughter and take pictures with her. Dinkins, like me, had succeeded against the odds. I knew that being the first black mayor wasn't easy, but, as a journalist, I could not allow myself to become too involved. I had to admire him from a distance. On this election night, I straightened my tie and reported on the mayor's loss. That night, as he went down in defeat, he stood proudly, but I knew that the loss had to be eating him alive on the inside.

Rudy Giuliani came into city hall on fire, with hard feelings for a lot of people. It was payback time in his mind, especially for New York 1 News. Rudy felt that New York 1 hadn't scrutinized Dinkins's record as much as he thought we should have. He refused to grant New York 1 a one-on-one interview for months, and he didn't allow his commissioners to talk exclusively to us during that period, either. He was petty, all right, and he was already known for his bravado, which I liked. I knew there would never be a dull moment while he was in charge of the city. Rudy did things his way, and whoever didn't like it would just have to get over their disappointment. To be blunt, Rudy had a huge set of balls, but so did I. And we were headed on a collision course.

In 1994, Israel had been hit with another wave of suicide bombings and attacks that left scores of innocent Israelis injured and dead. One infamous event occurred on a Number 18 bus, and more than a dozen men, women, and children were killed. So what did the mayor of New York City do? He decided to go to Israel and ride the Number 18 bus. He wanted to send a strong message of New York City's solidarity with Israel. Covering Giuliani's trip would be my first trip to the Holy Land. I found Israel to be a beautiful, ancient country even during a time of turmoil. We rode the Number 18 bus with the new mayor, and again I was putting my life in danger, but I had a job to do.

While in Israel, I saw the Israel Defense Forces up close. The majority of Israelis, both men and women, served in the military. But I couldn't get over how young the soldiers were. I stood near boys and girls who could not have been a day over sixteen and saw them wielding loaded submachine guns. They had a tough look in their eyes, but their innocent faces betrayed them. I had never seen anything like those young soldiers in my life. I could tell that Giuliani liked the fact we were there in Israel with him to report back to his voting base in New York, but he was extremely guarded with the media, and the trip did nothing to improve our personal relationship.

Back at New York 1 after the trip to Israel, I realized that the station was becoming better known. Our audience was growing, and we were no longer considered a rookie station. My career was being watched closely by the media. I found that the publicity could work positively and negatively. Journalists can sometimes lose their tempers, and fights in newsrooms were not unheard of. It seemed it was now my turn to garner some bad publicity.

One hot July day in 1994, I called our assignment desk and spoke with an assignment editor, Brian McLaughlin. Brian was one of the original New York 1 staff members and was a beefy guy with a loud, scratchy voice like mine. He liked to throw his weight around every now and again; otherwise, he was a decent person. On that day in July, he wanted me to do a story that I felt was not newsworthy. Our phone conversation got heated, and then Brian crossed the line. He abruptly told me, "Go f——yourself." And he hung up.

I called back to ask him what he had said, and he said it again.

I said, "Okay, we'll see who'll go f——themselves when I get back!"

A huge rage came over me, and I jumped into the news vehicle and flew through red lights, even zooming past the news director in his car. No doubt he wondered who the hell was driving like that. When I got to the newsroom, I rounded the corner into the assignment desk and headed straight for the assignment editor's desk.

I approached Brian like a ball of fire and tried to reason with him. He stood up defiantly to say, "Go f——yourself."

At this point, my street instincts kicked in. On the street, if you are disrespected, you have to strike back. Believe it or not, I forgot I was in a professional environment, a Time Warner newsroom, no less, and I tried to push Brian. Staff members jumped in between us just as we were about to come to blows. Then I looked around and threw the first thing I could find at him: a stapler. It narrowly missed Brian, and our fight didn't go unnoticed. And, of course, it was in the George Rush column of the *Daily News* days later.

> New York 1 Reporter Dominic Carter made a little news the other day when he clashed with assignment editor Brian McLaughlin. One source says Carter was so steamed over a story that he marched into the newsroom and got into a shoving match with McLaughlin and ripped his shirt—just as NY1 Veep Paul Sagan was giving a newsroom tour. McLaughlin denies it got physical, saying only, "We had a loud disagreement over an assignment. It's both our faults. A couple of hours later, we were out having drinks together."
> —New York *Daily News*

I was steamed that someone on the same team, a New York 1 staff member, had leaked the story to the paper. I thought it was the catty revenge of a few colleagues who had tried to damage my reputation. Perhaps they were angry that management took no action against me. Brian and I had no hard feelings about that incident. But we both had an understanding that there would be no more of that "go f——yourself" stuff.

That run-in with Brian was not the first or the last time a colleague said something insulting to me. One close staff member stood with me in a room as I hurried to make a deadline and casually said, "I think something's wrong with you."

I turned to her and sternly said, "What did you say? What do you mean?"

And she turned beet red and broke down in tears. She apologized, and I let it go. But I felt that she meant to offend me, even though I considered her a friend. I knew she wouldn't dare make the same statement to my colleague Andrew Kirtzman.

On another occasion, a manager said to me after a debate over the newsworthiness of a story, "I think you are just naturally lazy."

Hearing that remark, I marched directly up to Paul Sagan's office and reported the manager's comment. Fortunately, these incidents appeared to be isolated and few. Sometimes people say things they shouldn't say, but I have very little patience for demeaning remarks. Otherwise, most of the staff treated me as I treated them—with the utmost respect.

By November, I had made inroads with politicians in Washington. Harold Ickes was the go-to guy for President Clinton, and he liked me. Harold started to allow New York 1 access to federal officials. He and I had mutual respect, and Ickes put in a good word for me with Mark Gearan, the White House communications director. Ickes sent Mark a memo and me a copy dated March 26, 1994.

> Mark, Dominic Carter is the political reporter for NY 1
> News, a twenty-four-hour New York City TV station. He
> has given balanced coverage in the past. This is worth doing
> if you can fit it into the schedule.

Typically, local reporters had a tough time getting national interviews, which were usually reserved for the press out of Washington, DC. Thanks to that memo, Clinton cabinet members suddenly began appearing on New York 1. Health and Human Services Secretary Donna Shalala and Housing and Urban Development Secretary Andrew Cuomo appeared, to name a few. I also got an exclusive interview with Vice President Al Gore at the Waldorf Hotel in Midtown. Most federal officials who lived in Washington did not know what New York 1 was in 1994, about two years after our first broadcast, so they granted the interviews strictly because of Harold. When Al Gore walked into our interview, he said, "So, you're friends with Harold Ickes, huh?" Translated: he was doing the interview because of Harold.

I appreciated all of those interviews, but I was shooting for the big fish: Bill Clinton. Harold couldn't get me to the White House for the interview, but he got me a satellite interview with the president, which suited me fine. President Clinton was in Detroit, and I was in New York 1's studio. Clinton looked directly into his camera, and I looked directly into mine, and we could hear each other through our earpieces.

Our interview was about the midterm elections. I asked, "Mr. President, this has been a bitter, nasty campaign season across the country in which Republicans have made you the issue of local races in commercials linking you directly to the local Democrats. While many Democrats have held open arms to campaign with you, some have kept their distance. Do you feel that you are a direct target, your administration?"

The president said, "Well, they've worked hard on this for a long time. The Republicans tend to be a Presidential party, and they are unfortunately now very extremist, very negative, and that's what they've tried to do ... I would also point out, Dominic, ... there is beginning to be some division within the Republican ranks. People are recoiling; good Republicans are recoiling from this extremism and this negativism."

I was impressed that the president, who hadn't referred to some members of the White House press corps by name, was addressing a man who had grown up in the projects in the Bronx. The interview lasted approximately ten minutes. One of my career accomplishments is that our interview is transcribed as part of the "Public Papers of the Presidents," which is part of his official history of William Jefferson Clinton. Not bad for a poor kid from the Bronx.

6

My professional life was lights, camera, action, but no one could have imagined that my personal life was filled with despair, disillusionment, and health problems. My highs were very high, but my lows were also quite low.

In the mid 1990s, I was still torn between two worlds: one of privilege and the other of poverty. My mother suffered with high blood pressure and diabetes, which ravaged her thin frail body. I was called upon to be my mother's keeper and a dutiful son. Laverne's deterioration was eerily similar to my grandmother's final days about ten years before. As Laverne appeared to win the battle over her mental illness, her body grew weaker. Frequently, Laverne's poor health kept her hospitalized; she often spent one week at home and the next week at the hospital. Then her time at home would increase to two weeks, and she'd spend two weeks at the hospital. She was only in her mid-forties.

It was difficult for me to witness my mother's downturn. I didn't wish her ill, and I certainly did not want her to die, but I had a bad feeling that her death wasn't far off. I supported her on an emotional level during her illness, but I made sure to guard my heart so that my feelings would not be involved. I was afraid of having to confront those awful childhood memories. I had built a plate of armor around my heart to protect the emotions raging inside myself, but, as I aged, I encountered a serious problem. Nobody could get into my emotions, and I couldn't get out. Unwittingly, I had created my own prison and locked myself in. I initially closed myself off emotionally to keep Laverne from hurting me ever again, but many people found themselves outside my heart: my wife, my colleagues, my friends.

As articulate as I was on television, I could not explain to people who loved me what I needed. I couldn't tell my wife, who was so close to me, how much pain I was in. I could find many words to describe the political climate, but I couldn't find the words to describe what went on in my soul. And dealing with Laverne's problems made communicating my feelings that much more complicated.

At times, I visited my mother in her apartment in the Patterson Housing Projects at the corner at 143rd Street and Morris Avenue in the South Bronx. As in years past, the uninviting smell of urine in the elevators served as a pungent reminder of how sad my mother's world had become. She lived in her own two-bedroom apartment, but it might as well have been her prison. Her apartment had bars on the windows, and the doors were bolted shut.

She could come and go as she pleased, but she could travel few places aside from the hospital and the corner grocery store. She also visited her sister Inez and my mother-in-law, Ruby, from time to time. There was no beauty in Laverne's world except for her two daughters. The television was the only thing that brought some life into her world; other than that, her way of life seemed miserable. No matter how sunny the day was outside, a dark cloud always loomed over my mother's apartment. She had no plans for the future, no goals, no dreams. My mother simply existed from one day to the next.

I was racing ahead in my career while my mother's life stood still.

Laverne's main concern was her health. She had to take a large number of pills to control her high blood pressure, but she often refused to take her medications. She had Type 1 diabetes and had to receive insulin shots, which she detested. She was terrified of needles and taught my sister, Malika, who was now a teenager, to administer the injections. Laverne often said in a complaining tone, "My sugar is acting up again," or "These people are running up my pressure."

I was there for my mother in body, but not in spirit. We talked about a lot of things. Laverne was not very insightful and would often use her favorite catchphrases, with a raised voice, such as "Got to be more careful!" or "You win some, you lose some!"

Unlike most mothers, she rarely told me what to do, probably because she knew better than to try to direct my life. But she was a good listener and rarely interrupted me when I talked about my problems. Yet our conversations never felt like mother-and-son talks. In reality, we were little more than distant friends. Though Laverne was more stable mentally, I still resented her and her past actions in my life.

When Laverne needed medical care, she never went to Lincoln Hospital, which was across the street from her apartment building, because she considered city-owned Lincoln to be substandard. Most residents in the Patterson projects felt the same way. Laverne often said, "If I'm dying, don't take me to Lincoln Hospital." Instead, she went to New York Hospital, which is on Manhattan's Upper East Side.

That upscale hospital is frequented by celebrities and politicians; oddly, my mother felt right at home. When I visited her in the hospital, we always went through the same routine. I paid cash to have Laverne's television turned on. I consulted with doctors. Then I told Laverne that everything would be okay. Though we followed that routine, I always removed myself emotionally. I couldn't help thinking how unfair it was that I had to look out for the mother who had never looked out for me, but I remained by her side anyway, along with her sister Inez.

As I walked the halls of New York Hospital, I recalled how helpless I had felt when my grandmother Anna Pearl was on her deathbed at the same hospital—back in the times when I was a nobody. Fortunately, I was no longer unknown in New York City. The doctors and nurses knew who I was, and, as a result, they gave this poor woman, who lived in the projects on SSI and without a job, prompt medical attention. Laverne was on Medicaid, a public health insurance program, but she was treated as though she had private insurance. I was still a bit embarrassed that a high-profile television reporter needed the public's help to get medical care for his mother. I hoped one day to make enough money to get my entire family out of the ghetto, but I wasn't able to just yet.

At home, my wife still wasn't happy. As I tried to make her and my mother-in-law happy by keeping in touch with Laverne, Marilyn warned me about my friends. Although I rubbed elbows with some of the best and brightest in the city, all of my close buddies were still the same guys I had grown up with in the Bronx. Marilyn felt that I should've left them behind because they were a bad influence on me, but I did not agree with her at all. Even though some of my colleagues had gone to the best Ivy Leagues schools, and I was on par with my friends professionally, they could not truly relate to me or understand where I had come from. I'm not a jealous person, but I quietly wondered what my life would have been like if I'd had my friends' upbringing. What would my life have been like free of horrific memories of sexual abuse and poverty? What would my life have been like had I attended top-notch prep schools? What would my life have been like with a mother and a father who loved and supported me?

I could simply relax and be myself with my old buddies. They were proud of me, though I believe a handful may have been jealous. But I felt a sense of loyalty to them, and everywhere I went, they went. When I was escorted into popular restaurants and bars, I brought them along with me. When I was invited to concerts and sporting events, my friends' names were also put on the VIP list. Sure, some of the promoters gave my friends second looks, but the scrutiny didn't bother me and certainly didn't bother my friends. I didn't feel that I was better than they were. I had just seized certain opportunities in my life and had worked hard, refusing to take no for an answer. By the grace of God, doors had been opened for me. I never bragged to my buddies about my accomplishments, I didn't have to—they watched New York 1 News and saw my accomplishments for themselves.

Maintaining the friendships of men I had known since youth also humbled me because they reminded me of what my life could have been had I made the wrong choices. Most of my friends who had dropped out of high school deeply regretted that move and sometimes viewed my success as their success. I was the one who had done well, and I made most of my friends proud. A handful of my childhood buddies found good jobs in the private and public sectors, but many of my childhood comrades got lost in a world of drugs and poverty. Some of the women whom I'd known in my youth turned to prostitution.

One close friend of mine shared a lot in common with me. When he was young, my friend told me he'd been sexually abused by an uncle. Though my friend was smart and energetic, ultimately he pursued a life of crime. He was my best friend in junior high school, and, when I listened to his troubles as an adult, I realized that were it not for my sheer determination and will, as well as help from Aunt Inez, I would probably have suffered the same fate as he. He married a girl who had been raped repeatedly and viciously by her father when she was a child. She was my friend, too. She and her husband developed a close, dysfunctional, yet loving bond. They were happy that I had escaped the ghetto, but I sincerely empathized with the troubles they had endured. Many of my childhood friends felt trapped because, no matter how much they tried to fix their broken lives or where they moved, misery usually followed close behind them.

By 1994, I had moved out of the inner city. Marilyn and I finally purchased a home of our own, a real milestone for us. My salary was steadily increasing, as was hers, and we were finally ready to invest in a house. Together, we were making more than one hundred thousand dollars a year, which had been a dream of ours during college. Back then, we naively thought we would be *rich* if we ever earned one hundred thousand dollars a year. We didn't understand that, like most American families, the more you make, the more you are tempted to spend and the higher your taxes are.

Marilyn and I agreed to get out of the city and into suburbia for the sake of our kids. We headed north of Harlem, searching for homes in Rockland County. I liked the look and the feel of the hilly area that was just twenty miles outside New York City. Even though I had been raised in the city, I loved nature. My first exposure to Rockland had come from Elita DeValle, the mother of my childhood friend, Ty. I respected Elita because she had single-handedly moved her family out of a crowded Bronx apartment into a spacious home in the suburbs. She had been a single parent and worked nearly seven days a week to make ends meet, a Herculean task in those days when most families I knew never left the ghetto, certainly not for the suburbs. I also had tremendous respect for Randy Codrington's mother, Ronnie Codrington. Both she and Elita held jobs, and, when my grandmother didn't have anything for me to eat, Elita and Ronnie lent money to my dear grandmother. Elita and Ronnie were quiet women, but they had taken care of their families, and made me part of their extended families. Perhaps it is the actions of these two women that made me willing, now that I am grown, to do anything to help a friend.

After numerous visits with a Realtor, Marilyn and I finally found a home we could grow in, less than a mile from Elita's house. Our house was a three-bedroom, 1.5-bath, extended Cape Cod structure on a quiet tree-lined block in a racially mixed neighborhood. The house had been built in 1944 and had a two-car garage, a fireplace, a wood stove, and a bar in the basement. As a teenager, I had visited Elita's family and had loved the trees and the grass. The area had mountains and lakes, and the air smelled fresh.

The owners knew we were first-time home buyers, but I wasn't going into the transaction blindly. As New Yorkers, we were naturally skeptical and even fearful that we might be taken advantage of. I did a lot of research on the house and on the inspection process, realizing that I hadn't done enough research when I had purchased the brownstone in Harlem, and I didn't want to make the same mistake again. I had the home inspected not once but twice. Inspectors went over the home inch by inch and found flaws ranging from missing bathroom tiles to roof leaks. I asked that everything be fixed before we closed.

The first attempt at closing in October was a disaster. The owner acted as though I should be grateful to get his house and did not fulfill his end of the deal by completing the repairs we had agreed upon. I was furious and walked out of the closing. The deal nearly fell apart. Somehow our attorney and personal family friend, Ricardo Morales, managed to get everything straightened out, and we closed on our house shortly after Thanksgiving. I was the first homeowner in the Carter family, and Marilyn was the first in the Stevens family.

When we moved in just weeks before Christmas 1994, I pleaded with my mother-in-law to move in with us. She wanted to stay in Harlem and maintain her independence. As in most cases, whatever my mother-in-law wanted, she got. We moved north thirty miles from New York City to Rockland, and she stayed in Harlem.

During the cold winter months, we lit a fire in our new fireplace. Our two kids loved to rumble down the stairs early in the morning. Although I had once been part-owner of a tenement in Harlem, this house was altogether different. I was the king of my castle. I felt a tremendous sense of power. Most important, this was my first real home ever. As a child, I had always been tossed to and from places. I lived with my mother one minute, my grandmother the next, foster care, friends in Seattle, and finally my aunt. When I went away to college, my living arrangements changed from year to year. And when my broad-casting career got underway, I lived with my mother-in-law.

From birth until this day, I'd had no place to call home. But now I had so much going on in my life that I couldn't truly stop and exhale. I still worked long hours as a reporter, and I still partied late into the night, so I couldn't fully appreciate our house's large kitchen or its spacious backyard that wild animals like beavers and deer romped through. We had a garden in the front yard, but I literally could not stop and smell the roses. Marilyn was so proud of her new home that she put a wooden placard in the front lawn that read "The Carters." Indeed, it was home sweet home, but I still wasn't happy.

At this stage of my life, my television career was still going strong, and I gained a new title to add to my resume: anchor. The nightly political show, *The Road to City Hall*, which had been hosted first by New York 1 anchor Leslie Devlin and then by Roma Torre, proved to be too much for their busy schedules. Paul Sagan and Steve Paulus decided it would be better if the political reporters alternated hosting the show. This approach sounded unworkable, and I resisted doing the anchor spot at first, thinking it was a bad idea. I liked working as a reporter because I loved the action, and I wanted to remain a reporter.

Television anchors, I believed, were easily replaceable for those who had a face for television. Anchors usually stayed inside the studio all day, practically chained to a desk, a position that would have bored me to death. I liked being where the news was, and I liked being given the inside perspective on an issue rather than the usual spin. I couldn't get that insider infor-mation from the confines of a studio. But Paul and Steve insisted that I give the anchor spot a chance.

On several occasions after I started co-anchoring, I marched into Paul Sagan's office to complain about having to be part of the political unit. I apparently complained one time too many. When I plainly said that I did not want to host the show any longer, Paul put an abrupt end to my whine.

"Well, then, I'm sorry to hear that you're leaving New York 1," he said briskly. Sitting across from his oak desk, I retracted my complaint and said, "Wait a minute! We can work this out—" I finally crept out of his office, chastened for once by my own bravado.

Ultimately, anchoring a television show turned out to be a good career move for me. Field reporters may be in the thick of particular stories, but anchors become the face of every story. As a result of hosting New York 1's political show, my popularity and credibility increased tenfold. Now the entire show centered on me, not just on a two-minute news report. I hosted the show on Mondays and Tuesdays, and Andrew Kirtzman, the other political reporter, hosted on Thursdays and Fridays. We alternated on Wednesdays.

I was still bored at times, but anchoring was a cushy gig. On the political show, I did fifteen- to twenty-minute interviews live with the same newsmakers that I used to interview in the field. The newsmakers still gave me the inside information, this time in the hallways of New York 1.

With so much time to kill in the studio, I formed a closer bond with some of my colleagues, like Claire Brinberg, a former student at Barnard. She was among the first group of interns, and she had worked her way up in the political unit. Initially, she was very shy and sat alone reading newspapers in a cubicle off to the side of the newsroom. There she waited for someone to give her work to do.

She was about five feet seven inches tall, had sandy-brown hair, and wore trendy eyeglasses. A cross between a 1960s hippie and a 1990s punk rocker, Claire had a sing-songy voice and said things like, "Oh, Dominic, you are too much, dude." She idolized the Rolling Stones and Bruce Springsteen and never missed a Springsteen concert in New York. I had felt sorry for the young intern who didn't mingle with others, so I took her with me on assignments. She was a quick study. By the time she graduated from college, New York 1 scooped her up as a political news assistant.

Claire's boss and mine was Dan Jacobson, the executive producer of the political unit. I knew him back when he had been a wire service reporter for the now-defunct United Press International, and I liked his quiet style. He was a die-hard Brooklynite and was very open-minded and fair. He never panicked or raised his voice or held a grudge. He had close-cropped, reddish-brown hair and a pleasant countenance. Whenever we were pressured for time in preparing for the political show, Dan's tone never changed, and, unlike most producers, he remained calm. Still, I considered him a real character with a witty sense of humor, and he produced one of the most talked-about political shows in the city.

Attention from fellow media colleagues is welcome as long as the coverage is favorable. One television critic called our political show the *60 Minutes* of local television. I was a huge draw for viewers; perhaps that's why one of the greatest citations of my career soon arrived.

In September 1996, I appeared on the cover of the *New York Times* television guide. On that sleepy Sunday, I picked up a huge *New York Times* and fumbled through the sections. Sure enough, Anna Carter's grandson was on the cover. Marilyn sat nervously next to me and shouted, "I can't look!" Being on that cover was quite an accomplishment. I stared at the glossy television guide in complete amazement, seeing the color photo of myself with Mayor Giuliani. It was a full-body photograph showing me pointing the microphone into Mayor Giuliani's face.

Most journalists would give their right arm to have their name even mentioned in the *New York Times*. And in the paper of record, I had the entire cover to myself. If that wasn't enough, I was referred to in that article as one of the important journalists in New York City. Most journalists want to earn the respect of their colleagues, and this article accomplished that goal for me.

The cover story was brilliantly entitled, "Eyes on New York: NY1: An All-News Station with Home Grown Talent." On pages 4 and 5, there were four pictures of me working on a typical news day. One photo showed me carrying the tripod and the camera, a serious look on my face. The photo montage was called "A Day in the Life of Dominic Carter." The accompanying article by Robin Pogrebin focused on New York 1's growing popularity after three years on the air.

> After a typical day on overdrive—covering a news conference on adult protective services and acting as a host for the nightly talk program "Inside City Hall"—Dominic Carter was finally fast asleep when the telephone jolted him awake at 2:50 AM.

The story referred to the mysterious crash of TWA Flight 800, which had gone down off Long Island, New York, just minutes after takeoff on July 17, 1996, and how New York 1 got its staffers to the location. But I was the focus of the article.

> Mr. Carter, a native of the Bronx who grew up in Harlem and started his career in radio, has become something of a local celebrity. "Dominic is the most important black journalist now in the city," said [Mitchell] Moss of New York University."
> *New York Times*

I was humbled by the comment of Mitchell Moss, who headed the Urban Studies Center at New York University. However, I chafed at the "black journalist" remark. I thought his observation had put me into a box, and I do not like being pigeonholed. I was mildly annoyed that my race was even being taken into consideration and felt the comment should have been "one of the most important journalists" in the city. Why did I have to be the "black" journalist? The phrase felt like a backhanded compliment. Later, in other publications, I would be referred to as the best, period.

The news business is tough. Often, the clock is not on your side when you are rushing to file a report, and tempers can easily get out of control. Once, after following a massive protest march across the Brooklyn Bridge during the hot, humid days of August, I hustled back to the newsroom, rushing to make deadline and file a report. I was assigned to the lead videotape editor, who was well known for having a short temper with reporters. When I walked into his edit room, he started his antics before we even began working. Red-faced, he asked me if my tapes and material were ready. When I told him I was still organizing my materials, he slammed his fist down on the console and cursed to himself.

I tried to defuse the situation and told him to calm down because I wasn't in the mood for his attitude. I walked out to give both of us a moment to cool off. As I walked out, he said, "You'd better walk out because I'll have your f——job."

At that precise moment, I erupted in a blind rage. I turned around, headed back into the edit room, grabbed him around the collar, and threw him against the glass wall. I saw fear in his eyes. I did not want to hurt him, but I wanted him to know that he had crossed the line. In letting him know that fact, I crossed the line as well. My executive producer, Dan Jacobson, and the news director, Peter Landis, immediately ran into the edit room. I heard people screaming at me to put him down. I was furious and stepped out of the room, announcing that I was going home. The news director said, "No, you can't leave," but then he paused, looked at my face, and agreed that I indeed should go home.

This encounter clearly wasn't one of my finer moments, but I had zero tolerance for that kind of disrespect. This wasn't the first time I had been insulted, but it was the first time I had reacted so aggressively. I had spent the most vulnerable years of my life being harassed and bullied by my mother, and I wasn't going to take harassment and bullying from people who meant nothing to me.

Many of my colleagues were pleased that someone had finally stood up to the boorish editor, but I paid for my actions with a suspension. And to add insult to injury, the media accounts of the incident, including coverage in *New York Magazine*, used my name in bold print but left the editor anonymous. If this wasn't enough, just weeks before the altercation with the editor,

I had also been in the newspapers for taking an action I am not proud of.

During a press conference at City Hall Park for his reelection bid. Mayor Giuliani received the endorsement of emergency medical service workers. I wanted to ask the mayor about remarks made by his Democratic rival, Ruth Messinger, who at the time had been the borough president for Manhattan. But his communication director, Cristyne Lategano, allowed the press to ask the mayor only the questions that she thought relevant—questions about his endorsement. In other words, she wanted to control the message the mayor put out for the day. I wanted to ask the mayor about Messinger. I thought the mayor was a public servant on the public payroll, and as a journalist I had the right to ask questions. But every time I motioned for a question, Lategano rudely cut me off.

"Dominic, no! The mayor is *not* taking questions on any other topic!"

I ignored her and raised my voice to ask the mayor about Messinger's comments. She cut me off again. She was so disrespectful that I lost my cool right in the middle of the press corps. Without thinking, I said in a normal tone, "Keep it up, Cristyne, and I will single-handedly bring you down."

At that moment, Cristyne knew that she finally had me. Almost giddily, she said, "What did you say?"

I walked away, knowing instinctively that I shouldn't have said what I had said, but I didn't like her policy of restricting me from doing my job. A lot of reporters have said a lot worse to press secretaries and communication directors behind closed doors, but I would be singled out. This incident was reported in the newspapers, most prominently on page seven of the *New*

York Post. "Riled TV Reporter Warns Lategano: I'll Ruin You" screamed the bold headline.

> TV reporter Dominic Carter blew his top at Giuliani spokeswoman Cristyne Lategano yesterday, warning the communications director, "Keep it up, Cristyne, and I will single-handedly bring you down."
>
> Carter, who works for the NY1 cable-news station, was angry at Lategano because she wouldn't let him ask the mayor questions at a press conference where city EMS workers endorsed Giuliani's re-election bid.... Lategano cut off Carter, telling him that the mayor was only taking questions about the endorsement in City Hall Park. But Carter persisted and finally uttered his warning to Lategano. Lategano would not comment on the incident, but a senior Giuliani administration official blasted the City Hall reporter. "It's become apparent in recent weeks that he's been losing any objectivity," said the official, who asked not to be named.
>
> "This simply reinforces the fact that he's no longer an objective journalist when it comes to City Hall," the official said. "Everyone who heard him say this was shocked by it, including the professional journalists who witnessed this thing." Steve Paulus, the vice president for news for Time Warner-owned NY1 defended his reporter. "We stand by Dominic's journalism. I think what happened is that he lost his temper. He wasn't getting a legitimate response from City Hall to legitimate questions," Paulus said. "Dominic lost his temper. He regrets losing his temper. Obviously what he said, he shouldn't have said but he has no ulterior motives. We stand by the quality of his reporting."
> *New York Post*

I was pleased that Steve had stood by me during these trying times. But not everyone sided with me. The same day that the

Post article came out, my sister-in-law, Judy Buckery, phoned to tell me that some callers to the popular radio station WABC were furious. The show was hosted by Guardian Angel Curtis Sliwa, a man whom I knew rather well from my years of covering his leadership with the activist group. Members of that organization wore red berets and made citizen arrests to help reduce crime in and around the city.

I just shrugged the news off. Many reporters were so afraid of Mayor Giuliani that they didn't want to provoke him. But I wasn't afraid. This is the item that ran in the *Daily News* during that time.

> NY1 reporter Dominic Carter has been suspended for a week after a scrap with an editor, according to a source. Carter has been a particularly vocal member of the press pool in questioning Mayor Giuliani about his marriage … And he recently responded to months of behind the scenes strong-arming by mayoral aide Cristyne Lategano by saying, "I will destroy you." While Carter's tough stance had nothing to do with the suspension, says the source, his top boss won't say what [the suspension is] about or even if [Carter] will be off the air this week. "I really can't comment on internal personnel decisions," said NY1 News Director Peter Landis.
> New York *Daily News*

I was glad to see that the *Daily News* was fair enough to note that I was responding to months of Cristyne Lategano's pressure. Indeed, the *Daily News* put the incident in perspective. But all of the negative press didn't reflect well upon me, and I worried that people would think I was out of control, or worse, "an angry black man." One could assume from my behavior that I had a drug problem. The fact of the matter was I had made the critical, stupid mistake of starting to believe my own press. On the outside, I was still the same guy who went to work every day, but inside I had started believing I was untouchable.

Invincible no more, I had to accept responsibility for my actions. In most of these incidents where I lost my temper, I had been provoked. But I couldn't fully grasp what was going on in my life. For years I easily avoided such political land mines—but suddenly I was taking the bait over and over. Did it having anything to do with my mother and the pain I hid inside? Was all of the pressure finally getting to me?

Dominic as a child.

Grade School Photo.

A very proud moment in Dominic's life. His daughter's
(Courtney) High School graduation.

Dominic and then first lady Hillary Clinton at Staples Center
in Los Angeles.

Former NYC Mayor Rudy Giuliani and Dominic at performance for annual charity event.

Nelson Mandela and Dominic at Gracie Mansion in New York.

Dominic in Karate Class.

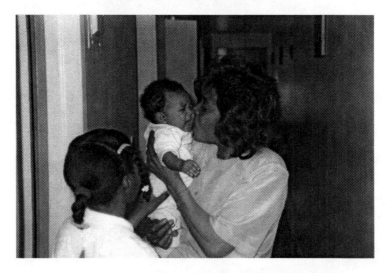

Laverne sharing a moment with her granddaughter Courtney.

Throggs Neck Housing Project in Bronx New York. Laverne
Carter and her sister Aunt Inez celebrate Mother's Day.
With toddlers (from left to right) Beatrice, Dominic's niece
and his daughter Courtney.

Military flight. Aboard a C-130 cargo plane. An exhaused
Dominic flys around the world to reach Somalia in Africa.

Dominic's daughter from her High School Days as a Cheer-leader.

The Carters at a Syracuse University Football Game.

A passion for Dominic Carter. Speaking to young people
around the country.

7

The new millennium was one year away, and, while the world prepared to celebrate the year 2000, I wasn't in a celebratory mood. Laverne was dying. She was no longer just sick; diabetes and high blood pressure had begun to overwhelm her system. Laverne's once-brilliant brown complexion took on an ashen tone, her youthful radiance long gone. She walked and talked very slowly, eerily reminding me of the time she had taken psychotropic drugs. Laverne still managed to smile and laugh, but she had a look of resignation in her eyes. I didn't ask her, yet I instinctively knew that she wasn't afraid of death. Laverne was tired. Life had beaten the hell out of her for fifty-six years, and she was ready to stop fighting. Her expression said, "Enough, already."

I hadn't called her mommy since I was about seven years old, but I suddenly didn't want my mommy to die. I didn't want her to leave me. Sure, I'd had moments when I had been frustrated and resentful toward her, sometimes even scornful of her, but those moments hadn't negated the fact that I didn't want her to pass away. She wasn't perfect, but she was mine. For the first time, I realized there was indeed a bond between us. For all of the pain and anguish, I still had compassion and empathy for my mother.

When I was young, I had wished a million times that she wasn't my mother, but wishing couldn't make that relationship different. I had gone through a roller coaster of emotions because of her actions, but I still wanted Laverne to live and to be happy. Yet she wasn't happy any more, and neither was I.

When I greeted my mother, awkwardness always stood between us. I never hugged or kissed her, and she never hugged or kissed me, either. She would greet me with a smirk and would say, "How you doing, Mister Carter?" and I would reply with a tender punch on her upper arm. She would say, "Ouch, boy." And we'd giggle. That was our salute to one another, our mutual expression of goodwill. In hindsight, I know our exchange was the way we ignored a painful past and avoided any form of affection or tenderness.

We remained in our warped land of make-believe, pretending that our many wounds were healed, though they clearly had not. Our wounded past had healed into a nasty keloid, and we simply tried to hide it as best we could and to keep moving. We played our roles quite well, even pretending that I had never confronted her about her sexual abuse of me. After she had rebuffed my direct questions more than two years prior, I had almost given up my wish to ask her the questions that would reveal the truth to me. I would never confront Laverne again, though I had many opportunities. I figured that we had to be somewhat disingenuous about our past, for, if we were honest about it, the shame alone would never permit us to speak to each other at all. But the tension between us steadily increased. It apparently affected my mother physically, and it ate at me emotionally.

I lived in two distinct and very different worlds. One bright, with the promising lights of an increasingly successful television career, but the other was a dark, frightening world, rotten with sexual abuse and abandonment. For more than thirty years, the secrets I held inside nearly ate me alive. At work, I was all smiles, but inwardly I was unhappy. Almost nothing I did could help me become fully happy. Nothing—not a home in the suburbs, not an exciting television career, not a devoted wife and beautiful children, not even an ever-increasing salary—nothing could make me happy inside. My pain ran so deep that nothing external could fix it. I was a pressure cooker about to blow. On October 13, 1999, I finally exploded.

My action could have served as a classic case of acting without thinking. For days, I had been trying to renegotiate my television contract at work, and Steve Paulus and I were not seeing eye to eye. In New York City, the number-one media market in the nation, most reporters and anchors sign contracts for their services. Such a contract details the length of employment and the salary, and lists numerous stipulations that are contingent upon one's conduct. If you're good at what you do, your contract will likely be renewed. If you're not good, most news directors allow your contract to expire, and then you're no longer an employee at the station. My work had been good at New York 1, and I was not in danger of losing my contract, but Steve and I had problems over the salary.

After several stalled meetings and a nasty argument with my executive producer, Claire Brinberg, I woke up one autumn morning, and I didn't want to deal with the stress any more. I was tired of living a double life. I was sick of the snake pit of New York City politics, and I was tired of fighting Rudolph Giuliani's city hall. My telephone at work rang nonstop because everyone expected me to deliver something. If I delivered a big, exclusive interview, I thought the reward was for the bar to be raised even higher.

That day in October 1999, I reached a hasty conclusion as I got dressed for work. I said to myself, "I'm gonna quit." With that thought, I felt a weight lift from my shoulders. I felt that for the first time in my life, I would be free. My feeling was false, but, when you live in emotional bondage, freedom can disguise itself as almost anything. I planned to walk straight into the vice president's office, which now belonged to Steve Paulus, the guy who had been promoted from news director several years before. I would tell Steve that I was quitting.

I phoned my wife before I left home. "Hi, hon," I said. "Listen, I'm gonna quit today." I was abrupt, direct, and to the point. My wife was so disgusted by my mood swings that I could almost feel the tension between us.

Marilyn snapped, "Go ahead. Quit." She sounded more than a little sarcastic and probably assumed I wouldn't dare do such a thing.

She should have known better than to dare me. I hung up the phone, packed up the company-issued laptop computer, and headed out the door into my car. I planned to resign quickly—do a "quit and run," if you will.

I took my usual route from Rockland County to the station's headquarters at 460 West Forty-Second Street in midtown Manhattan. I felt enormously liberated. I parked my new SUV at a meter and put one single quarter in the meter because I didn't plan to stay long. My heart beat quickly as I rode the elevator up to the fourth floor. I prayed that I wouldn't see anyone whom I really cared about, because I feared that anyone I spoke to would try to talk me out of quitting. One such person was Esther Nazario, a secretary with whom I had worked during the Dinkins Administration at city hall. Esther is a very hard worker, and, when Dinkins lost his race for reelection, she was out of a job. At that time, I personally appealed to Steve Paulus to hire Esther. She had a cubicle just outside Steve's office, and I knew that, if I took one look at her, she would stop me at the door. As I approached Steve's office, I was relieved to see that Esther was away from her desk.

I also worried about running into the personnel director, Elisabeth Fanfant. Like me, she was also one of the original staff members, and she knew me quite well. She had become like a surrogate mother to me. She had a witty sense of humor and often tried to keep me in line. She had a calm voice when things got hectic. Entering the office, I saw that Elisabeth was not in the office yet, so I knew my mission would succeed.

I walked right into Steve's office. He could tell from the look on my face that I was not happy. He had seen that look many times before when I had been frustrated over story assignments. I felt beads of sweat forming on my neck and forehead.

"Here's the computer, Steve," I said, holding out my laptop.

He looked straight into my eyes and stood up. Steve had a fairly large office with an oversized desk, and off to the side was a small, round table with five chairs. "Dominic, sit down," he said, heaving a sigh. His face showed that he was tired of playing this game with me.

"Steve, I quit," I said.

Steve looked more nervous than I did. He hesitated as he spoke. "Dominic, I like you, and I worry about you. You have to think about your family."

I could barely look him in the face, so I scanned the room instead. In his office were about a half dozen television monitors, tuned to all the television stations in town. At the top of his wall, overlooking his desk, were five clocks. Most national newsrooms have numerous clocks to keep track of various time zones around the nation and the world. Steve's clocks registered the same times as they tracked the hours in Manhattan, the Bronx, Staten Island, Brooklyn, and Queens. Visitors to Steve's office always chuckled about the clocks. But this time as I stared at them, I found nothing to chuckle about. I felt that my time at New York 1 had run out.

I had great respect for Steve, and I knew that he was sincere, but I didn't want to be talked out of quitting. I stood up abruptly and left him sitting at the table. He didn't try to stop me, and I surely couldn't stop myself. I dashed down the spiral staircase, then down the hall, through the double glass doors, back down the elevator, and onto the street. When I returned to the car and checked the meter, I saw that barely nine minutes had passed.

For a moment, I felt a huge sense of accomplishment. After nine years of working at New York 1 News, I had finally done it. I felt like yelling, "I quit my job today." Finally, no one controlled me.

But within moments, reality slapped me in the face. The fog I was in quickly cleared away. I asked myself how I would pay the mortgage in the coming months, the car payment on the brand-new SUV, the private school tuition for Courtney, and the food for my wife, my children, and myself. What was I going to do to support my family? What about my reputation, which I had worked so hard to build up as a tough-as-nails reporter? I was certain that the local newspapers would be reporting my abrupt resignation.

I went from feeling like a king to feeling like the court jester. How foolish I had been! My critics hadn't been able to take me down, so I had done it for them. The more I thought about my resignation, the more tears wet my face. It was clear that I was hell-bent on thwarting my own success. City hall couldn't stop me; jealous colleagues couldn't stop me; my own mother couldn't stop me; and neither had poverty or the projects. But I had managed to stop myself. Everything that my grandmother Anna Pearl and Aunt Inez had worked for seemed to be going up in smoke.

I cried during the whole ride home. My vision got so blurry that I couldn't see the highway. I traveled home north on the Palisades Interstate Parkway, one of the most scenic highways leading out of New York City toward New Jersey and Rockland County. I had been on this narrow, winding, two-lane road many times, but this time it looked different. Through swollen, teary eyes, I noticed the hilly landscape that framed the parkway. Fall foliage was just beginning to show, and it was a breath-taking sight. I could identify with the changing of nature's guard. I, too, was changing; my emotions imitated the leaves preparing to fall from the trees. All of my bottled-up emotions wilted inside me.

As I turned into my driveway, I came to myself almost as if I had been unconscious before. I ran into the house and called Steve Paulus to take back what I had said and done in his office. This time, Esther, Steve's assistant, picked up the phone, and I could tell from the sound in her voice that she was alarmed. "Dominic, what did you do?" she asked.

I was so choked up that I couldn't speak. Esther transferred me to Steve, who spoke in a somber tone. "Dominic, listen," Steve said. "I don't know what I'm going to do with you. I've already put out a memo to the staff, announcing your resignation. It's too late."

"Listen, Steve," I said in a panic. "I'm under a lot of pressure. I didn't know what I was doing."

"Dominic, give me a call in a couple of days, okay? Bye-bye."

And with that, I was officially unemployed for the first time since I was eighteen years old. Steve had finally called my bluff. I had backed him into a corner, and this time, he'd found a way out.

Sitting in our living room at home, I called my wife at her job and blew my top. I directly blamed her for the whole thing.

Marilyn was stunned that I blamed her for resigning my own job. "How could this be my fault?" she screamed into the telephone.

Desperately seeking to absolve *myself* of any blame, I tried to explain to my wife why she was responsible for my behavior. "You knew I was distraught," I said, "and you didn't talk me out of it." Deep down, however, I knew that I had screwed up royally.

As was customary, Steve's memo to the staff was distributed to the mailbox of every employee at the station. The memo was blunt and to the point. "Dominic Carter has resigned from New York 1 ..." Steve had written before briefly mentioning some of my accomplishments in a paragraph. He ended the memo with "Please join me in wishing Dominic well."

Within hours, the phone rang. Elisabeth Fanfant, Claire Brinberg, and Esther Nazario and others—it just didn't end. As I spoke to one colleague, another rang in through call waiting. Then newspaper reporters began calling for comment. I had no comment, but they didn't need one to publish this story, and there were several resignation stories published. The *Daily News* featured me in their gossip section the following day. The popular columnists George Rush and Joanne Molloy gave my story the headline "Carter Signs Off at NY1."

NY1 political reporter Dominic Carter has left the city's all-news channel. Buzz is that Carter may have locked horns with his bosses.

Three years ago, the co-anchor of *Inside City Hall* was reportedly suspended for a week after a scrap with an editor.

Carter, who distinguished himself as a tough questioner of the mayor in his seven years at the station, didn't return a call. NY1 spokesman Ed Pachetti said his departure "was sudden in our eyes."

"Dominic left for personal reasons," said Pachetti. "We wish him well. We're hoping that if he resolves those personal issues, he might return." Asked what those personal issues might be, Pachetti said, "That's Dominic's personal life."

New York *Daily News*

The official company response made me even angrier. I knew I was fair game as a public figure, but it was very easy to conclude that I had a drug problem. I did not use drugs of any kind, but I knew that "personal issues" for those in the public eye often meant an illegal habit of some kind. I was furious with the tone of the company's official statement, and New York 1 management told me not to offer any comment on the record. I told some columnists who called the house that my mother was dying, but the damage had been done. My resignation was the talk of the town.

I didn't realize who my true friends were until after I resigned. One staffer called and told me that she was certain she could change Steve's mind and told me to sit at my computer and write a letter of apology. I was so emotionally drained that I couldn't think of what to write, and she dictated the letter for me. The next day, she met me around the corner from the news

station and made me sign the letter. Then she took it directly to
Steve and made a special appeal on my behalf. Her kindness
helped to calm my nerves.

One of New York 1's anchors, Lewis Dodley, also reassured
me. To many at the station, Dodley often seemed a bit distant,
but he surprised me with his compassion. "Dominic, trust me,"
he said. "Everything will be all right. We'll work this out. You
cannot go down like this."

Two other staffers who had met in the newsroom and subse-
quently married also stepped in to help me return to the station.
Michael O'Looney, one of New York 1's original reporters, and
Annika Pergament called and promised to help mediate the situation because they were personal friends of Steve. An associate
producer and now a reporter, Sandy Endo, called me at home.
Another colleague who always stood in my corner, Anchor
Roma Torre, called with words of support, as did my political
producer, Jamie McShane. I liked his laid-back style and his
newshound instincts. Jamie had become a close friend of mine.
He was my friend when I was on top, and he was still my friend
when I was at the bottom. He said he would do anything to get
me back on the job.

I also heard from many people outside the television industry, such as Rafael Martinez Alequin, who published a small,
monthly newspaper called the *Free Press*. Rafael's claim to fame
was that he took pride in asking Giuliani difficult questions that
others journalists wouldn't dare ask. Of course, we all used
Giuliani's answers, but Rafael was the one who did the dirty
work. Rafael called and told me to hang in there. I also had a
call from my longtime friends, Joe and Barbara Bragg. As I have
mentioned earlier, when I began my career in radio news, I

replaced Joe, a highly respected reporter at WLIB and WBLS after Joe went over to WRKS, also known as KISS-FM.

Jules Martin, Esquire, and Ruby Ryles got in touch with me. They had worked together during the Dinkins administration, Ruby as one of Dinkins's press secretaries, and Jules, a lawyer, as a member of the New York City Police Department. Jules was assigned to the Intelligence Division as head of the Municipal Security section in 1990. In other words, he was in charge of Mayor Dinkins's security detail. To Jules's credit, although we are very good friends, he had never leaked or confirmed a single story to me. Ruby also took part in a letter-writing campaign to New York 1 asking that I get my job back.

I also received a call from Bronx Borough President Fernando Ferrer. The popular Latino politician told me to hold my head high. The one person who made me laugh during this distressing time was the Reverend Al Sharpton. This civil rights leader, no stranger to protests, offered to start a protest immediately in front of New York 1's studios on 42nd Street, and he was deadly serious. This action would have been against his own self-interest. New York 1 was a major media outlet that Sharpton needed to get his message out when he held news conferences, and he held many news conferences that New York 1 covered regularly when other stations did not. I told him that the protest would not be necessary.

All of the support made me realize that people cared about me. Sometimes I had felt alone in my battle to make a name for myself. The saying is a cliché but is so true: it's very lonely at the top.

Just days after my departure memo, the political show that I had anchored, *Inside City Hall*, was prepared to put my resignation on the air. After the announcement was made public, viewers made numerous calls to the station to ask when I was coming back. One of the political reporters who filled in as anchor for *Inside City Hall*, David Lewis, was prepared to read a story about my resignation live on the show. Because of my popularity, managers concluded that they should make an official, on-air announcement that I had decided to leave the station. Fortunately, Jamie McShane and managing editor Dan Jacobson pleaded with management to delay the announcement until it was certain that I wasn't going to return to the station.

It wasn't an easy fight. Some in management—actually one particular person whom I had an unpleasant history with—wanted to put the final nail in my coffin, but Jamie knew that I regretted quitting and wanted to return. The story about my departure was all set and ready to go, but Jamie and Dan won a delay, and fortunately that story never aired. But not everyone was sorry to see me leave. One staffer said in the middle of the newsroom, "F——, Dominic. We don't need him, anyway." Another staffer stormed into a top managers' meeting and declared that he was the only conceivable replacement for my anchor slot on the political show. The managers, I was told, laughed the moment he walked out of the office.

When the phone finally stopped ringing, I had to face my family. My wife was supportive, but she did not appreciate taking the heat for my resignation. Still, I refused to change my story because I didn't have the courage to admit that I'd chosen to resign, so I made Marilyn the scapegoat. My approach wasn't fair to my wife, but it was my coping mechanism at the time.

I felt weird being at home when our daughter and son returned from school. They were as surprised to see me as I was to see them. One positive result of my resignation was that I had a chance to know my children better. Because of my busy career, I hadn't been at home much during the day. By the time I woke up, the children were usually at school. When I returned home in the evening, they were already asleep. After my resignation, I had time to talk to them about their schoolwork and their social lives. I didn't realize how much I had missed by working so hard. I never wanted my kids to know what ghetto life was like, so I had worked hard to make sure they would get the best of everything. But my full schedule caused me to miss something special in the meantime—their development. Now I realized that I couldn't help them with their homework, and I didn't know most of their teachers. Yet because I was home now, I wanted to show them that I truly did care.

Before I could appreciate my family, I needed to get reinstated at work. I felt miserable without the security of a job to protect my family. My instincts told me that my reputation as an award-winning journalist would lead to a call from New York 1. I was right. Several days later, the personnel director, Elisabeth Fanfant, called to alert me to meet with the news managers. She said this discussion would determine my future with the company. On the day of the meeting, I walked into Steve's office—the same place I had walked out of days before—to see all of the power brokers at New York 1.

Sitting in a semicircle were news director Peter Landis, managing editor Dan Jacobson, personnel director Elisabeth Fanfant, and assistant news director Bernadine Han. I sat in a chair and had to eat a big plate of crow. One by one, they said that my behavior had been outrageous, and a few of them made comments that I thought were intended to provoke me to anger. I remained calm. They asked me how I felt about getting therapy to control my anger. I agreed and told them I would cooperate fully. I had come to terms with my mistake and had begun to see that my anger was having a negative impact on my job. I was prepared to be humble.

Steve Paulus was conspicuously absent from the meeting. He was tired of my games and, I guessed, wanted to teach me a lesson. I had always turned to Steve when I was in a jam, and this time his absence sent me a message, loud and clear, that I was on my own. When the meeting ended, I left humbled. I knew I had screwed up so badly that I had put myself in a demeaning position. At the same time, I refused to grovel. I had helped make New York 1 News what it had become. My aggressive reporting style gave the station credibility, and they could not afford to let that go easily.

Two days later, Elisabeth Fanfant called me and said the managers had voted to reinstate me, but I would have to stay out for two months without pay and get counseling. My wife was working, and I had some money saved, so I wasn't that worried. The newspapers had another field day with my return. The *New York Post* included a comment from Steve Paulus, who said that I would return to New York 1 on December1. Paulus was quoted as saying that I'd been on a leave of absence for what he termed "personal problems."

The *Daily News's* television section also covered the story, but this time I felt that I had to give a comment to stave off any ugly or false rumors.

> Almost as hastily as he left his anchor slot at cable's New York 1 News, Dominic Carter has changed plans and will return to his post on December 1.
>
> "Sometimes you do things in haste, but then when you have time to reconsider, you work it out. I like working at New York 1," says Carter, who has served as a political reporter for the channel since its launch seven years ago.

Carter also hosts the nightly *Road to City Hall* political news segment.

Carter cited personal reasons for leaving the network this month, but he also said things became a bit tense before he left. "I did get a bit hot under the collar," he said.

Carter turned his resignation into a leave of absence after NY1 general manager Steve Paulus 'worked out the details with management for my return.'

New York *Daily News*

Even though I was set to return to work, the letters of support kept coming, like the one I received with the letterhead "Congress of the United States, House of Representatives, Washington, D.C." It was dated November 19, 1999.

Dear Dominic,
Welcome back.
You've never made it easy for me, but I've missed you.
Most of all, New York has been missing one of its toughest and most savvy reporters.
Look forward to working with you.
Sincerely,
Charles Rangel
Member of Congress.

The charismatic congressman Charles Rangel had gone through a lot in the public eye over the years, but I had always treated him fairly. I had interviewed him repeatedly on live television, and I was pleased to know that he wished me well.

I essentially had two months to kill, salary-free. Those two months weren't pretty financially, but they marked a turning point in my life. After years of living in a whirlwind, I was forced to reexamine my life. I spent a lot of time at home with my wife and kids. After all, we had been married almost fifteen years, and Courtney was ten, and Dominic was six. All of a sudden, the lure of the nightclubs meant nothing to me. After my humbling mistake, I started to see that the clubs meant nothing in comparison to my family. And also during this time my mother began to fade away.

I made frequent visits to the hospital, and Laverne looked worse than ever. She had suffered a stroke and spent more time in hospital beds now than in her own bed. One week she'd be in New York Hospital, and the next she'd be in a rehabilitative hospital for the indigent. This was the first time in my adult life that I began to see clear signs of her mental illness. She would lie in the bed, hooked up to monitors, with a terrified look on her face. She periodically cried and mumbled under her breath. It was sheer torture to witness this sad spectacle. Water spilled from her eyes and stained her thin blue and white hospital gown, and I tried not to show my pain. I didn't know what to say or what to do. She was practically an invalid, and I had to feed her. To make matter worse, Malika and Antoinette were living in Laverne's apartment. Malika, barely twenty years old, had been thrust into the role of an adult with the responsibility of taking care of her baby sister. I had to keep an eye on their well-being. I stopped by Laverne's apartment every other day and took the two of them food shopping.

One time, I fed Laverne applesauce and had a flashback that almost made me throw up. I saw her putting me into bed with her and sexually abusing me. I saw myself taking off my pajamas and following her every command. I tried to swat the image from my mind and continued spooning applesauce into her mouth. My, how the tables had turned, and I wasn't at all pleased about the change. Every time I raised the spoon to her mouth, I looked at her lips and her tongue and her very sad eyes. When the applesauce dripped down the side of her mouth, I took a napkin and gently wiped it away. I wished this woman no ill, but I was about to explode from years of holding back my emotions. Dealing with her death was just too much for me. I felt grief, and to say I was angry would be an understatement.

As sad as this episode was, I refused to cry in front of my mother. In a weird way, I didn't want to give her the satisfaction. It was very important that I not appear weak. Whenever tears welled up in my eyes, I would abruptly leave, and she mumbled and cried again.

I rarely stayed at her bedside for more than half an hour. When I left, she was so weak and I was so heartbroken that I kissed her on the forehead and said, "Everything is going to be okay, Laverne. *We* love you." Interestingly, I couldn't bring myself to say, "I love you." I tried, but that phrase wouldn't come out. I had to pin my love on the whole family. How could I tell her I loved her? Before I kissed her forehead, I searched for alternatives. I couldn't playfully punch her in the arm, like we used to do because I might've hurt her. I couldn't shake her hand because that would seem almost too formal, even rude. I didn't want to hug her, and I didn't want to kiss her on the cheek. So I deduced that the safest place for me to kiss her was on her forehead.

Even during these sad final days, there was something about her that repelled me. My response wasn't vindictive; it was more like an awkward emotional reflex. I did not want to hurt her feelings, but I had to protect my own feelings at all costs. If I didn't protect myself, I feared that I would fall apart, and that was not an option. Self-destruction was one thing; a nervous breakdown was quite another. I could always fix my mistakes, even if I had to eat crow, but if I broke down completely, I might not be able to put myself back together again.

I was a complex individual with a complex history. I wasn't an easy person to figure out, and I knew that. I viewed most people with suspicion, though I treated them with the utmost respect. To many, I was as harmless as a pussycat, but to others I was a raging tiger. Sometimes I was moody and impulsive; other times I was gentle and thoughtful. However, I was consistently loyal to people I loved and trusted. I would do anything for my family and even friends, especially friends I had grown up with—like Ty.

While I was off work, Ty and I drove through nearby afflu-ent communities like Montvale, New Jersey, to help me to stay motivated. We envisioned owning million-dollar homes. I dreamed of being wealthy and driving up a spacious driveway on a sprawling estate. Ty reminded me how close I was to realiz-ing my dreams and said that I was too close to turn back.

I also took a road trip to Atlanta to visit another friend, John Williams, who had once lived in New York City. Atlanta is a lively city, and the visit was a great way to escape from New York. As I relaxed, I finally stopped blaming my wife for my res-ignation and owned up to my faults.

After my return home, I decided to take my family to the Poconos in Pennsylvania. I held my wife's hand as we took long walks through the forests and kicked dried leaves that would soon be covered with snow. It was November 30, the day before my return to work. I was a little nervous about my return. I had already resumed my demanding schedule. We left the Poconos at about 7:00 in the morning to make it back to the Big Apple. My relationship with Marilyn was getting better. I'd had time to reflect on what really was important—not the job, not the glow of the media, but rather those closest to me who gave their love unconditionally.

New York radio legend Hal Jackson wanted to interview me on his popular radio show *Sunday Morning Classics* on WBLS, where I once worked. The show plays a wide spectrum of black-oriented music from jazz to soul to R&B. It was my first trip back to the radio station since I had left in 1992. It brought back a flood of memories. I took my kids inside the studio as Hal interviewed me live at around 11:00 AM. We talked about my brief resignation from New York 1 and my accomplishments in broadcasting. We also reminisced about my days in radio when I used to get coffee for Frankie Crocker. Mr. Jackson, as I called him, was very proud of me and urged all of his listeners to watch New York 1 the following day. I told him I would be back reporting on city hall as ferociously as ever. He liked that and wished me well. The interview was an effective way to prepare for my first day back.

On December 1, I returned to New York 1. Many people hugged me, and others shook my hand. I just wanted to get back into my routine, but as a new-and-improved Dominic without the temper. I knew I had to lie low and not create a disturbance. But, fortunately, I had been getting therapy while I was off from work, and it had proved to be very helpful.

The therapist's name was Penny Nash. Her office was on 34th Street in Manhattan, across from the Empire State Building. She was about forty years old and was firm but soft-spoken. She was a stylish dresser. She focused on ways for me to manage my anger. I initially walked into the office with an attitude of "What can *you* possibly tell *me?*" She quickly disarmed me with her kindness and compassion. She said something that was simple but very profound to me: "Dominic, you have to think before you act." And it suddenly occurred to me that I rarely thought before I acted. I was very impulsive at times, and I often made moves without thinking them through—and was forced to deal with the consequences later.

Sometimes my impulsiveness worked in my favor, but other times it did not. When it didn't work, I usually paid dearly. In my mid-thirties now, I was getting too old for angry outbursts. At Penny's urging, I decided to at least try to restrain myself. She taught me how to count to ten, walk away from provocations, think about the possible outcomes beforehand. Had I used these techniques just one year before, I would never have quit, I would never have told off the mayor's communications director, Cristyne Lategano, in full public view, and I would not have attacked my colleagues. I often had taken the bait when it dangled before me, and at last I had a way to stop myself in my own tracks.

I had not had a mother or a father who taught me how to check my temper. Although my grandmother and two aunts did one hell of a job turning me into a man, they could not teach me everything. They taught me how to be independent and self-sufficient, but they couldn't teach me how to control my bravado. There were times I was like a runaway train, and I would hear the women in my life say, "He's just being a man," or "That's just Dominic." I now see those comments were just excuses for poor behavior.

Counseling went better than I expected. However, as much as Penny and I talked, I never told her that my mother had sexually abused me. I was too ashamed. I felt that my anger was my anger and that my mother was a problem from the past that I didn't want to revisit with her or anybody else—especially as

Laverne lay dying. How could I even begin to explain that there was any type of sexual contact with my mother? I didn't feel there was anything Penny or anyone else could say about that situation that could make me feel better. Unless they had a way to erase it from my memory, I didn't believe that any amount of therapy could help me overcome the pent-up emotions related to that horror.

When I stepped foot in the newsroom, it was truly like I had never left. I was back in the thick of the political world—only this time, I tried to visit my mother before my work day started at noon. I wouldn't stay long, but the emotional impact lasted for days. I could feel it in my heart. I got flashes of my ailing mother while I was in city hall. And the closer my mother got to death, the farther away from her I wanted to be. Sometimes my mother would call my mother-in-law's home, and she couldn't speak well, so she mumbled enough to barely get my name out.

My mother-in-law knew that Laverne was crying out for me. "Dominic, you go see your mother," she said. "I'm not playing with you!" I begrudgingly did so, but no one—and I mean no one—understood the emotional toll it took for me to witness my mother's decline. Sometimes my wife accompanied me to the hospital, and I still couldn't stay long enough to sit down. I used every excuse to walk out of the room. One minute I went for the newspaper, and the next minute, I went to pay a hospital bill. I dragged minute errands out to eat up time. No one understood that this was a horror show for me. It wasn't just sad; it was horrifying, devastating, and scary. Everyone wanted me to be there for my mother, but who would be there for me?

I felt very alone during this time, even though I was surrounded by family and friends. It was the loneliest time of my life. I wanted to scream, but who would hear me? I wanted to cry, but who would wipe away my tears? My pride would not allow me to break down. I refused to cave in. I had never given up before; I wasn't going to give in now.

In spite of my ongoing family drama, I was increasingly recognized as a major force in the journalism industry. This was confirmed when I, along with several of my colleagues, received one of the biggest honors of my career. In the mail I received an elegant invitation from Bill and Hillary Clinton to join them for a holiday reception at none other than 1600 Pennsylvania Avenue. I had visited the White House before, but only in the press room, never for a social event. To my surprise, this affair was held not at a hotel but at the White House. Imagine that! Dominic Carter, a boy who at times hadn't had enough food to eat, had been invited as a guest to the White House! The invitation allowed me to bring a guest, and that was an easy decision—my wife.

I owed this to her. She was, after all, largely responsible for my success. They say behind every successful man is a good woman—and it's true—especially in my case. I probably would have dropped out of college when I got cut from the football team, but Marilyn helped me stay in school. Marilyn and I started as a team, and I believed you should "dance with the person who brought you." So Marilyn and I jumped on a shuttle out of New York's LaGuardia Airport the day before the festivities. My wife was so excited that she bought me a new suit and tie for the gala.

The event included many members of the national media like Helen Thomas, whom my wife took a photograph with. There were military choirs decked out in their crisp uniforms as they sang in front of giant Christmas trees in every room. We were given a tour of the White House and snapped pictures to bring back home to Courtney and Dominic. The White House was more majestic and beautiful than I had imagined. The portraits of the presidents, from George Washington to George Bush, graced the mansion. We took tours of everything from sitting rooms to dining rooms, even the bathrooms, which had hand towels embroidered with the White House seal. We even saved some disposable hand towels as souvenirs. I simply put them inside the inner pocket of my suit jacket.

The high point of the evening was meeting the president and the first lady. These were their final days in the White House, as Clinton had served two terms, and they were leaving for New York. We stood in a long line to greet them and have an official White House photograph taken with them. When I walked up to the president, he gave me a warm greeting. "Hey, man, how you doing?" I smiled and chuckled at his familiarity. He was so confident and at ease that I felt comfortable greeting the most powerful man on earth.

It should have been a great way to end a year that began with such despair and sadness. My highs were extremely high, but my lows were very low. But just days after this elegant fete, all hell would break loose—just in time for Christmas.

My mother somehow persuaded the doctors to let her go home for the holidays—why, I'll never know. She was still gravely ill, but they let her go home anyway. She asked me for money during Christmastime to purchase some gifts. I gave it to her without hesitation. It seemed to cheer her up. She wasn't strong, but she suddenly had a burst of energy and was looking forward to Christmas. Laverne had this remarkable ability to see-saw from being functional to being near death. One week she'd lie helpless in a hospital bed hooked up to monitors, and the following week she'd be back on her feet.

I, on the other hand, was constantly drained and tired. My wife and I didn't celebrate Christmas at our home in Rockland; we took everything to my mother-in-law's apartment in Harlem. We did that often because Ruby's house was the center of activity during the holidays. We even spent several nights there with other relatives. We just enjoyed being together. I opened my gifts, but I remember feeling somewhat numb. I couldn't get excited, no matter how I tried.

A couple of days after Christmas, I found out that my mother had taken some of the money I had given her and had had the audacity to use it to buy a present for my sister Malika's boyfriend. I went through the roof. This was the ultimate slap in the face. She had given Malika's boyfriend a Christmas gift instead of me? I was beside myself with anger. First of all, she had never given me a gift as an adult. Not a birthday gift, not a Christmas gift, not a graduation gift—*nothing*. Not even a gift for my children.

But she had given Courtney a birthday card when she was two, a card that we managed to save. On the front of the five-by-seven-inch card are six children on a roller coaster. Each child bears gifts, balloons, a cake—even a puppy. Inside it reads, "Just think, you're two! How fast you grow. You're twice as old as a year ago! And hope you're twice as happy, too. And having fun the whole day through!" My mother signed it in script: "With love from Laverne, Malika, and Antoinette." A grandmother signed a card to her granddaughter "Laverne" instead of "Grandma." It was yet another subtle reminder that Laverne felt like an outsider; more important, she knew I considered her an outsider. Thus she treated her own flesh and blood accordingly.

But Laverne should have tried harder to show more love to us, especially after I stood by her in the hospital, fed her applesauce, and wiped the sweat from her brow as she lay dying. None of that helped her see me as a worthy individual. I had tried with all my might not to hold a grudge about her abusive treatment of me, and this is how she thanked me? And just who was Malika's boyfriend, anyway? Who was this guy compared to me? Did he give Laverne money when she needed it? Did he have Laverne's television turned on in the hospital when she could not afford it? I was flabbergasted that my mother thought more of him than of me. And to top it off, what she gave him was bought with *my* money. She couldn't even take the money *I* had given her to purchase a gift for her only son or her grandchildren.

Dammit, for once, I wanted this woman to acknowledge me, to show me some measure of respect and affection. What did I have to do to earn her love? I had tried all of my life with no success. I was tired of being her victim. These hard feelings finally gave me just the ammunition I needed to ignore her from then on. On December 29, the telephone rang at my mother-in-law's apartment. It was Laverne, and she asked to speak to me. I flatly refused to take her call. My mother-in-law gave me a stern look. But now I stood on principle, and I wouldn't budge. My wife tried to get me to answer the phone. I just gave her a look, and she backed off. I listened to my mother-in-law explain to Laverne in a diplomatic way that I couldn't come to the phone. This time I was going to have the last laugh, or so I thought.

The very next day, December 30, Laverne lost consciousness. Malika thought Laverne was just sleepy and listless that cold winter night, but Laverne was near the end. Throughout the day, she would not eat and did not have the strength to take her insulin. Then, not long after sunset, Malika shook Laverne, and she didn't respond. Malika got worried and called 911. My mother always told us that she did not ever want to go to Lincoln Hospital even though it was directly across the street from her apartment building. She hated Lincoln Hospital. She hated how the staff treated poor people; she hated the long waits and even the smell of the place. The hospital was smack in the middle of one of the poorest communities in the city, and my mother wanted nothing to do with it. She went there only in an emergency and got transferred out as soon as she could. When the ambulance arrived at the apartment, Malika told them not to take her to Lincoln Hospital, but the emergency medical service workers said they had to because it was snowing, Lincoln was the closest hospital, and Laverne was in a critical state. And she was. The ambulance report read, "Fifty-six-year-old found unresponsive … trach in place."

She was admitted at 7:45 PM and was so sick, weak, and in and out of consciousness that she was unable to sign the general consent for treatment form. The primary admitting diagnosis, according to the medical records, was hypoglycemia and hyperkalemia. This diagnosis posed a twin danger for Laverne. Hypoglycemia is an abnormally low level of glucose in the blood, and hyperkalemia is an abnormally high level of potassium ions in the blood. Both of these put her at risk for a massive heart attack. Malika called me in a panic, but I didn't panic. Laverne had been in and out of hospitals so much that I decided I was going to wait a couple of days before I visited her. I was still seething, and I wasn't going to run to her rescue this time, since she obviously didn't appreciate me. Besides, I wanted to ring in 2001 in peace. It was not to be.

On New Year's Day, Laverne went into full cardiac arrest inside Lincoln Hospital. She was supposed to get round-the-clock medical care, but apparently she did not because an undetermined amount of time passed before nurses found her lifeless body. The hospital report read, "Patient found unresponsive, pulseless, diaphoretic, no blood pressure recorded, code called … CPR initiated."

In essence, Laverne was dead. She had suffered a massive heart attack and slipped into a coma. Most of her organs gave out. Her heart failed, her kidneys failed, gangrene set in to her legs, she was on a ventilator, and she did not respond to anything. CPR did manage to revive her, but she was essentially in a vegetative state. When I got the news, I was shocked. I didn't know what to think or do. When my wife and I went to the hospital, I wasn't prepared for what I was going to see.

I suddenly felt as if I were walking in slow motion as I entered the hospital room. There was my mother with her eyes taped shut. The white tape had the shape of an X. It looked so gruesome that I had to hold onto the bed railing so I wouldn't faint. I had never seen anything like that in my life, and I thought I had seen it all. I stared at her taped eyes for so long that my mouth fell open. Her eyes were taped shut because there had been some seizure activity, but the taping looked so cruel. She couldn't open her eyes even if she wanted to. It was, without a doubt, the worst thing I ever witnessed in my life. There were tubes running into and out of her body. She'd had a tracheotomy, which left an apparatus seemingly bolted into her throat. Both of her arms had numerous tubes and wires attached—it was a ghastly sight.

In a low tone, I spoke her name, and she didn't move a muscle. She looked dead, and I assumed the doctor was going to come in and tell me to expect the worst. To my surprise, a young intern came in and started talking about surgery. Laverne looked like she was beyond help. The doctor did not suggest or imply that she would make a full recovery, but he did talk to me about consent as her next of kin. I also had to sign an informed consent for transfusion of blood and for treatment of dialysis. I felt so helpless seeing my mother like this. My empathetic nature somehow wished I could save her. My mother had made my life hell, but I didn't wish her ill, and I could do nothing more than watch the inevitable ending. I regretted that we hadn't had a normal life—whatever that is—but I couldn't undo our past, and I could no longer pretend it had not happened.

Many people at the hospital recognized me, so I tried to be strong. I would give them a quick hello and try not to make eye contact. My mother was fighting for her life, and I certainly did not feel like talking. I was too busy trying to make sense of all the medical jargon associated with my mother's condition. In addition to her heart failure and diabetes, she had hypernatremia, or sepsis, arteriosclerosis of the extremities which progressed to gangrene in the lower limbs, anoxic encephalopathy, end stage kidney disease, lung disease, and anemia. Laverne, age fifty-six, also kept a very high fever of 105.2. A CAT scan showed extensive brain damage. In a last-ditch effort, the staff pumped close to a dozen drugs into her: Timentin, gentamicin, metoprolol, Pepcid, Tylenol, Amphogel, albuterol, Atrovent, insulin, and aspirin. They also fed her intravenously and administered fluids.

By January 7, 2001, Laverne was showing no spontaneous or voluntary movement and no corneal response. I usually went to visit my now-comatose mother with family members, either my wife or Malika. Both were good buffers for me because I knew I wouldn't break down if there were other people around.

One day in mid-January, I intentionally went alone to see Laverne at Lincoln Hospital. I walked into the room, and she looked the same way I had left her days before—comatose and unresponsive, her eyes taped shut. I stood over her and for a split moment I wished I had the power to raise her from her vegetative state. I knew I couldn't. I was as helpless as she was. I stared again at her eyes taped shut and wished I had answered her last phone call. Who knew that she was calling me for the last time? I had let my pride prevent me from having one last conversation with my mother. It hurt so much that I had to put it out of my mind. I looked at my mother's feet. They were very dark. The toenails were very long, thick and yellow. She had gangrene in her legs, so, if she survived, doctors would have to amputate them. The fact that they didn't remove them indicated that they knew she wasn't going to make it.

The doctor came into the room and was very respectful but to the point. "Her CAT scan shows very little activity," he said. "It's not looking good. We're doing everything we can."

This was me with Grandma Anna Pearl all over again in her final days. I had mixed feelings because I couldn't understand why my mother had suffered a massive heart attack while in their care. It really bothered me. I felt that if she had been properly attended to and hooked up to a heart monitor upon admission, they would have possibly caught her heart attack before she slipped into a coma.

I looked at my mother in a daze. I didn't know why she had lived the life she had lived. I don't know why she had inflicted pain on me. There was so much that I didn't understand. And this final chapter made things even worse. This was not a life well lived; this was a tragedy.

From the beginning to the end, her life was filled with adversity, a tale of great sorrow. I don't know if Laverne was ever truly happy at any point in her whole life. There was trouble, always trouble. Laverne had not been a happy child because she believed that her parents didn't want her, especially considering she lived apart from them. To my knowledge, no one had ever given Laverne a birthday party. She hadn't gone to the prom, and she had never married. No one had celebrated Laverne's being on Planet Earth—ever. When I, her firstborn, came into the world, she went from the maternity ward and months later to the mental ward. Every man she loved beat or betrayed her. She undoubtedly wrestled with memories of straitjackets and mental institutions. She probably lived with a near-paralyzing guilt of her abuse and abandonment of me. And she lived in public housing, owning very little and having no means of making an independent living.

She didn't even use my success to buoy her life. She never told me she was proud of me, though a twinkle in her eye made me believe that she truly was. She showed interest in my career, but only from afar. It essentially had rained every day of Laverne's life, and I was deeply saddened that my mother was leaving this world essentially the way she came: helpless, unable to communicate, and dependent on others for her survival.

"Laverne," I said, wondering if she could hear me. I was in the room alone, and my voice bounced off the sterile hospital walls.

"Laverne." A cold chill began at my spine and shot down my legs and then up to my head. The tears came so quickly that they didn't even well up in my eyes; they just tumbled right out of my eyes and down my cheeks.

"Laverne, listen, I love you. Please pull through. I love you, Laverne."

Suddenly, it wasn't hard for me to say those precious words to her. I did love my mother, warts and all. I was finally expressing my heartfelt emotions, but it was too late. I tried to touch her hand, but I couldn't get to her for all of the wires. I wanted to kiss her cheeks, but now I couldn't because of the tubes running down her throat. The only thing I could do was kiss her forehead. I was intensely angry and sad at the same time. I felt that nobody should die like that. I quickly walked out, hoping for the best, yet prepared, sort of, for the worst.

Football still had a way of picking up my spirits. I am a big football fan, and a local team, the New York Giants, played the Baltimore Ravens in Super Bowl XXXV. Giants' coach Jim Fassel had an incredible year, leading Big Blue to the NFC Championship. Back in November, Fassel had brazenly told the press that his team would make the playoffs. That was some prediction, considering the Giants hadn't made the playoffs in a few years. But he called it right, and New Yorkers went nuts. I had been following defensive end Michael Strahan's career, and he was red hot. I was sure the Giants were going to win.

During the NFC championship, the Giants whipped the Minnesota Vikings 41 to nothing. I told my family not to bother me on January 28, Super Bowl Sunday, because I wanted to watch the game in peace—alone. I turned off my cell phone, and I enjoyed my chicken wings and dipping sauce. My wife kept the kids out of the house for most of the day because I wanted to sleep late and get up to watch the Super Bowl pregame and the post game all night. I sat on the love seat and started eating hot wings. The phone rang. It was my mother's doctor from Lincoln Hospital.

"Hello, Mister Carter. I don't think your mother has much time. You may want to get to the hospital as soon as possible."

My heart sank. I had a feeling that she was already gone. Truthfully, I was scared to face her death. I felt like a little boy being told that his mommy was dying. I would have run from her death if I could have, but there was nowhere to run. So I slowly got up from the couch and threw on my jacket, leaving behind my hot wings, potato chips, and the Super Bowl. My body trembled as I went into the January nighttime air, started the car, and made my way to the South Bronx. I turned my cell phone on and called Aunt Inez to brace her. Throughout everything over the years, Aunt Inez had been my maternal figure, but she had never turned her back on her sister. Ever. I couldn't get in touch with my other aunt, Joann. Aunt Inez started crying on the phone, and I told her that I had to go. I couldn't handle her tears. I called my wife, who was at her mother's house, and she asked to come along, but I told her this was something I wanted to do by myself. I wanted to face my mother's final hour by myself.

I parked my vehicle and rushed to the nurses' station, thinking I still had time to say good-bye, even if Laverne couldn't hear me. As soon as the nurses saw me, they said, "Mister Carter, please have a seat in this room." A nurse led me to a small, dingy conference room with worn chairs along the wall. I didn't know what they were going to tell me. I was shaking so much at this point that even my hands shook. I was very anxious as I sat in that room alone. I knew that my mother was somewhere in that hospital; I just didn't know if she was in a hospital bed or in the basement morgue. Was she still lifeless in her room, or was it too late? I heard footsteps coming toward the conference room, and then I heard the door handle turn as the door slowly opened.

As soon as I locked eyes with the doctor I knew what he was going to say.

I had seen similar scenes on television dramas a million times, but this time there would be no commercial break. The doctor said, "Mister Carter, I'm sorry. Your mother didn't make it. She's gone."

I wanted to cry, but I choked back the tears and stood up to leave. I said, "Thank you for doing everything you could do."

I was quick and to the point. I didn't have any questions, and I didn't want any explanations. And I had no desire to see her one last time. I knew what my breaking point was, and, had I viewed her corpse, I might have collapsed for good. I walked to the elevator a broken and torn man. I was relieved that my mother's tortured, hellish life had finally come to an end, but I didn't know what my life would be like on an emotional level without her. As I waited for the elevator, I truly began to weep. I didn't simply cry—I wept. I learned the difference between crying and weeping on that miserable day. You can cry about anything. You can cry when you're happy or sad; if someone makes you laugh hard enough, you can cry. But when you weep, that's altogether different. And on this day, January 28, 2001, I wept. It was a day that should have been all smiles because it was my daughter Courtney's birthday. My head was bowed and my shoulders nearly folded into my chest as I walked into the empty elevator and made my way to the lobby. I heard a tiny television broadcast sounds of the Super Bowl—and it held no meaning for me.

When I got into the car, I let it all out. I was inconsolable. I wept for everything that I had held in. I wept for my past and my mother's past. My mommy, bless her soul, died all by herself with her eyes taped shut. She couldn't cry out for help because she had a trach in her throat. She couldn't motion for help because she was in a coma. And with all of my political clout, I couldn't do a thing about it. Where was the justice? Didn't anybody care? Life seemed so cruel, yet again.

I banged on the steering wheel as I wailed. When my head began to throb, I abruptly stopped. I felt like I was about to come unglued, so I forced myself to stop. I said to myself, *what is done is done.* As I drove, I thought about the consequences of her death. She had no insurance, no will, no assets, nothing. Malika and Antoinette were still unable to care for themselves, and now I was responsible for them. I had to arrange to have my mother cremated. Whatever unfinished business my mother had left was now my problem. My grief turned to anger. My emotions swung from "I can't believe my mother is dead," to "Why am I being dragged into this—her final drama? Why can't people just leave me alone?" It was a cry for help. In essence, I didn't want to face her death. It was unbearable.

By the time I got home, my wife was hysterical. I have never seen my wife cry like she did that day. She sat on the steps and said, "Laverne did not deserve to die alone like that." And my wife turned her anger on me. She kept repeating it over and over. It broke her heart that nobody was at the hospital when Laverne passed away. My wife felt that I had turned my back on my mother at her time of need. Marilyn was also hurt because she thought my lack of emotion meant I did not care about my mother. Her reaction broke my heart, too, but I did not cry with my wife. I walked into the bedroom, closed the door, and turned on the television. The Giants had lost, 34 to 7.

This was also the first time I had to tell my children that someone they knew and loved was dead. Courtney and Dominic both knew that Grandma was sick. I gathered them together in Courtney's room upstairs. I looked into their faces—full of joy and life—and said, "Grandma Laverne is gone. She's in heaven looking down at you two."

I hated to tell them, but I had to. I was choked up as I spoke to my two children, who fortunately knew nothing of my own childhood. They looked back at me with wide eyes, not fully understanding why I was so remorseful. They didn't cry, perhaps because they hadn't spent as much time with Laverne as they did their other grandmother, Ruby, who they had lived with when they were very small. But they still understood that their grandmother was dead and appeared somewhat shaken by my words. I took them in my arms and embraced them both. I was very sorry that their grandmother was dead, but now more than ever, I was grateful that my children lived a happy life, free of poverty, abuse, and neglect. If I did nothing else in my life, that alone was a major accomplishment. I had broken a vicious cycle, and my children were free.

The following morning, I had to figure out how to take care of my mother's body. I went through the phone book, found a crematory, and made the arrangements. I didn't want to have a funeral or a memorial because I didn't want to suffer any further. I just wanted to cremate her and be done with it.

It wasn't that I was being mean, but I needed to have some closure immediately. The whole world had failed my mother, and I didn't see any cause for celebration or remembrance. With the exception of my aunt, my sister, and my wife's family, no one had cared about Laverne when she was alive, so why should they care now that she's dead? This attitude infuriated Aunt Inez. She wanted to memorialize Laverne, and I refused. It turned out that Inez went ahead with a tiny memorial at a local church near where Laverne had lived, even though Laverne had not gone to this church. I didn't go. Actually, I couldn't go. On an emotional level, I couldn't go.

After she was cremated, I took bereavement time off from work and tried to get on with my life. It was time to focus on Dominic, not Laverne. There was nothing I could do to bring her back. I couldn't keep looking behind me; I had to look at what lay ahead of me. Everyone tried to get me to talk and grieve with them, but I didn't want to talk about it. I wanted to be left alone. I wanted all of my troubles to go away. I did a lot of soul searching. As the days wore on after my mother's death, I wondered which day my mother was actually being cremated. I told my wife that I didn't want to know. It would have ruined my day to know that this was the day my mother was going into a fiery furnace.

I thought about what it meant that I would never see my mother again. Did this mean that those awful memories died with her? I could only hope they would.

Did this mean I was free? I didn't realize it at the time, but I felt emotionally bound to Laverne in many ways. Some ways were good, but others were bad. I felt bound to her as a son—the maternal bond. But I was also bound to her by anger. In the end, I wasn't exactly angry at her; rather I was angry at what had transpired between us. And, at times, that anger was all-consuming. Even my therapist couldn't help me calm my mind, but she tried as much as she could, given that I had not told the therapist everything.

When I was a child, I had wanted my parents to protect me, and neither one of them could help me. They had both hurt me in many ways. They had not affirmed me. I had to console myself and survive the best way I knew how. All I had really ever had was my grandmother and Aunt Inez. They were my mother and father. While I can offer no explanation as to why my biological father rejected me outright, I do have a better understanding about my mother. She was hurting in many ways, and she unwittingly transferred that pain to me. I do not believe my mother was a vicious, mean, or evil person, but she had her faults.

Obviously Laverne was impulsive, too. She gave little thought to her actions and did not consider the consequences of her behavior. She had to live with that, as did I. It was not easy living without my mother's love. I was by no means a momma's boy. I remember my boyhood well. I have always been a tender-hearted, good person. I wanted to please my mother and wondered why she didn't like me. What did I do that was so wrong? At any point, I would've forgiven my mother's lapses, even the sexual abuse. I didn't turn on her until it became painfully obvious that she was trying to spite my beloved grandmother. I stopped trusting my mother, but I still loved her, even though I didn't want to admit it to her or myself.

As an adult, I have a better perspective. When my mother wasn't around, she was probably in a mental hospital, or maybe she was wrestling with an abusive relationship. Maybe she was hallucinating on the psychotropic drugs she was given. Or maybe she was simply depressed. But she never expressed any remorse for breaking my heart. My mother never said she was sorry. To her dying day, Laverne never told me she was sorry. Laverne never healed physically or emotionally. And now that she was gone, just one question remained. Would I ever get closure, or was the past doomed to torment me for the rest of my life?

8

Whether there was emotional healing or not, life *had* to go on. Laverne was no more, and I had to keep living without her. However, I wanted closure. I needed closure.

Normally, when a staff member's parent dies, a manager sends out a memo. But I told my executive producer, Claire Brinberg, that I wanted nothing of the kind. Many of my colleagues sent their condolences and fruit baskets. But I just wanted everything to go away—to vanish. I didn't want memories of any sort. But during the winter following Laverne's death, there was still no closure. The rope that had kept me tied to the ghetto was finally gone. I had hoped for a quick fix so that all of my pain would die with her, and I could finally go on to live a life free of shame and guilt. I tried to tell myself that Laverne was better off dead; now, at least, she was out of her physical and mental pain. Her death was good for me, too, I thought. No more calls in the middle of the night to rush to the hospital—no more awkward or embarrassing moments. She couldn't hurt me any more.

I told myself one story after another to ease the pain, and, to my surprise, my feelings only worsened. I tried to be strong, like I always had, but I was weak. I put my best face forward to my colleagues and the public and concealed the turmoil I was feeling inside. Indeed, my flesh was willing but my spirit was quite weak. But I made a critical error: I underestimated the importance of grief. I wept for a short time, but I didn't truly grieve. I didn't respect the grieving process, in part because I didn't understand it and also because I felt that I didn't have any energy to spare. I didn't have time to cry. My television career was more important, or so I foolishly thought. But there was so much pain inside of me that it practically screamed to get out. I stood five feet eight inches tall, yet I was still that same small, wounded child.

It turns out that I was afraid of the dark. And for me, darkness was made of the disappointments of my life. I didn't want to face the pain, the heartache, and the abuse because I didn't know how to handle such feelings. What do you do with such emotions except cry like a baby—and who wants to do that? When faced with the option of crying from the pain or running from the pain, I ran. But the past was gaining on me. The faster I ran, the faster it ran, right on my heels. I was afraid to even look pain in the face. I was afraid of death, of sickness, of anything bad. I wanted the sunshine without the rain, but life would have none of it. It beckoned me to face the different seasons of my experience—the summers as well as the winters. But I couldn't let that happen.

I began to withdraw without even realizing it. First, I cut off social activities like the annual black tie event where the press and city hall officials put on a show that lampooned the mayor. The event is called Inner Circle. In New York, it's considered a major social affair. I had participated in the show for nearly twenty years, but suddenly I didn't want to go. I skipped many social events that winter because I just wasn't in a celebratory mood.

My painful childhood started to come into full focus, and I could no longer run from it. And the more the memories flooded back, the weaker I became. Then, suddenly, in spring of 2001, my whole world came crashing down on me. Seemingly from nowhere, all of my horrific memories came flooding back in a tidal wave. I was negative about myself and my past. I stayed in bed for days on end and cried. Just as I had suspected, the tears started one day and didn't stop. I was in the throes of a nervous breakdown. I hadn't had time to grieve my mother's death, but grief had made time for me.

Aunt Inez and my wife kept telling me to take time to go through the grieving stages, but I felt that I could shake grief off. My mother and I had not had a traditional relationship, so I honestly believed there was no need for me to go through any so-called grieving process. Even though I was an amiable, vibrant person, I started feeling tired and listless. I began missing a day of work here and a day of work there. Some days, I just couldn't get out of the bed, and I would sleep all day long. The next day I would struggle to wake up and force myself to go to work. It would be the same process the next day. I felt like I was standing on quicksand. I tried to keep going, but with every step I felt like I sank a little deeper. First sorrow was up to my knees, then to my waist, then to my neck, and finally I was totally submerged in grief.

I cried a few minutes one day, then an hour the next day, and a little more every day. Before I knew it, I was in bed for four days straight. I didn't even have the energy to brush my teeth or shower. I barely ate, though I usually had a ravenous appetite. Now I took twenty minutes to eat two pieces of toast. Nothing wanted to go into my mouth. Those four days in bed seemed like an eternity. Every day just gelled into the other days, and I couldn't tell one day from the next. I would briefly wake up in the morning and go back to sleep. I would wake up again at about three o'clock in the afternoon. Maybe I'd get a glass of orange juice. Then I'd go back to sleep and wake up at eight or nine o'clock that night. I slept at least twenty-one out of twenty-four hours. I might nibble at my wife's dinner and then go to sleep overnight, and start all over again. I would cry, sleep, cry, and sleep. It became a tormenting cycle.

When I cried, I wasn't solely sobbing for Laverne. I accepted that she was dead. I guess I wept for nothing in particular and everything in general. I bemoaned the past, the present, and the future. My tears didn't have an agenda. I released everything that I had bottled up over the years. As I lay in bed and thought that my life was over as I knew it, I thought back to how I had worked so hard for so long in a cutthroat industry, only to get lost in my own sad world. My life just wasn't fair.

So many scenes ran through my mind. Had I, in fact, turned my back on my mother as she lay dying in a city hospital? Should I have attended the tiny memorial service in her memory? Could this torment be related to my deepest darkest secret—the fact that my mother had sexually forced herself on me as a child? Or was the pressure of being a high-profile television reporter finally pushing me over the edge?

The worse part was that I couldn't hide my breakdown from my kids. I was embarrassed that my children saw me reduced to an emotional pile of rubble. Courtney, looked at me sympathetically even though I was not the big, strong daddy that she was used to having. She said, "Daddy, it'll be all right." I looked back at her with red, swollen eyes and didn't say a word. I would cry even harder when she left for school. I was at an all-time low.

My family knew that something was wrong, but I, as the leader of the family, couldn't explain this sudden change in behavior because I didn't know myself. For the first time in my life, Dominic Carter was down for the count. I was weak, and I was scared. As far back as I can remember, I had cleared unimaginable hurdles. Here I was, a poor, neglected, and abused kid from the Bronx, being embraced by the rich, powerful, and famous. I was on a first-name basis with billionaire Donald Trump, who had lauded me and, without my urging, wrote a letter of recommendation to the president of CBS, calling me a hard-hitting and fearless journalist who really does his homework. The Donald also said I was his sole reason for watching *Inside City Hall*, New York 1's daily, hour-long political show. He urged many of his friends to watch the show, as well.

Notwithstanding Trump's commendation and the accolades of being called the most important television political reporter in New York City by other respected print organizations, I was at the mercy of my mind, which started playing tricks on me. I felt guilty about my mother, though I knew her physical and mental heath issues were beyond my control. What would I do now about Malika and Antoinette? I wanted to save my family, but I could hardly save myself. Would I be able to go back and host the hour-long television show, interviewing some of the most powerful people in the city and nation? The show was not taped. It was live, and, mentally, I had to be sharp.

Would I be able to go toe to toe with America's Mayor Rudy Giuliani during the final months of his term and cover the upcoming race for mayor? This was the same mayor who had single-handedly beat down the notorious New York press corps and who knew how to exploit a reporter's weakness. Viewers who watched the show every night had no idea of my mental anguish or my traumatic childhood experiences. I tried to sugar-coat my breakdown, but there was just no explaining away my abrupt leave of absence from work. I would have no other choice but to tell a handful of my colleagues the embarrassing details of my downward spiral.

It was time to get help. I had always thought of myself as too strong to see a psychiatrist. I had lived through hell and back and always had a smile on my face, but this time my smile was frozen. The twinkle in my squinty eyes was gone. My hearty, giggly laugh was reduced to a whimper. I was not the same person. One day when I managed to struggle in to work, I went to the personnel office and looked up the number to the employee mental help hotline. I was too embarrassed to ask anybody, so I quietly flipped through the pages of a personnel book and got the 800 number. Looking up every few seconds to make sure no one was around my desk—which was rare—I called the hotline.

I felt relief as the phone rang. The first thing the person on the other line asked was, "Do you think you might want to hurt yourself?" I wasn't offended because I knew it was a mandatory question. I firmly answered no. The only reason why I felt comfortable calling was that I figured it was a national number, and the person likely would not recognize my name. The person immediately gave me the names and numbers of several professional counselors in my neighborhood.

My visits to psychiatrists humbled me; I felt like crawling into their offices on my hands and knees. It took every ounce of my courage to keep my appointments, but my depression rendered me incapacitated both personally and professionally. The first doctor told me I was depressed and suffering from anxiety. He gave me drugs, the beginning of what would become a mélange of pills that promised to make my blues go away. Were these the same drugs, I wondered, that my mother had taken when she had had her breakdowns? Was I following in my mother's haunted footsteps? Day after day, I took the pills with a large glass of water, praying that this dose would be the one to do it. After sixty days, against the advice of my doctors, I stopped taking the antidepressants. I just decided on my own that they had to go. I felt that the pills were a liability to my television performance. I did not feel that I was in full control of my mind.

While on the medication during my live show, as guests responded to my questions, I often felt I was in a daze, sort of like a dream state. Other times, it was like an out-of-body experience where I was watching myself screw up the interview. I felt like I was operating at 70 percent at best. Depression proved to be a formidable foe. This was the first time that I had been knocked off my feet, and, once I got back up, I realized that I was not the superman that I had considered myself to be. When I began my career, I concluded that the long hours of work and personal sacrifice would amount to my selling my soul to the devil. Was he now finally getting his due?

I've always felt that I fought with one hand tied behind my back. Every time I crossed a finish line in my life, there were many who stood and cheered. But few saw how bruised and battered I was in the end. No one could see how I ran and cried at the same time. No one could see how emotionally handicapped I was. Many at the finish line who cheered me on seemed to forget that I had started from the back of the pack and had fought my way to the front. I didn't have the best equipment, like an Ivy League education, but I made the distance. I didn't have the traditional support, like the love of a mother and a father, but I stayed in the race. And when I crossed one finish line, there was always another race waiting for me. I felt as though I could never rest.

And as I lay in bed for days on end, I guess not getting up was my body's way of saying "I need to rest." But this "rest" period was scary. I stayed in my house with the blinds sealed shut. I had no fresh air, no sunlight, nothing but a television that aired background noise. I couldn't even concentrate on what show was on. I had gotten very good at playing games with myself. I was able to tell myself a lie and believe it. I would say that my mother's sexual abuse didn't bother me as an adult—when it clearly did bother me. As far back as I can remember, I told myself to get over the abuse—when I clearly could not recover from it. I would tell myself to stop thinking about it—but I would not stop. I couldn't put a bandage on this trauma, no matter how I tried. I had to root out this pain, face it, accept it, and move on. But it became painfully clear that I could not do this work by myself. I had tried to recover by myself at first. I would tell myself, Okay, tomorrow you're going to be your old self. Yet tomorrow would never come. One blue day would just fade into the next.

I officially had to tell some people at the station what was going on because I feared they would think I was being irresponsible by not showing up at work. I told the human resources director, Elisabeth Fanfant, and she was very supportive and gave me time off from work. My boss, Steve Paulus, called me at home to reassure me that he understood, but I didn't think he or anyone else could relate to the full extent of my situation. Paulus said, "You're one of my guys. I'm with you, so don't worry about it."

But I was very worried. I wanted the pain to end immediately, and it didn't. I wanted a doctor to say something else or give me something to make me feel better because I scared myself. One day, I drove myself to another psychiatrist not far from my home. After taking an assessment of my emotions, he stared at me and with a deep, baritone voice said matter-of-factly "What you're going through is depression." Like an addict, all I wanted was a quick fix. As I focused on the psychiatrist's degree on the wall over his head, all I cared about was a magic bullet that would help me snap back into real life.

I felt like the real me was trapped inside this sad, pathetic person who was fighting to get out. And I wanted the real me to get out before I lost him forever. Of all the fights I had ever fought, this was the toughest one yet. I was fighting for my sanity. Secretly, I had always feared this would happen, so I carefully guarded my emotions at all times. This is why I was so careful when my mother was dying. I knew that a breakdown was a possibility. I knew, with everything I had been through, that I would be susceptible to emotional collapse. And that's exactly what had happened.

I wrongly assumed that picking a psychiatrist and drugs would be as easy as going to a general practitioner. I was so far off base. But what truly scared me to death was the fact that, within a matter of a few short weeks, I would end up with a medicine cabinet full of antidepressants. On March 30, 2001, a psychiatrist gave me alprazolam, also known as Xanax. All of a sudden, driving became a challenge. The anti-anxiety drug made my body feel at such ease that I had difficulty concentrate on the road. Then the so-called occupational hazards associated with the drug, as stated on the pharmaceutical company's own website, turned out to be correct.

> As with other CNS depressant drugs, patients should be cautioned against activities requiring mental alertness, judgment, and physical coordination such as driving or operating machinery, particularly in the early phases of treatment and until proper adjustment to side effects has been established.

Now I was fully tired and depressed. I still felt miserable and annoyed that I wasn't myself. I wondered what the drug had done to my overall health. I was deeply concerned that antidepressants had serious side effects, some of which were sexual. The doctor and I didn't hit it off. I didn't like his line of questioning, and I felt that he was detached. I thought he should have been more compassionate, considering that I felt I was losing my sanity.

I was reluctant to tell the doctor about my troubled past, and I never told him or any other doctors about the time my mother sexually abused me. When I was seeing him, I did not know the full extent of my mother's mental illness. Receiving her psychiatric records would be a few years down the road. Of course, it probably would have helped if I told the doctors about the sexual abuse, but I wasn't ready to bare my heart and soul. I just wanted to feel better, plain and simple.

Sensing my frustration that the drug was not working quickly enough and considering that I had to get back to hosting a live, one-hour television show, the doctor wrote a prescription for another antidepressant, Effexor, which didn't work for me, either. Every time I was given a drug, I got on the computer and checked out its side effects. And there was one side effect that Effexor had that Xanax did not: "abnormal ejaculation." When I saw that phrase, something in me just froze. It petrified me to consider that these mind-altering drugs were so powerful

that they could even change a man's sexuality by greatly pro-
longing the ejaculations. That may sound like a fantasy for
some men, but when you're in that situation, it's embarrassing,
especially when your wife is asking you what's wrong. Now, my
mind and my penis were playing tricks on me.

Three days later, I found a new doctor and a new drug. I was
frustrated. Where the hell was the magic bullet that would get
me back in front of the camera? I felt frustrated not because I
missed the limelight, but because I had been away from work
for a couple of weeks, and I feared that the longer I was away,
the more it might raise the suspicions of a tabloid gossip colum-
nist. My new doctor was a woman, and we had better rapport. I
drove an hour to Connecticut to her office, but she was worth
the trip. Each time I drove up Highway 95 North to see her, I
felt that I could relax. I would give myself a little extra time so I
could visit the nearby state park and look at the ocean.

Fourteen days after my first encounter ever with an antidepressant, I began yet another new drug. Serzone, a white pill
with six sides and a slit down its middle. Serzone definitely
made me feel better, and I could work without experiencing
panic attacks. But I noticed that its effects would wear off very
quickly, and the anxiety would creep up again. Even though I
temporarily felt better, I felt as though I was being controlled.
The drug made me feel dependent. I just wanted a drug that
would effortlessly make me feel more like myself. After I complained about that drug, the psychiatrist pulled out that familiar
white prescription pad and wrote directions for another drug:
Wellbutrin.

The first thing that attracted me to this drug was that I could
take it once a day. That was a major plus. It also had a risk of
sexual side effects and weight gain. Many antidepressant drugs

affect you sexually, not only by delaying ejaculation, but also by causing impotence. I was lying on the doctor's couch, just like in the shrink scenes in the movies, explaining my concern. The doctor said, "Oh, that's not a problem. I'll just give you a prescription for Viagra." She didn't mean to offend me, and she was really trying to help. But I was not amused.

After a couple of days, I was frustrated again—so frustrated that my psychiatrist suggested hypnotism. I have to admit that I knew going in that hypnotism wouldn't work. As a journalist who is skeptical by nature, I realized that a mind over matter approach would not work for me. The doctor meant well, but as I lay there on the couch, supposedly in a semi-sleep state, listening to her tell me to repeat "Dominic, you will come out of this," I thought to myself that this treatment was not working. I had one embarrassing moment with this psychiatrist, who was well known in the industry and had a second office in Manhattan. When I visited her Manhattan location, which is on busy Thirty-Fourth Street near the East River, the doorman and the building's staff recognized me from television and asked for autographs. I didn't know if I was coming or going, and these people looked up to me and called out my name in admiration.

About one month later, when I finally returned to a regular work schedule, I could see from the tapes of my shows that I still wasn't myself. I couldn't quite put my finger on the differences, but something wasn't right. I felt like I wasn't responding as quickly as I had before my breakdown. I'm sure no one noticed this but me, but I am my harshest critic, so the change mattered a lot.

I wanted a milder drug. On May 11, my psychiatrist gave me Paxil, another once-a-day drug. Fearing it would leave me feeling sleepy, I decided not to take it. I began to realize that it wasn't the drugs: it was me. I had always been an independent, strong person, and I was going against my very nature and personality by taking anti-depressants. Deep down, I was repelled and embarrassed by taking drugs, but I felt so desperate that I kept doing it. Finally, in mid-May, I just said, "To hell with it." I gathered all of the drugs together, having never finished an entire bottle, put them into a yellow plastic supermarket bag, and put them in a closet. I declared I would have to beat depression on my own.

I built up the nerve to face my fears. I had some temptation at the beginning of each day to reach for that yellow bag. But I figured that if I didn't have any drugs to reach for, I would be forced to give up the pills. Though I did not feel completely back to normal, I decided to keep going. One afternoon, I chickened out a little bit. I felt a wave of anxiety come over my whole body, so I went to the corner drug store and bought a bottle of St. John's Wort, an over the counter herbal supplement. Every day, I felt a little bit better. I could again look at people eye-to-eye. My confidence level went up, even though some mornings I felt the urge to cry. But I would almost literally swing my arms at an imaginary punching bag in the air and resist that urge. I was quite literally fighting the temptation to go back into the abyss of depression.

Eventually it became easier to resist, and the old me came back to life. Even in the midst of my mother's demise and all that was going on in my life, I was still being honored with various awards, most notably an award from the New York State Associated Press Broadcasters Association for my interviews with Amadou Diallo's parents. Diallo was the young African immigrant gunned down in a hail of forty-one bullets by New York City police officers who mistook his wallet for a gun.

I had no idea of what was about to come in the first year of the millennium, but I was about to receive the test of a lifetime. The year 2001 saw the beginnings of the mayoral race in New York City take shape. With a public referendum that instituted term limits, Mayor Giuliani was wrapping up his second and final term as mayor. The fiery Republican mayor was leaving city hall in January 2002, and the big question was whether New York, typically a Democratic town, would return to its roots and elect a Democrat. The front-runner was Mark Green, a silver-haired politician who happened to be consumer affairs commissioner during the David Dinkins administration. Green had made quite a name for himself by cracking down on consumer fraud and had earned his consumer stripes alongside Ralph Nader as a "Nader Raider" in the 1970s. Green honed his liberal credentials working on campaign of Senate wannabe Ramsey Clark and presidential-hopeful Gary Hart.

The race for mayor was Green's sixth run for office. His first serious attempt was against New York Senator Alfonse D'Amato in 1986. He lost that race but raised questions about D'Amato's ethics and led to a senate investigation. Green ran again against D'Amato in 1998 but didn't make it past the primary. Green's campaigns helped raise his profile, and he was finally elected as public advocate for New York City, which made him one of the city's most recognizable figures. Now Green was shooting for the top prize in New York City. He ran a cautious primary campaign, unveiling broad proposals and avoiding confrontation with his three Democratic opponents. Though he was the front-runner for much of the campaign, by primary day Fernando Ferrer was breathing down Green's neck. The popular Bronx Borough president, who had successfully built a black-Latino coalition, was determined to become the city's first Hispanic mayor.

But there was another candidate on the political radar. After being fired from Salomon Brothers, a local businessman named Michael Bloomberg used his own money to start a new media company, and it paid off handsomely. Even though he wasn't exactly a household name, he spent a lot of money introducing himself to voters. Money was no object. But he had to learn how to handle the press because he could get testy and snap on a moment's notice. The media was very skeptical of the man that many Democrats accused of attempting to buy city hall. Bloomberg attempted to counter such criticism by using television ads to illustrate how he was a self-made man who had built his company from scratch.

Less than one month before the primary, my career was in the news again. The *New York Times* profiled me again, this time with my colleague Andrew Kirtzman. Reporter Randy Kennedy gave a flattering commentary of our respective careers in a story called "For This Two-Man TV team, Politics, Vaudeville Style." The story featured a photograph of the two of us atop the spiral staircase at the Forty-Second Street studios with two blue and white New York 1 logos in the background. The article focused on how the mayoral candidates dealt with Andrew and me as "forces to be reckoned with." It said, "The mayoral candidates elbowing their way toward November do not have many things in common. But here is one: they could probably describe to you, in some details, the inside of a small, modestly decorated room on the fourth floor of a former bus terminal on West Forty-Second Street." That modestly decorated room was Studio B in New York 1's newsroom, where we did our show every night at seven o'clock.

It was one of the few articles that probed into my family history, and I was delighted. The article noted that Andrew grew up on the Lower East Side with a grandfather who owned a news stand. The article said, "Mr. Carter, in contrast, seems like the kind of kid who grew up doing air microphone instead of air guitar in front of the mirror. He was raised in Harlem and in the Bronx, in two tough housing projects. For parents, he had his grandmother and two aunts. 'I saw my dad maybe four or five times growing up,' he says, and he learned early on that to survive in his neighborhood, he had to speak up, loudly and frequently."

When Randy asked me about my family and upbringing, a flash went through my mind. What if I sat here and told the truth? I wondered what would happen if I said, "You know, Randy, it's a miracle that I'm here because my mother sexually abused me when I was a kid, and if it wasn't for my grandmother and my aunts, it is quite likely that you would be writing something very different about me—something like 'Bronx man shot and killed during prison escape.'" But I toed the line and only scratched the surface of my troubled childhood.

Interestingly, I had no problem indicting my father for his wanton neglect, but I did not say a thing about my mother. I was thankful that Randy didn't ask. Perhaps Randy, like most people, sensed that the subject was off limits. I didn't mind talking about poverty, the father that I never knew, or the projects, but I didn't want to be asked about my mother. I didn't tell the truth to myself, so I certainly couldn't tell it to anyone else.

One sunny morning, I was sleeping late because I knew I was in for a big day. Elections are New York 1's bread and butter, and this was primary day in New York City. I would be reporting live all night until the election results were in, typically between 9:30 PM and midnight. I had the windows open wide in my bedroom and reams of newspapers and research about the candidates on the floor. I planned to wake up about 10:00 AM. Traditionally on election day, I try to force myself to sleep late for what always is the big night when I report live and analyze the election results. I had to be sharp. But a phone call awakened me and left me in a state of shock and disbelief. A longtime friend, Ron Johnson, called to ask me if I was okay. He wanted to know whether I had heard what had happened.

Before he could finish talking, I turned on the television and stared at the World Trade Center's twin towers ablaze. Initially, I didn't know what to think because there was a possibility that a plane had accidentally slammed into the Trade Center. But the moment the second plane circled the tower and shot into it, obviously, this was no accident. I knew the newsroom had to be turned upside down because I did not receive a phone call telling me to get down to the scene, as is the case with most stories of this magnitude. I jumped quickly into the shower and turned up the volume on the television full-blast so I could hear it from the bathroom. I showered and shaved quickly, sensing that the primary election was minutes away from being cancelled.

As I tightened my tie around my neck, the situation got worse. The first tower collapsed. I knew there had to be thousands of people inside that one tower, including rescue workers. I sat down on the edge of the bed and put my head in my hands. I was all alone in the house, and I could feel my body shaking. I had been in the Trade Center more times than I could count. I remembered that during the World Trade Center explosion in 1993, I was the only television reporter traveling with the mayor in Japan and had broadcast his reaction live back to New York City. But I never imagined that the towers would be targeted a second time. At that very instant, I knew that my day, indeed my life, would never be the same again. I picked up my cell phone and could not get a signal at all. I started up my car and the radio almost simultaneously. A radio reporter, clearly shaken, announced that the second tower had collapsed.

I was numb with shock. I rode into work, but I wasn't sure how far I would get because the city was quickly shutting down the tunnels and bridges leading into Manhattan. I made it over the Tappan Zee Bridge, about twenty miles from the tip of the Bronx. But just barely. Once I arrived on the border of the Bronx and Manhattan, I parked at 207th Street and Broadway, but there was no way to get to work. As a native New Yorker, I had never seen anything like this before in my life. The subway was shut down, police officers were blocking the entrance to the highway, and when I called New York 1 to find out how to get to work, I was abruptly told that I was on my own. I could not get a cab of any kind with traffic at a standstill. After about an hour, a Mexican man and his wife pulled up to me in a pickup truck. They spoke little English, and I was reluctant to get in. But the driver said, "C'mon, Dominic, we'll take you wherever you need to go." The three of us squeezed into the front seat and made our way slowly down Broadway.

Once we got to 168th Street near Columbia Presbyterian Medical Center, I noticed there was a subway station still open. The scene was like something out of a movie. People were dazed, apparently not knowing where to go, and there were perhaps five people in the subway station. Everyone appeared to be in shock. Finally, a train pulled up, and I got off at 42nd Street. When I walked out of the subway, I saw a scene like the Twilight Zone. There was no traffic or cars, and people were walking the streets by the thousands, probably trying to figure out how to get home. When I arrived at New York 1's offices, staff members were frozen in shock. Some were crying because they knew some of those lost in the towers.

As a senior staff member, I tried to console some of my colleagues. Then I was called out to an assignment that would cause me nightmares for weeks to come. I was sent to Bellevue Hospital, a level-one trauma center and the place where the city expected many injured patients to get treatment. Sadly, there were very few people coming in and even fewer bodies being recovered because many people had perished. But I witnessed a spontaneous outpouring of grief that haunts me to this day. Families of victims gathered by the thousands, clutching pictures of their loved ones, hoping to get some information on their whereabouts. Relieving my colleague, Jeff Simmons, I continued interviewing these people one by one and began doing live interviews with them. Many survivors were openly weeping as they described their loved one whom they feared dead. I had to choke back tears and still maintain a degree of professionalism as well as compassion.

Those grieving families were one of the most powerful images of a catastrophic day. Before I knew it, dozens of reporters were alongside me, covering the same, heart-wrenching stories. There were parents looking for children, children looking for parents, brothers looking for fathers, brides looking for husbands—the flow of seekers went on and on and on. My producer, Jamie McShane, had people lined up down the block, all of them hopeful that their loved ones had lost consciousness and had been spotted wandering aimlessly around the city.

I continued to do these live interviews, one about every twenty minutes, for ten hours straight. In my heart, I wished that every one of these family members would get the good news they were hoping for, but deep down I knew that most of them would never get the news they wanted to hear.

New York 1 put up all of its staff members at a hotel because the city was locked down, and the managers wanted to keep all of us close by in the event something else happened. As I lay down, I saw the eyes of those family members, desperate and shocked, as they prayed for someone who would answer their prayers. I closed my eyes and tried to force myself to go to sleep. But few New Yorkers or Americans got a good night's sleep that night.

The primary election had been cancelled on September 11, and the mayoral contest was thrown into chaos. The city was still reeling from the worst domestic attack in the history of the United States. Who could think about politics? Rudy Giuliani, in his final months in office, became a beacon of hope for New Yorkers and, indeed, all Americans as he helped maintain calm during a period of utter turmoil in New York City. For a week and a half, city council speaker Peter Vallone, another Democrat candidate, was the only visible mayoral candidate, often sharing the stage with the mayor and the governor at their frequent televised press conferences, which drew some criticism from Vallone's rivals.

Weeks later, Giuliani had the Republican candidate Michael Bloomberg join him at press conference, subtly invoking images of Giuliani's heir apparent. About two weeks after September

11, the primary election was rescheduled for September 25. The World Trade Center site was still ablaze, and bodies were still trapped, but politics had to continue. But this election was, by no means, business as usual. The city's campaign finance board told the participants in the program for city matching funds that the candidates could not spend any more money in the primary except for things they would have spent on the original primary day and for equipment to replace equipment damaged in the terrorist attack. Now candidates had to face a new twist: how to get elected after September 11, 2001, without campaigning.

I faced a new challenge as well—how to cover the politicians who were now severely limited in spending funds. Many of the council members, in particular, could not get to their campaign offices or their apartments located downtown. And the Board of Elections was in the most unenviable position of all: the mix of more candidates than usual, a prediction of many close races, anticipated low voter turnout, and a collection of outdated voting machines—all this seemed to be a recipe for disaster. And I had to report more bad news. There would be no polling sites open west of Broadway, so the people who usually voted in that area had to request absentee ballots from the Board of Elections, and the Board's central office just blocks from the World Trade Center was still not back to operating normally. No one could control the fallout from the events of September 11. As a reporter, I reported the facts and tried to stay focused on the outcome, which was surprising but expected.

Michael Bloomberg easily won the Republican nod, but the Democratic race was too close to call because no candidate received a required forty percent plurality. What was shocking was that the frontrunner Mark Green, found himself in second place as Fernando Ferrer won the primary. So amid the chaos, Ferrer and Green had to have a runoff election. No one was happy. The city was still in mourning and still very anxious, and many people wanted politics to go away for a while. It didn't. It couldn't. As much as the city and the nation admired Mayor Giuliani for his leadership during the attacks, someone else had to take over city hall on New Year's Day. On October 11, Mark Green won the runoff in a close election.

One month later, the city endured one final election between Green and Bloomberg. By November, the debris at the World Trade Center site was still smoldering, but Green and Bloomberg had to make their case to voters, and the contest got nasty. Green told reporters, "I'm running against a man with absolutely no experience in government to get anything done. He is spending more money per capita—sixty million dollars in five months—than anyone has spent in American history. It's my accomplishments against his ads." By now, the nation was riveted on the question of who was going to replace Giuliani, now called "America's Mayor" and widely credited with keeping the city together after September 11.

In December 2001, I emerged from one catastrophe into another. As the ruins of the World Trade Center were still piled high, my beloved mother-in-law's health had reached an all-time low because she was dying of cancer. Laverne had not been dead for one year, and now Ruby Stevens was preparing to leave us, too. Besides my Aunt Inez, who had raised me, Ruby was the only person I felt I could trust. She knew everything about me, the good and the not-so-good. I could trust her with my innermost secrets, and I knew she would never betray my confidence, not even to her own children—not even to her own daughter, my wife. From the moment I laid eyes on her, I called her Ms. Stevens because I considered that name a sign of respect. Even though her family called her Ruby or "Ruh," she was always Ms. Stevens to me.

Once when my wife had gotten mad and thrown me out of the house, I had ended up at my mother-in-law's apartment, and Ms. Stevens had taken me in. She hadn't chastised me; she had only embraced me. When the sun had come up early the next morning, she had made sure I made it back home to see my son off for his first day of school. She would tell me, "That's your family, so you do what's right. I don't care how mad your wife is." Ruby was a quiet woman, but when she laid down the law, that was it. When I began my career, Ruby got up early with me on those early, frosty days when I had to awaken during the pre-dawn hours to head to work. She was my biggest fan, and I was her biggest fan, as well. When I lost my cherished grandmother Anna Pearl, I gained Ruby. That's how I liked to think of it. They were both gems in my eyes. Where would I have been without Anna Pearl, Inez, and Ruby?

Ruby was also special to me because I was not her flesh and blood, as I was to Inez and Anna Pearl, yet Ruby truly treated me just the same. She commanded respect, but she acted with real style and grace. It was hard not to love Ruby, and it was even harder to see her go. She had battled cancer of the esophagus for years, but as hard as she would fight, cancer would have the final say.

Like my mother, Ruby hadn't taken care of herself when she was young. She didn't have regular doctor visits, and she didn't take preventive measures as she aged, which was especially dangerous because she was also suffering from lupus, a disease discovered when my son, Dominic, was a toddler. The births of

Courtney and Dominic, Jr., inspired Ruby to take better care of her health. Perhaps their youthful energy had inspired her, and better care gave her a new lease on life. But this care was too late. Slowly but surely, her soft voice became hoarse, and she had more and more difficulty in swallowing. In the fall of 2002, it was hard to witness her steep decline. She suffered with loss of appetite, fatigue, indigestion, and acid reflux.

Ruby was eighty-four years old, and doctors tried to treat her condition with drugs, but when the drugs didn't work, they resorted to the dreaded chemotherapy treatment. The family agonized over whether to allow their elderly mother to undergo this risky regimen. But the family took a chance because everyone wanted to save Ruby and see her well again. As is typical with chemotherapy patients, Ruby became weak and nauseous as cancer-killing agents were infused into her frail body. Initially, chemotherapy worked, but it had a wicked side effect: it made my mother-in-law not want to eat. Ruby couldn't keep her food down, and she became afraid to swallow for fear of throwing up. She would often vomit, which hurt her throat tremendously.

As a result, she developed a sort of fear of swallowing, which was so painful that she preferred to spit rather than swallow. After Ruby had steadily lost weight, doctors recommended surgery to insert a feeding tube into her stomach. The procedure was done at Mount Sinai Medical Center in Manhattan, the same hospital where I had been born in and where my mother had been a mental patient. While I was at work, minutes before going on the air live, I often got phone call after phone call, telling me that Ruby had fainted and passed out cold in her apartment. Then she would be rushed to Mount Sinai again.

Just as I had felt with Laverne, I didn't want to see my mother-in-law lying on a hospital bed, but I did so numerous times. By now the grief, denial, and pain were sadly familiar, and I didn't want to revisit these scenes, especially after recovering from my recent bout with depression. I just wanted everything to go away, except my mother-in-law, whom I wanted her to stay.

And for a while her cancer did go away. Once Ruby got the feeding tube, the frail, physically weak matriarch of the Stevens family started putting on weight. The cancer was in remission, and she started going out in public again. I tried to send her on a trip to her hometown of Savannah, Georgia, but she didn't want to go. She had never boarded a plane in her lifetime. She did, however, make the trip up to our house in Rockland County for my son's birthday party on September 28. It would be her final visit to our house and her final visit outside her own house.

Soon, the cancer returned with a vengeance. There was talk of putting her back on chemotherapy, but this time even Ruby refused. The doctors agreed. They knew the end was near for her, and they told the family to let her rest at home and enjoy the time she had left. But the time was anything but enjoyable. Ruby started losing weight again, but this time her health took a turn for the worse. Her voice was very hoarse, and she lost her appetite and her strength. She became bedridden in the last weeks of her life. The family showered Ruby with love until the very end. Marilyn's sister and two brothers alternated days being with Ruby so that she was never left alone even though she had a home attendant named Betty.

I was moved by my wife's complete devotion to her mother. Marilyn was always at her mother's side, helping around the house, cooking her meals, and buying her clothes. Marilyn's love for her mother was unwavering, and in the end, Marilyn literally lifted her dying mother in her arms to wash her sapless body. Marilyn combed her withered hair and she sat shoulder to shoulder with Ruby in the bed and watched television, trying to coax a laugh from the woman whose body was wracked with pain. My wife was much stronger than I. I loved Ruby with all of my heart, but I couldn't bear to see her like that. I didn't want to cry in front of her, so I stayed in an adjacent room and helped out whenever needed. After Laverne, I just couldn't subject myself to this again. Once again, I feared I couldn't handle it.

The Christmas tree was up at Rockefeller Center. People in the city could hear the holiday jingles everywhere. Christmastime was near, and just like the year before, the family was on a deathwatch. Last year we had watched Laverne. This time it was Ruby. Though bedridden, Ruby promised the family she would live to see Christmas Day, and she kept that promise. We all gathered not at our respective homes, but at Ruby's apartment that Christmas Day. Her final gift to us was surviving to see one more Christmas.

But on Christmas Eve, Ruby's son, Larry, called our home in Rockland and, in a calm yet nervous voice, informed us that the end was near and that we should get down to Harlem immediately. We rushed there, and when Marilyn looked at her mother, then my wife, a woman of tremendous pride, held her own head up, walked past everyone into the bathroom, closed the door, and cried. Even though she loved her mother dearly, that would be the first and only time Marilyn cried.

December 25 was definitely somber, but everyone tried to keep the day jolly. Even though Ruby could no longer talk, we tried to include her in all the excitement. The door to her bedroom was kept open so she could hear young kids running back and forth. As family members arrived, they went into her room and showered her with presents. It's interesting how when a person is about to die, money is completely useless. My wife gave her a framed photo of herself as a young woman with her kids around her. My mother-in-law loved dolls and collected them. Our niece Stephanie bought her a doll and had to deliberate whether to give it to my mother-in-law early, fearing she would not make it to Christmas Day.

As was a family tradition, Marilyn planned and cooked for the entire family on the holidays. The menu was traditional Southern fare—ham, turkey, collard greens, and macaroni and cheese. At least this time preparing the Christmas dinner would keep Marilyn's mind off what was inevitable. My wife encouraged me to go into the room and talk to my mother-in-law. I tried, but it was just too difficult for me to see her so ill.

Even on her deathbed, I think my mother-in-law knew how tough her death was for me. She knew I loved her dearly, but this was unbearable. Ruby was still tough, and she was able to look at her visitors even as she drifted in and out of consciousness and as her eyes slowly opened and closed. She could squeeze a person's hand and nod her head. I went into her room on Christmas Day and thought to myself, "Be a damned man." How in the hell could I cry in her presence when she was the one dying?

My kids had taken all their gifts from Rockland down to Grandma's house to open on Christmas, but as the head of the household, I had to tell them about Ruby's impending death. I had to explain that Grandma was not going to be with us any more physically and that she was going to heaven." It's interesting how smart children can be. My son immediately replied, "Grandma is going to be with Grandpa," and, sort of relieved, I said, "Yes, Dominic."

Ruby survived through Christmas, but we knew she wouldn't make it to the New Year. The day after Christmas, everyone in the family was officially on deathwatch as my mother-in-law faced her final hours. Hospice workers came to the apartment to provide comfort for Ruby, who was in such intense pain that the nurses suggested giving her morphine as her organs began to fail. One son, Tony, overwrought with grief as his mother faded away, did not want his mother injected with morphine for fear it would speed up the death process. But he was overruled as other family members couldn't bear seeing Ruby writhe in pain. They wanted her to go in peace.

Ruby started having anxiety attacks and breathing heavily, and Marilyn tried to soothe her mother by putting ice on her lips. On Ruby's final night, we were all in the Harlem apartment in different rooms. All of the men were in one bedroom. Her son, Larry, was on the couch, and her grandson, Rowan, slept on a mini-couch. Dominic Jr., and I slept on an air mattress. Marilyn stayed at her mother's bedside until the end.

At about five o'clock in the morning, Ruby leaned forward and took her final breath. My daughter, Courtney, and my niece, Stephanie, stood at the doorway of our room, crying. I sat up and looked as tears rained down my daughter's face. Courtney said, "Grandma's gone." At age fourteen, my daughter was especially distraught because Ruby had been her caretaker when she was a baby. I sat straight up on the air mattress and fought back the tears, though my first instinct was to cry like a baby.

Then I got up and went into the kitchen. The one image I knew I could not endure was seeing my mother-in-law's body taken out in a body bag.

Like a child, I hid in the corner of the kitchen between the yellow stove and the refrigerator, where so many times my mother-in-law had reached up into the cabinet for coffee. I closed my eyes tightly and forced the tears back. I had cried enough after Laverne. I had to be strong for Courtney and Dominic. I checked on my wife, and she was a rock. I don't know how she did it. She watched her mother's spirit leave her body and didn't break down at all. I worried about Marilyn because she was suppressing her grief. Grief and I were well acquainted. I had spent a lifetime suppressing grief, but not Marilyn. I almost wanted my wife to cry over her mother's passing, but she didn't. As she awaited the caretaker to remove her mother's body, she washed Ruby for the final time. It's a Southern tradition for the family to wash the dead. I marveled at Marilyn's strength, but I was also perplexed by it.

As the sun rose that day without shining on Ruby, I thought of those old, furry slippers that used to shuffle down the hallway to wake me up at three in the morning and send me off on my new career in radio. I would never hear those slippers again. I wanted to disappear, but there was nowhere to run. I had to face death—again.

There were some eerie similarities between my mother and my mother-in-law. They were both born on October 19, though not in the same year. Both suffered for a long time before finally expiring. Ruby died on December 28, 2002. My mother had died on January 28, 2001.

In that year and eleven months, I had found myself in the depths of despair and somehow found the strength to pick myself up and start again. I had learned that suppressing my feelings was the equivalent of building an emotional powder keg, but I had no alternative. To keep from weeping about Ruby's death, I reverted to my childhood coping mechanism, just blanking everything out to keep from breaking down. I had to pretend death didn't exist.

Five days later, we attended Ruby's funeral. This was the first time I had attended a traditional funeral for a close family member, as most of my loved ones had been cremated. We rode in a limousine to Benta's Funeral Home on 141st Street and St. Nicholas Avenue in Harlem. It was a dreary day, cloudy, cold, and rainy. The family members sat in the back of the limousine. I sat in the front seat next to the driver, and as he parked in front of the funeral home, a taxi in front of us dropped off my colleague, Andrew Kirtzman. I was astonished, and the sight of Andrew caused me to choke up. Andrew and I had worked together for ten years, and he had recently left New York 1 News to join WCBS News. People perceived us as rivals, but we had mutual respect for one another. Andrew and I never had a single fight. And even though he had moved on, I was deeply touched by his support during this difficult period in my life. He was joined by another colleague, executive producer Claire Brinberg, who would soon leave for Washington to join CNN. Claire even brought her mother along. I will never forget how Andrew and Claire supported me during that difficult time.

As I entered the funeral chapel, I was distracted by many people who were greeting and consoling the family. But eventually I had to face that salmon-colored casket for the final time. The family marched in, and I walked slowly, holding the hands of Courtney and Dominic. Courtney starting crying, and I wanted to cry as well, but I had to stay strong for my family. If I broke down, then the rest of the family would crack. Marilyn was calm, but I knew her heart was broken. Ruby looked beautiful. She was wearing a pink dress and a dainty pink hat. That was my Ruby, pretty as a picture. She had a peaceful look on her face. The only thing that consoled me was that she was free from pain. But that was of little consolation as I prepared to say a few words during Ruby's funeral.

My niece, Shanai Harris, a newscaster in Columbia, South Carolina, had made the trip to New York for the funeral to officiate at the funeral. Ruby's children decided not to speak at their mother's funeral. I decided I had to say something, but didn't know if I could build up the courage to do so. I prayed that I could stand at my mother-in-law's casket without collapsing in grief. As I walked up to the podium, I felt my emotions take hold. I couldn't speak for about thirty seconds and just stared at the crowd. I couldn't see any specific face—not one. I was fighting back the tears so much that my face started trembling. But all I had to do was look at the long faces of my daughter and son, and then I knew I had to be strong for them.

It was tough to hold back the grief, but it was easy to find the words. I said, "Ruby stood by me no matter what. She didn't birth me, but she might as well have, because she always treated me like a son. I'm gonna make sure she'll never be forgotten." I really loved Ruby and I truly did not want to see her go. And I didn't want Ruby to be just another dead person. I wanted the world to know that Ruby had been here. I wanted her legacy to live forever. Ruby had eleven children and had buried seven of her boys. Just four of her children survived to bury her: Marilyn, Judy, Tony, and Larry. Ruby had seen more than her share of loss and sorrow, just like me. I became her son, and she became my mother.

When we went to the cemetery, we each put a flower on Ruby's casket. I was relieved that they didn't lower the casket into the ground in front of us. It had rained earlier in the day so that the dirt caked on my shoes and looked like clay. I know that death is a part of life, but I really wondered why God took my mother-in-law away from me. I was comforted knowing that she was back with the man she'd married. Her husband, "Big Al" as he was called, preceded her in death, and his grave was next to hers.

As we left the cemetery, I thought that there were two people whom I desperately want to see again when it is my time to go. And those two people were my grandmother Anna Pearl and Ruby—my two precious jewels who lit up my life. So I didn't say good-bye as we were whisked away from the gravesite. I told Ruby that I would see her later.

9

To hell and back! That's where I have been, but I am no longer ashamed of myself or my experience. That's the major reason why I decided to lift the veil and expose my life story. And, in the process, I freed myself from the emotional chains that bound me. I never thought in a million years that I would be the one to say this, but telling the truth set me free. I feel better, and my soul is better, and I even look better. Every morning when I lean over my bathroom sink to shave my round face, I look in the mirror and can't help but notice that my eyes are wide open now. For some thirty years, I could barely look at myself in the mirror. Nowadays you can't get me away from a mirror. I like myself—no, I love myself. I really do. I'm proud of myself. I am amazed at what I have accomplished, given the circumstances against me. I really was set up to be "dead or in jail" as that misguided guidance counselor predicted during my youth.

It's also a tremendous relief not having to hide any more. What an exhausting way to live! As a journalist, so much in my life is public, that it seemed almost hypocritical to conceal my dirty little secret, however calamitous it was. It's a terrible feeling to live with a secret like the one I lived with. Subconsciously, a small part of me always wondered if somehow the abuse had been my fault, even though I honestly knew it was not. I now realize that children are unable to properly process abuse and guilt. Most of the time, we abused children just accept it wholeheartedly. As a vulnerable and tender hearted little boy, I emotionally convicted myself for crimes I had not committed. I was not to blame for my father's negligence, nor was I to blame for my mother's mental illness and her sexually forcing herself on me. Yet somehow, I took all of their sins and put them on my little shoulders. I carried it until I began to write this book. And the sad part is that I didn't even realize I was carrying it. Through months and months of soul searching, I have finally accepted that I was not responsible for them; they were responsible for me.

We abused children are innocent. And we need not live our lives repaying debts that we did not incur. The debts belong to the abusers, and that burden is one they have to live with, not us.

It takes a lot of energy to live a lie. You can't always cry when you want to, and you can't always laugh when you want to. Something deep inside is stifled, and often you cannot explain why. I set myself free by exposing the shame. Although every abuse victim may not be able to write a book, I would strongly advise that they tell somebody and talk about it until they feel better and until they are no longer ashamed. They should tell it until they are free.

I have learned that talking about issues that shame you is like giving CPR to your soul. Keeping issues to yourself is a form of self-mutilation. In my view, it's therapeutic to speak openly and honestly about where we've been. For many of us, shame sets in because we fear what someone would think about us. Yet we often find that people don't view a situation as harshly as the victim does.

I can be forthcoming with my present life as it relates to my past. Many are probably wondering if I have a normal sex life. The answer is an unequivocal yes. And when I am engaging in sexual relations, I do not think of my mother or of the sex abuse. I was so skilled at blocking out those images that I do not allow them to affect my current relationship with my wife of twenty years. Had I never told a soul, no one would ever have guessed that I survived such abuse. I could have continued fooling the world, and no one, not even my family, would have figured it out.

There is one residual effect that I am still working on, and that is trying to understand the world of sex abuse victims and my induction into that group. I knew my own wretched history, but I never saw myself as an abused child. I was just Dominic, a kid with a troubled past. I never wanted to buy the labels. And I'm still not thrilled about them. Initially, when I started with this project, I rejected descriptions such as "incest victim" and "rape victim." My psyche absolutely could not handle such admissions.

When reviewing the initial rough drafts of this book, I repeatedly struck and deleted those words. "Sexual abuse" was the phrase I preferred. My mother did not rape me, for heaven's sake! Can a mother rape a child? Can a mommy rape a son? Can a woman rape a boy? I didn't want to believe it. Something deep inside me still doesn't want to believe it. Rapists are big, bad men with unshaven faces, aren't they? And incest—the very implication of the word disgusts me. Dominic, the incest victim? No way! My mother just had a bad night, lost her mind, and abused me. It happened once, right? There's no label for that, is there? I am still struggling with this—but I can finally admit that my mother raped me, and I am a victim of incest.

Rape is rape. Incest is incest. It doesn't matter who the perpetrator is.

The *American Heritage Dictionary* defines rape as "the crime of forcing another person to submit to sex acts, especially sexual intercourse or abusive or improper treatment; violation." That definition definitely matches my experience. I also rationalized that because my mother "knew" me, she couldn't have possibly raped me; we were not strangers. Laverne had beckoned for me and I had responded; so I figured that I was pretty much a willing participant—even though I had no idea what I was doing and followed my mother's directive. I was not only a minor, but I was not aware of the consequences of our actions. As a child, I had had nowhere to run and nowhere to hide. I had not even been in a position to say no.

I have learned that rape is not exclusive to the boogeyman. Sometimes the person you trust the most in the whole world can rape you. Sometimes you can be raped and not realize you've been raped until years after the act. Sometimes you follow what appear to be simple orders and later learn that you've been raped. Sometimes, your mommy can rape you.

As for incest, the *American Heritage Dictionary* defines it as "the statutory crime of sexual relations with a near relative." What relative is nearer than your mother, the one who gives birth to you? It was also difficult to accept the notion of incest because the media widely portrays incest as a father forcing himself on a daughter, or a sibling on a sibling. I had never heard of a mother forcing herself on her son. Now, after researching the topic, I see that my experience is not unique, though it is still not common. Our society deifies mothers. Fathers may come and go, but mothers are expected to be above reproach. I never wanted to indict my mother by viewing our experience as a matter of incest or by castigating her as a rapist. But I suppose she was. Though I was victimized, I wanted to go easy on my mother. Honestly, I almost saw her as a victim, too. And when I assess her whole life, she was.

What I find most disturbing is that I am not alone. Through my research, I found that about one third of all children are sexually abused before the age of eighteen, and that figures includes thirty percent of males. I found that the vast majority of abused children are under the age of seven, just like me. Abused children are more likely to have lower IQs and have an increased risk of suicide and depression. I also learned that the preconceived notions I held about sex abuse are common myths. Abusers are not always men; at least five percent are known to be women. Abusers are not always strangers, as I believed as a child. Amazingly, statistics indicate that more than 70 percent of abusers are immediate family members or someone very close to the family. And another myth that I embraced in my youth is that "abusers are always hated or look bad." My mother wasn't hated, nor did she look bad. Laverne fit right in with her surroundings except when she was heavily medicated with psychotropic drugs.

Other misconceptions bring tears to my eyes: "some survivors even into adulthood will deal with the abuse by minimizing it; they make the abuser and the events 'okay' to make it feel that they're 'okay.'" This is my experience in a nutshell. I just wanted everything to be okay. When I had confronted my mother years ago, I hadn't wanted to shame her—I essentially wanted her to apologize and tell me that everything was okay—to clear the air, if you will.

Probing into my troubled past also gives me further clarity on my school performance. Statistics indicate that young victims rarely do well in school: "as students they are likely to get angry, refuse direction from teachers and lack enthusiasm ..." That was me to the letter. At one point in high school, I lost interest in academics altogether, not unlike many of my peers in some substandard public schools. I was entirely distracted by football, and academic excellence during my teens meant very little to me. Fortunately when I went to college, my attitude changed. I have my wife to thank for that. Marilyn's pursuit of academic excellence was a huge inspiration for me, and I am forever in her debt. Watching my wife, who was then my sweetheart, read book after book and keep copious notes motivated me not to give up. She helped me see that there was genius and brilliance in me. I knew I was special, but I didn't know how to mine the wealth inside me. Marilyn helped me develop my potential.

Marilyn was also patient with me as I struggled with my suppressed feelings. A hallmark symptom of abused people is the blocking of memories, a skill that I mastered as a child and continued well into adulthood. I am not sure how I acquired this skill. It's like I had an internal shovel that scooped up the abuse and trauma and buried it somewhere in a hidden corner of my mind. But the truth never remained camouflaged for long. It would rear its ugly head every so often, and when it did, I would rush to squash it. This is why I feel that living with such secrets is so exhausting. I feel like a major weight has been lifted since I've decided to live in the light.

As details of my autobiography began to leak out, most people looked at me in sheer amazement. Many exclaimed, "And you seem so normal." I found those comments especially interesting. First of all, what is normal? Second, what exactly is expected of us incest victims?

Overall, I am a gregarious person. I like to laugh, and I have inviting eyes and a peaceful countenance. Are people with experiences similar to mine not expected to have those qualities? My secrets and my pain expressed themselves in rage and self-sabotage. During every misstep of my life, I was my own worst enemy. Perhaps it was my way of punishing myself. Thankfully, my rage never destroyed me, but I came frightfully close at times.

My way of dealing with the pain has been to declare to those closest to me that I would never live past the age of forty-five. I assumed that my ailments—heart disease, diabetes, and high blood pressure, combined with the stresses associated with being a high profile television reporter—would kill me sooner rather than later. But that outlook that was my way of relieving myself of my inner torment. I looked toward death to set me free, not by my own hand, but by God's hand.

Now, after completing this book, I want to live. If my health permits, I'd like to live to be one hundred. But however long I live, I am now trying to live well. I have this book to thank for that. I must admit, however, that when I opened the Pandora's box of my mother's medical records, I had no idea what I would discover. I knew that my mother had sexually abused me, but I had no idea that she had physically abused me as well. That was the most shocking discovery of all, and it has forever redefined my life.

My mother told her doctors that she had wanted to kill me! That was one of many bitter pills I have been forced to swallow. I was completely choked up when I read my mother's medical records. Some nights, I couldn't sleep after reading them. I kept getting images of being in her sole custody as she lost control of her mind. I have no recollection of the beatings, but oh, how I cried because of experiences that were buried somewhere deep in my soul. Sometimes, I cried as I got ready for work. Other times, I cried on the way home from work. These were the only times in my day when I was alone. I knew that my childhood was bad, but I had no idea it was worse than I remembered. I thought I knew myself, but now I realize that I didn't know much about myself at all.

I spent hours sending letters to mental hospitals to request my mother's mental records. I also had to get over my embarrassment because many of the hospital workers who received my requests knew who I was, and some were even big fans of mine. When I received those big, bulky envelopes, sometimes weeks or months later, I would brace myself for what was inside. I might learn that my mother was suicidal and had stepped out into traffic as a young teen. That discovery broke my heart into a million pieces. It meant that my mother was so despondent that she saw no way out. I could hardly believe I was reading about my own flesh and blood. And when I read that my mother was institutionalized as early as age sixteen, I was simply stunned. What kind of hell on earth must that have been for Laverne?

I still look at my daughter sometimes and use her as reference point for my mother's age at that time. Courtney's life is the opposite of her grandmother's. Courtney's life revolves around a Big East college, MTV, makeup, the Internet, and chatty girlfriends. As a youngster, she attended the NASA space camp in Florida. I also sent her to Paris a few summers ago, and she had the time of her life. She's developing into a sassy, independent, and beautiful young lady. For her sweet sixteen party, I rented a stretch limousine to meet her in front of her school when the final bell rang to take her and her girlfriend to rap mogul Sean "P. Diddy" Combs's restaurant in lower Manhattan called *Justin's*.

Courtney has lived a charmed life, but two generations earlier, her grandmother Laverne couldn't even imagine that her granddaughter would live such a life. At sixteen, Laverne was imprisoned in a mental ward getting shock treatment. Her sixteenth birthday was anything but sweet; it was more like sad sixteen. She felt isolated from her family, who had migrated north to New York City. I stepped in between Laverne and Courtney and made sure the circle of despair would be broken. It didn't happen by accident. I made a concerted effort to break every link of low self-esteem and low self-worth so that it would never see the light of day in another generation. I destroyed it with a vengeance. Courtney is on the fast track to peace and happiness.

While I was writing the rough drafts of this manuscript, I still held a grudge against my mother, even her memory. As a youngster, my inappropriate guilt turned to a smoldering resentment and I had hard feelings for quite some time, though I was respectful of my mother. Until midway through the manuscript I couldn't even admit that I resented her. But the medical records set me free. I have finally been liberated. As horrifying as it was to read about my mother's life, doing so forced to me see her differently. And that was a good thing. My only regret is that I didn't uncover this information earlier. Had I known how my mother had suffered, I most certainly would have treated her differently. Perhaps I would have spent a bit more time talking to her. I might have tried to get her to open up more without making her feel guilty. Laverne Carter could not help herself and while that was not my fault, it was not entirely her fault either. Who is *ever* to blame for mental illness? I would have sent her, and possibly a friend on trips around the world.

My mother obviously carried a lot of shame, as well. Had she told me about her history of mental illness, we could have had an entirely different relationship. Though she never said it, she probably carried a great deal of guilt on her shoulders, too. What I did not fully understand was why my other family members didn't tell me about Laverne's past. Aunt Inez, who was never entirely thrilled with my tell-all book, says she and my grandmother wanted to protect me from such revolting information. They had great expectations for me, and revealing my past and my mother's past may have hindered that. As a grown man, I can barely handle the few scant memories I have, so anything more very well may have pushed me over the edge had I learned the truth as a child.

Also, Aunt Inez says she was unaware of much of what I learned from the medical records. She, too, was moved to tears when I told her of my mother's suicidal and homicidal impulses. Initially, she didn't want to believe those truths. Further, Inez didn't understand why I wanted to dig into the past. To this day, she adamantly refuses to look at Laverne's psychiatric records. I have explained to her, over many lunches and dinners, how the truth would set not just me but our whole family free. Still, my aunt does not want to hear it. She feels that what was in the past should stay there. She has enormous family pride and would prefer that the world know only the story of Dominic Carter's success. I disagree.

There were some accounts that Inez was able to confirm, such as the time when my mother threatened to kill somebody while she was wielding a knife on a fire escape. Inez was an eyewitness to that incident. But she says the family did not know of the sexual abuse until I told my grandmother during the custody battle between her and my mother.

And even as I neared completion of the book, I was still getting more information about Laverne. It took more than seven months to obtain her grade school records. They, too, were heartbreaking. I viewed her school records from the first grade in the Richmond County Board of Education in Augusta, Georgia. My mother entered the segregated school system in the first grade, according to records, on September 4, 1951. I'm sure she was just like any other youngster, doing finger painting and learning the alphabet. From grades one through seven, she received either P for pass or S for satisfactory. She did not receive one grade of E for excellent, but at the same time, she earned no unsatisfactory grades. She was presumably a normal student.

But by the time Laverne entered the eighth grade in 1959, something started going wrong. She became a solid D student. She received four *D*'s—in English, math, social studies and music. She flunked health. Could this have been the time my mother sat straight up in bed and had to be taken to the hospital for the first time for psychiatric problems? I'm not quite sure. She was promoted to the ninth grade, but clearly she was on a downward spiral. By the time she entered tenth grade (1961), she had no grades recorded at all. By then, I'm fairly certain, she was institutionalized. The school records were further confirmation that my mother's mental and emotional anguish began when she was young.

If it wasn't so sad, it might be funny. When my mother was alive, I showed little interest in her, and now I am fascinated with her life and her many stays at mental institutions in New York and Georgia. Ironically, I live two miles from Rockland State Psychiatric Institution. Two miles. I have to pass it every day on the Palisades Parkway. There's not a single time that I don't think of my mother even if it's for an instant. I will probably never know what happened to my mother at Rockland State Psychiatric Hospital. In a file labeled "Confidential and Privileged. For Professional Purposes Only. Not to be used against the patient's interests," Laverne Carter was patient number *91 78 13*. I only know that she was admitted there on May 23, 1962, and I don't know how long she stayed. These documents indicated that my mother had an interest in nursing. One of the paragraph says, "Patient had worked in various hospitals and nursing homes as a practical nurse and appeared to derive a great deal of satisfaction from this type of employment."

My mother also spent time at Bellevue's renowned mental institution. Bellevue administrators informed me that her 1960s records were destroyed. Because of a lack of storage space, hospitals are required to keep records for only a certain length of time, and then by law the records can be destroyed. However, psychiatrists from Bellevue transferred information to Rockland State. Those records noted that the "patient is a chronic schizophrenic who has auditory hallucinations; somatic complaints, is disorganized with disturbed thinking. She admitted to auditory hallucinations."

Mind you, before I began writing this book, all I knew was that my mother had some kind of mental problem and that she sexually abused me. Other than that I didn't know much else.

She didn't have a career, she didn't have a husband or an ex-husband and she didn't own anything. She didn't have any hobbies or interests. I learned about my mother's life through the scrawled penmanship of psychiatrists and social workers. These "strangers" had no idea that they would one day be the scribes for my mother's life story. Some of the doctors were very detailed in their analysis—and I am grateful for that. Some of the doctors described Laverne as pretty, and others described her as retarded. From these observations, I have painted a picture of my mother that shines a harsh spotlight on Laverne's life.

Of course, I found it intensely interesting that my beloved grandmother, Anna Pearl, gave her daughter away to her husband's grandmother to raise. I still cannot understand why Anna Pearl raised her two other daughters separately from Laverne, especially considering that they all lived in the same town, just minutes away from each other. Why did Grandma give up her first born? Aunt Inez cannot provide a reasonable explanation for this either. Could this separation have triggered my mother's mental illness? I guess I will never know.

I will also never know what entered my mother's mind when she sexually molested me and how that act affected her throughout her life. I have to believe that my mother was taking some psychotic medication that caused her to hallucinate. While she admitted to more than one psychiatrist that she had thoughts of killing me, she never admitted that she had sexually molested me—at least, such an admission does not appear not on the records in my possession. To my knowledge, she never touched another child in a sexual or harmful way. Just me. My sister, Malika, had it good compared to me. Laverne had stabilized by the time Malika was born. Fortunately, my sister was never tossed into a court custody battle and never had to live with relatives.

One thing Malika and I did have in common was poverty. My mother depended on SSI benefits to take care of herself and Malika in the same housing project in the South Bronx. Malika, who is in her late twenties and has a steady job in New York City, has a sweet spirit and is a gentle soul. When I told her about my undertaking, she practically whispered, "I don't want you saying nothing bad about Laverne." Her statement touched my heart. Antoinette graduated from high school and has a full time job, too. She also misses Laverne.

My mother's medical records revealed she aborted a couple of children between Malika and me. I don't know why. The records did not state her motivation for terminating her pregnancies other than to detail the procedure, which was dilation and curettage. Did my mother end those pregnancies because of me or because of the fathers involved or because of her mental state? These answers I will never know.

I also wonder how my mother related to men. She and my father apparently got along until I came into the picture, and then he was nowhere to be found. He died sometime in the 1970s. I had no desire to find out his story, and I'm certain he has a lengthy one, too. He dismissed me. To my knowledge, *he* was not mentally ill. If he had been a real man and a real father, he would have been a part of my life. I don't know what my mother did to him, if anything, but it doesn't matter what she did or did not do. He was responsible for me, and he dropped the ball and kicked it away. In his mind, I guess I didn't exist. Now, he doesn't exist to me. I have no reason to commemorate or celebrate my father.

But, in spite of her tragic life, I do celebrate my mother, Laverne, for this one thing: she was a survivor. And I say with the utmost sincerity that I am not ashamed to be called her son. Truthfully, I wasn't always proud, but I am now. My mother could easily have given up, especially when she was sick. I don't know how my mother fought her way out of the revolving door of mental institutions, but she did. And for that, she should be applauded. Somehow, she found the courage to become a mother again and to live. For Laverne Carter, that was a major accomplishment.

I am proud of my mother for resisting the urge to give up. Suicide would have been an easy way out for her, yet Laverne had not given in, though she had many reasons to do so. Life did not offer her much to laugh about, but she did manage to laugh almost to the end. My dear mother made some serious mistakes in her life, some of which she could control, some of which she could not. I've often talked about the race that *I've* had to run, but Laverne had her *own* race, as well. Though hobbled and hampered, she staggered to the finish line. And she may not have had much in life, but she had me. I am her living will and testament to the fortitude of the human spirit. My mother was a survivor, and I inherited that same tenacity to overcome adversity. What a gift she gave me!

When my mother died, I was annoyed that she had left nothing material for me. I was so wrong. My mother left a legacy worth more than any insurance policy. My mother lost her mind and managed to take it back. I am quite humbled by that achievement. There was a time when my mother believed she saw little people tugging at her clothing and talking to her. My mother overcame that hallucination. My mother once saw only suicide as the way out of her misery, and she even attempted to drink poison. But one day she found a will to live. What a victory!

There are so many things that we take for granted that my mother struggled mightily with. Laverne struggled, fought, and won. I now know that winning in life is not measured by the amount of money in your bank account, or the number of homes or the degrees on the wall. You become a real winner in life when the winds of fate knock you down, and you manage to get back up. Many people, rich or poor, cannot get back up, but my mother did.

Had my mother lived, I would have hugged her more. I would have said, "I love you" more, rather than saving it for a time when she was on her deathbed. If only I could have gotten her to talk about her past, I would have listened without judgment, forgiven her, and moved on. We could have been friends. If I could only have one more day with my mother, I would love to just sit, hold her hand, and be her friend. I would have been the ear she never had, and I would have given her the compassion she never felt. Even without knowing the full extent of her past, I could have turned a corner with her had she expressed her love for me. Being able to accept my mother has been a cathartic experience that has taught me how to how to have compassion for myself and how not to be ashamed of my own tears.

These days, my kids are my life. My daughter, Courtney Ann, has stars in her eyes. One solid generation removed from poverty and mental illness, she has lived a charmed life. During her years in high school, she excelled beyond our wildest dreams. The spitting image of her father, she was elected president of her junior and senior class, the first African American to ever win such elections at the school. With a flair for drama, she took on the role of Muffie for her school's Mystery Dinner Theater. I sat on the edge of my seat as I watched my little girl, donning a black wig and bright red lipstick. She was drop dead gorgeous.

Courtney has inherited her mother's intelligence and my charisma. Courtney's girlfriends think I'm a cool dad—partly because I listen to rap music as they do. Often I joked around with my daughter and her girlfriends and drove them to school dances and sleepovers. I was tickled pink when my daughter got her first job at McDonald's. She modeled her Mickie D uniform around the house with great flair, and I drove through the drive-thru window just to watch her in action. These days Courtney is truly all grown up and has decided to follow in my footsteps. She is a college student at Syracuse University and is a broadcast journalism major at the SI Newhouse School of Public Communications—the very same school that I had to claw and fight my way into. But my daughter was accepted on her first try. She writes for the *Daily Orange*, Syracuse University's student newspaper, and she has completed several high-profile internships at local television stations, for she wants to be a television anchor like her dad—maybe even a politician. Her future is so bright that it burns my eyes.

My son's future is just as bright, but he has a few more obstacles in his way. Dominic Junior has epilepsy and requires strong medications to prevent seizure activity. It's a constant struggle. Due to the epilepsy and the anti-convulsant drugs, academics for Dominic Junior does not come as easily as it does for his sister.

Otherwise, my son is pretty much just like any other kid He enjoys playing video games and sports. In the spring of 2003, he was on a Little League baseball team called "The Mets." The coaches assign all the kids to play various positions, but I truly never thought I would see my son pitching one day. Sure enough, young Dominic Carter, number 42, was put in to pitch. He slowly walked up to the pitcher's mound in front of a group of teammates and adults and gave it his best shot. At that point that I realized how lucky I am. At that moment, I didn't give a damn about being on television. I was a proud father. His mother, sister, Uncle Larry, and Aunt Judy were watching, too, and I'm sure his two grandmothers, "Ruby" and Laverne, were looking down on him and smiling with pride, too.

Dominic's baseball team went on to make the playoffs and won first place in their league. We keep his championship trophy above our fireplace. It reads, "East Ramapo Little League AA champions 2003." During the off-season, I teach my son the tricks of the trade by taking him to the batting cage to hit some fast balls. When it's too cold to play, we stay inside and fire up the PlayStation 2 games, or he'll help me do repairs around the house. I got choked up when he took part in a ceremony for DARE (Drug Abuse Resistance Education), which teaches young people about the dangers of drugs. He had to deliver a few lines in front of several hundred people, and at first he was shy, but then he did great. I was so moved that I hugged him right in front the audience before he could sit back down. One parent looked at me and said, "Congrats on your son. You must be so proud." Indeed, I was. I was prouder than anyone could imagine.

I'm still at the top of my game, but time is passing quickly. I never thought I would say this, but I'm getting old. While once I was the new kid on the block, now I'm a veteran journalist with twenty years experience under my belt. Those veterans who came before me in the news business slowly but surely retired—veterans like Bob Caper of WABC Radio; Mary Taylor of WCBS Radio, who passed away; Bob Teague of WNBC-TV; and my longtime friend Joe Bragg of WRKS.

I firmly believe in giving back to the community because the community gave me, a young poor kid from the Bronx, more than I could have imagined. For example, I am involved with the organization the Police Athletic League, also known as PAL. I spent a lot of time at the PAL community center in the Bronx when I was a kid. A lot of people gave their time and resources to the children at PAL, and I was one who benefited from this enormously. So when PAL asks me to speak at their events, I do so with pride. I enjoy inspiring kids and explaining to them how I can relate to where they are in life. They see me as this big anchorman television guy, but I let them know that I am just like them. All they have to do is believe in themselves and be willing to work hard to pursue their dreams. Had I not believed in myself, I would have never made it the news business or any other business. This is what I try to drum into the heads of today's youth.

One of the top officials in the Police Athletic League's New York branch was a man named Felix Urrutia. He is a smart and savvy man who could easily make big bucks in the private sector; instead he dedicates his life to children. He is source of inspiration for me. On June 12, 2003, just a few days shy of my thirty-ninth birthday, Felix asked me to spend the afternoon with some PAL kids. I happily obliged—even though it meant taking part of the day off from work. To me, that was a small price to pay to galvanize twenty-five teenagers who are trying to stay out of trouble.

First, Felix brought the teens to the newsroom for a tour and my boss, Steve Paulus, foot the bill for pizza and soda as he always does with no public fanfare. Some TV stations have huge promotional campaigns, claiming to be part of the community, but would never pay for such items.

After the tour and lunch, Felix insisted that I ride with him in the PAL van back to the Webster-Giannone PAL Center—the same center I played in as a kid. It's located at Webster Avenue and 183rd Street in the Bronx. During the ride there—he kept radioing back to the center—giving them an estimated time of arrival. I didn't understand why he kept giving them our estimated arrival time, but I figured they were in some kind of rush to get the daily afternoon activities started for the kids. When we pulled up, I felt right at home. The center looked the same. The side street of the center was closed to the public, just as it was when I was a kid—and a new generation of youngsters was playing in the street. Those were happy times for me.

When I got out of the van, I got the shock of a lifetime. About a hundred kids between the ages of six and twelve pulled out poster boards in a rainbow of colors saying "Welcome Home Mister Carter." And they gave me a rousing homecoming—cheering and clapping wildly. A DJ who was set up outside played the theme song from the show *Welcome Back, Kotter*: "Welcome back, to the same old place that you started from …" Young people surrounded me and hugged me saying "We love you, Mister Carter, Thank you for making us proud." Felix turned to me and said, "Surprise, Mister Carter, and welcome home, Dominic, we are sooo proud of you!" I looked around and there were flyers everywhere with a photo of me on top of the flyer that said: "Come and join us as we welcome

back a local hero, New York 1's own Mr. Dominic Carter."
Other flyers said: "Join us as we celebrate the return of Mr.
Dominic Carter to the Webster-Giannone Center." It was
impossible to fight back the tears, and I didn't even try.

Some of the kids were confused and asked me why I was crying. I tried to explain but I couldn't get the words out. I had
received a hero's welcome in my community where I started out
as a nobody. I was considered a nobody, my mother was considered a nobody, my grandmother was considered a nobody, and
on and on. Now I broke the mold—I became somebody. I also
cried because I remembered how hard I had worked my entire
life, and seeing the kids reminded me of my own innocence as
well as theirs. I cried because I couldn't control my beginning,
but I could damn sure control my ending. I cried because their
reception proved that all of my efforts were not in vain—that I
was making a difference and giving back to the community. I
cried for all the Carters that day. I cried because I was no longer
ashamed to cry.

Notes

1. Meier, Barry. 1988. "Blacks in New York: Reported Tuned into Listeners". Newsday. 7-8.

2. Gay, Verne. 1992. "I-Witness News; The City's First All News Channel Features A Controversial Cost Effective Concept: The reporter and the camera operator are the same person. Newsday. 68-70.

3. Carter, Dominic. 1992. "Somalian Update". New York 1 News. Taped broadcast report.

4. Lambiet, Jose. 1993. "They Fought Slum, Then Bought It." New York Daily News.

5. Carter, Dominic. 1993. "Dinkins Reacts to WTC Bombing." New York 1 News. Live Broadcast from Osaka, Japan via Satellite.

6. Chiles, Nick. 1993. "All Choked Up; Liz loses composure during taping for TV." Newsday. 5.

7. McKinley, James. 1993. "Holtzman Breaks Down at Interview." The New York Times. B1.

8. Holtzman, Elizabeth. "Who Said It Would Be Easy: One woman's life in the political arena." New York, New York. Arcade Publishing. 1996.

9. Rush, George. 1994. "Gossip". "The New York Daily News. 12.

10. Clinton, William Jefferson. 1994. "Interview with Dominic Carter of New York 1 Television, New York City." Public Papers of the Presidents. 30 Weekly Comp. Pres. Doc. 2217.

11. Pogrebin, Robin. 1996. "Life at NY1; Where the News and Reporters Never Seem To Stop." The New York Times. TV Section Column 1 4-12.

12. Hardt, Robert. 1997. "Riled TV Reporter Warns Lategano: I'll Ruin You." New York Post. 7.

13. 1997. "Signing Off For Now" New York Daily News. 10.

14. Rush, George and Molloy, Joanna. 1999. "A Little Hardball Politics." New York Daily News. 18.

15. Petrozzello, Donna. 1999. "Television." New York Daily News. 108.

16. www.xanax.com. 2002. Pfizer Inc.,

17. Kennedy, Randy. 2001. "For This 2-Man TV Team Politics Vaudeville Style." The New York Times. B2-3.

18. Bogorad, Barbara. 2005. "Sexual Abuse: Surviving the Pain." The American Academy of Experts in Traumatic Stress. www.aaets.org/article.

978-0-595-42839-7
0-595-42839-8

Printed in the United States
104686LV00002B/61/A